THE MONSTER MOVIES OF UNIVERSAL STUDIOS

THE MONSTER MOVIES OF UNIVERSAL STUDIOS

James L. Neibaur

ROWMAN & LITTLEFIELD
Lanham • Boulder • New York • London

Published by Rowman & Littlefield
A wholly owned subsidiary of The Rowman & Littlefield Publishing Group, Inc.
4501 Forbes Boulevard, Suite 200, Lanham, Maryland 20706
www.rowman.com

Unit A, Whitacre Mews, 26-34 Stannary Street, London SE11 4AB

British Library Cataloguing in Publication Information Available

Library of Congress Cataloging-in-Publication Data

Names: Neibaur, James L., 1958– author.
Title: The monster movies of Universal studios / James L. Neibaur.
Description: Lanham : Rowman & Littlefield, [2017] | Includes bibliographical
    references and index.
Identifiers: LCCN 2016048428 (print) | LCCN 2017007474 (ebook) | ISBN
    9781442278165 (hardback : alk. paper) | ISBN 9781442278172 (electronic)
Subjects: LCSH: Universal City Studios—Catalogs. | Monster films—Catalogs.
    | Horror films—Catalogs.
Classification: LCC PN1999.U57 N45 2017 (print) | LCC PN1999.U57 (ebook) |
    DDC 016.79143/75/0973—dc23
LC record available at https://lccn.loc.gov/2016048428

∞™ The paper used in this publication meets the minimum requirements of
American National Standard for Information Sciences—Permanence of Paper
for Printed Library Materials, ANSI/NISO Z39.48-1992.

Printed in the United States of America

To a great pal, Kelly Ann Parmelee.
And to her late father, who inspired her love of movies.
Thanks, Charlie!

CONTENTS

ACKNOWLEDGMENTS

Special thanks to my son Max Neibaur for collaborating closely on this book. He's been a fan of these films since childhood, and his assistance on this project meant a great deal to me.

Thanks always to Terri Lynch and Katie Carter, who live every book with me and continue to be invaluable on every project.

Thanks also to Ted Okuda, Kelly Ann Parmelee, Charles Parmelee, Tracy Nelson, Chris Costello, Elena Verdugo, Gregory Allen Mank, Tom Weaver, Bill Warren, Scott MacGillivray, and Barb Fellion.

PROLOGUE

During the golden age of Hollywood in the 1930s and 1940s, Universal Studios produced many films in several genres, including comedies, musicals, dramas, and westerns. But it is best known for its films of the horror genre, especially those featuring noted monster characters. Frankenstein's monster, Dracula, the Invisible Man, the Mummy, the Wolf Man, and the Creature continue to be iconic figures in popular culture and also continue to be identified as per their presentation in the Universal horror movies.

Count Dracula has been played by such actors as Christopher Lee, Frank Langella, and Gary Oldman, but whenever anyone mimics the character, they will invariably do the voice and mannerisms of Bela Lugosi. Lugosi played this character on film only twice—in the 1931 Universal classic and the 1948 comedy parody *Abbott and Costello Meet Frankenstein*. But his performance—and these films—left an indelible mark and continue to define our perception of the character. The image of Frankenstein's monster is identified as the way Universal makeup artist Jack Pierce depicted him.

This book examines, discusses, and provides information about the monster movies made for Universale Studios during the 1930s, 1940s, and 1950s and featuring Frankenstein, Dracula, the Mummy, the Invisible Man, the Wolf Man, and the Creature. Every movie featuring one of the previously mentioned monsters, including the initial film and all sequels in the series, is represented.

Beginning in 1931 with the films *Dracula* and *Frankenstein*, chronological chapters on the horror movies discuss the studio's progression, the importance of the first films and how they saved Universal from bankruptcy, their eventual relegation to B movies, and how they finally fizzled out by the end of World War II. A resurgence with *Abbott and Costello Meet Franken-stein* (1948) resulted in re-releases of the older movies, and a move closer to science fiction in the 1950s with *Creature from the Black Lagoon* (1954) and its sequels is also included.

However, this is not a book about the horror films as a genre. We do not discuss such Universal films as *The Old Dark House* or *The Black Cat*. These are the monster movies, featuring noted monster characters as central to the narrative.

The monster movies produced by Universale Studios have extended beyond the context of their era of release and have lived on over time and generations. The iconic characters and enduring stories continue to resonate. Their highs and lows, classics and misfires, impact when first released, and continued significance are all discussed in these pages.

A VERY BRIEF HISTORY OF UNIVERSAL STUDIOS

Universale Studios was founded by Carl Laemmle, Mark Dintenfass, Charles O. Baumann, Adam Kessel, Pat Powers, William Swanson, David Horsley, Robert H. Cochrane, and Jules Brulatour in 1912 with Laemmle as the president. Laemmle would eventually buy out the others, purchase a string of nickelodeon theaters, and, in 1915, open what was then the largest production facility for moving pictures. He bought a 230-acre farm, and Universal was the first truly "big" movie studio and remained the largest in Hollywood for a decade.

Laemmle was a very careful businessman, and rather than open theater chains like other big studios, he would finance and distribute his own productions. This was fine for the lower-budget westerns and serials, but Erich Von Stroheim's enormous budgets for films like *Blind Husbands* (1919) and *Foolish Wives* (1922) almost bankrupted the studio. The silent era is, in fact, the first time that horror movies saved the studio. Actor Lon Chaney was a master of theatrical makeup and a brilliant actor. His films, including such noted classics as *The Hunchback of Notre Dame* (1923) and *The Phantom of the Opera* (1925), were extremely lucrative for the studio and helped it survive the large budgets of the Von Stroheim dramas.

Much of the reason for Universal's success was due to Laemmle's secretary, Irving Thalberg, whose vision as a producer was so effective in producing better movies more efficiently that he was promoted to studio chief. However, Louis B. Mayer of MGM lured Thalberg away with the promise of more money and greater creative control. After Thalberg left,

Universal began struggling and was soon a lower-tier studio than the others. They were sustained not by their feature releases but by their popular Oswald the Rabbit cartoons that had been originally created by Walt Disney and Ub Iwerks. A discrepancy with Universal over their salaries resulted in Disney and Iwerks going off on their own to create the iconic Mickey Mouse character. The studio retained the rights to Oswald the Rabbit, and Walter Lantz was hired to head an animation department. He continued with the Oswald series until 1943. Lantz would grow with the company as a cartoon producer, eventually offering such favorites as Woody Woodpecker and Andy Panda.

By the end of the 1920s, Laemmle's son Carl Laemmle Jr. was head of production. Junior Laemmle was more innovative and daring than his father, buying theaters and equipping the studio for sound production during the early days of talking pictures. Junior's more progressive ideas resulted in the studio producing the first all-color musical feature *King of Jazz* (1930) and the Best Picture Oscar winner *All Quiet on the Western Front* (1930).

Buoyed by this success, Junior decided to arrange for some top-level horror movies to be produced by the studio. Recalling the success of the Lon Chaney features, Junior decided to once again use literary sources as inspirations for some new sound horror films. Recalling that his father was interested in filming Bram Stoker's novel *Dracula* as early as 1914, Junior set out to make that the studio's first sound horror film. Plans were to produce a lavish production based on the novel and to secure the acting talents of Lon Chaney for the title role. Chaney was in declining health but continued to be active and agreed to play Count Dracula. His longtime director Tod Browning was hired to helm the project. Inspired by the German expressionist horror films of the 1920s, Junior secured the services of German cinematographer Karl Freund, who shot such movies as *The Golem* (1920) and *Metropolis* (1927). Freund was already noted as being among the most innovative cameramen in movies, having invented the dolly shot and consistently exhibited a real understanding as to how to help the director command the pace of each film.

When the Depression hit in 1929, the lavish plans Junior had for *Dracula* to be a big-budget production had to be pared down, so instead of shooting the novel, the decision was made to base the film on Hamilton Deane's stage play, which was enjoying a lot of popularity in New York. Standing sets from Lon Chaney's earlier movies were being considered for use, and preproduction was concluding when Chaney died in August 1930. Several actors were considered to replace him, including a young Universal contract player named John Carradine, who would essay the role years later.

The actor who appeared in the New York play, Bela Lugosi, had done several films in his native Hungary and a few in America. He lobbied hard to get the role in the Universal movie, even arranging for Hamilton Deane and Bram Stoker's widow to take less money for the cinematic rights. Eventually, he was hired to reprise his biggest stage success in the film version of *Dracula*. Junior Laemmle didn't likely realize it at the time, but this film launched a series of horror movies that would define the studio.

DRACULA

(1931)

Director: Tod Browning
Screenplay: Garrett Fort, based on the play by John L. Balderston (from the novel by Bram Stoker).
Producer: Carl Laemmle Jr., Tod Browning. *Cinematography:* Karl Freund. *Editing:* Milton Carruth. *Art Direction:* Charles D. Hall.
Cast: Bela Lugosi (Count Dracula), Helen Chandler (Mina Seward), David Manners (Jonathan Harker), Dwight Frye (Renfield), Edward Van Sloan (Professor Van Helsing), Herbert Bunston (Doctor Seward), Frances Dade (Lucy), Joan Standing (maid), Charles Gerrard (Martin), Geraldine Dvorak, Dorothy Tree, Cornelia Thaw (Dracula's wives), Josephine Velez (Grace), Michael Visaroff (innkeeper), Anna Bakacs (innkeeper's daughter), Moon Carroll (maid), Anita Harder (flower girl), Carla Laemmle, Donald Murphy, Nicholas Bela, Daisy Belmore (coach passengers).
Released: February 14, 1931.
Running Time: 85 minutes (re-released in 1936 at 75 minutes).
Availability: DVD (Universal Home Video).

When F. W. Murnau produced the German film *Nosferatu* in 1922, the widow of *Dracula* novelist Bram Stoker sued and won. Carl Laemmle Jr. purchased the legal right to film the novel, avoiding any such repercussions. Horror master Lon Chaney was hired to play the title role. Universal chose Tod Browning to direct due to his having had experience doing horror films and had worked often with Chaney, while German cinematographer Karl Freund was hired to shoot the film. Chaney's plan was to play the title role in the same manner as Max Schreck in *Nosferatu*. He was going to create elaborate makeup for the character, and the production was going to have a large budget and follow the original novel. However, the stock market crash forced Laemmle to limit the budget, and Chaney's death forced him to recast the title role.

The plan was to adapt the Hamilton Deane stage version to film. However, the play's star, Bela Lugosi, was not originally part of the deal. The play was being performed at a theater in Los Angeles at this time, so Lugosi was nearby and able to negotiate for the role. He served as a liaison for Laemmle's purchase of the film rights from Stoker's widow and from Deane.

Junior Laemmle, however, was not interested in using Lugosi for the role. Although the actor had appeared in many films, he wasn't as much of a name as Chaney would have been. Laemmle considered such noted actors as Paul Muni, Chester Morris, Ian Keith, John Wray, Joseph Schildkraut, Arthur Edmund Carewe, and William Courtenay. Lugosi ended up being hired when he agreed to the very small salary of only $500 per week for seven weeks.

Bela Lugosi's acting career began onstage in his native Hungary around the turn of the twentieth century, and he started his movie career in 1917. Lugosi emigrated to America in 1920 and was appearing in American silent movies soon afterward. The character of Count Dracula gave him his greatest stage role on Broadway in 1927 in Hamilton Deane's adaptation of the Bram Stoker novel. During the play's three-year run, Lugosi appeared in the occasional movie, including one film directed by Tod Browning, *The Thirteenth Chair* (1929), for MGM. This was his sound film debut and the first time audiences heard his very distinctive voice.

Some accounts indicate that when Lon Chaney died, Tod Browning lost interest in the *Dracula* movie project and contributed little, leaving it to cinematographer Freund's vision. However, despite these production troubles, *Dracula* was an enormous hit with period moviegoers and has lived on as one of the quintessential horror films in American movie history.

The story deals with Renfield, a solicitor who travels to Count Dracula's castle in Transylvania on a business matter. A carriage driver warns him of vampires inhabiting the castle, but Renfield dismisses this outrageous notion and insists on being taken to the castle. Renfield's response to the warnings of vampires is dismissive, but in an era with less globalism, the idea of different occurrences in a foreign country fits comfortably in the narrative. The driver takes him only as far as the Borgo Pass, where another carriage brings him to the castle. This carriage is driven by Dracula himself in disguise as a driver.

Bela Lugosi as Dracula.

The entire opening sequence does a nice job of building suspense by informing the viewer that there's something dangerous ahead but allowing Renfield to be naive and head straight into it. Lugosi's power in the role and the effectiveness of both Browning's direction and Freund's cinematography are immediately evident. Bathed in darkness, the shot of a disguised Dracula as the carriage driver rests on his stern, unblinking face. Browning carefully held his shots of Lugosi just so long, never allowing him to blink on screen. Further emphasis on his eyes is made by pencil flashlights shining on them. Renfield appears to be only slightly unsettled, even after the carriage driver disappears and he discovers that a bat is leading the vehicle to the castle.

Adding to the macabre proceedings are shots inside the castle of various creatures scurrying about the coffins that contain the remains of Dracula's three wives. The creepiness of rats, possums, armadillos, and insects culminates with a medium shot of a coffin slowly opening and a hand emerging—

the skinny fingers creep out as if they are one of the other creatures. Even in the twenty-first century, the effectiveness of these images remains.

Renfield's response to the Count once they are in the castle is all business. He appears to find Dracula eccentric, but his focus is on their business transaction, as Dracula plans to purchase a castle in London. Dracula speaks in a deep, affected manner that is alternately charming and chilling. Renfield is charmed. He appears to be reasonably relaxed, even comfortably indicating that the bed he is to use that night "looks inviting." He does not realize Dracula is a vampire, even after he accidentally cuts his finger and the Count approaches it with interest. A piece of jewelry containing a crucifix that Renfield is wearing stops the vampire from attacking. When Dracula backs off, Renfield ironically concludes he is bothered by the blood, stating, "It's nothing serious, just a small cut." It isn't until Renfield opens a window and faints at the sight of an aggressive bat that Dracula attacks him. Renfield is thereafter a raving lunatic under the Count's spell.

Actor Dwight Frye, who plays Renfield, had been in films since silent movies and appeared with James Cagney in *The Doorway to Hell* (1930) but truly established himself in this movie. He is controlled and secure at the outset, and his metamorphosis into the moaning, giggling character who preys on insects for their blood and is an undying servant to Dracula is one of the more impressive performances in the movie. Renfield goes from calm and settled to wide-eyed and maniacal, actor Frye offering a completely uninhibited performance that was strong enough to result in his forming a niche for playing such characters in subsequent films.

Renfield and Dracula travel to London by schooner. When the ship arrives, he appears to be the only one alive. Dracula has destroyed the entire crew. Renfield is put away in a sanitarium headed by a Dr. Seward, while Count Dracula continues to hide in plain sight. He meets Seward, his daughter, her fiancé, and another female friend at the theater and introduces himself.

The attraction of Dracula is utilized most effectively here. Just as Renfield responded to him as eccentric but essentially harmless, the same goes with Seward's group at the theater. Seward is accepting. His daughter, Mina, is friendly and engaging. Her fiancé is also friendly but more distant. Lucy, their friend, is noticeably attracted to the Count, even to the point of reciting a rather creepy poem about death. Dracula's response, "There are worse things than death," only enhances her attraction to him.

In an era where quick edits and several shots often lasting only seconds are the norm in mainstream filmmaking, *Dracula*'s brevity is exhibited in its narrative. A more modern take would offer a great deal of backstory about

Seward, his daughter, her fiancé, and Lucy. Instead, the narrative moves quickly while shots are held longer. Browning often rests on Lugosi's serious face. Lugosi's movements are slow, deliberate, and controlled. But the story goes from Dracula's attack of Lucy, who dies the next day despite several transfusions, and quickly moves to his attack of Mina. We know little about these characters except for their basic introduction within the narrative structure. It is all we need to know.

Dracula's attack of Mina is an especially effective scene. Lugosi is shown in close-up, and as he approaches Mina, his entire head fills the screen. It is a frightening image that was said to cause moviegoers to scream and flee the theater during its initial release. Some reports indicated that women actually fainted.

From this point, the narrative moves even more quickly, buoyed by artful shots that further enhance the cinematic structure. Dracula visits Seward the following evening as Mina is talking about the attack, which she remembers as a dream and that the image who bit her was blurred by fog. Lifting a cigarette case that has a mirror on the inside cover, Van Helsing and Mina's fiancé see that Dracula has no reflection. When Van Helsing approaches the Count with the mirror, he angrily slaps it out of his hand, breaking it.

Mina reads about a woman luring children in the park and biting them, recognizing it as Lucy. She then realizes that she is also under Dracula's power and reveals this to her fiancé, indicating they must no longer see each other. Meanwhile, Dracula announces to Van Helsing that Mina now belongs to him and warns him to stay away. The movie concludes with Dracula impaled by Van Helsing with a stake through his heart as he attempts to escape with Mina, who thereafter returns to her normal state of being.

Although the writers are said to have studied *Nosferatu*, Dracula in this movie has no fangs, is stately and attractive, and can hide in plain sight. He is a Count who exhibits the manner of aristocracy despite an underlying eeriness crowded by a discernible charisma. There has been some discussion that Browning was distraught after the death of Lon Chaney and lost interest in this project. He would leave the set for long periods of time, and Karl Freund would take over the direction. There is some contention as to this story's accuracy, but whoever was in charge of the succession of shots and the framing of each scene certainly did so in an effective manner. Many of the medium shots present the character off to the side, allowing a great deal of negative space to frame the action. The expanse of such shorts effectively conveys the emptiness surrounding the proceedings.

The idea that Dracula really preys only on women is also established here, and it's something that we see carry over into other versions of

Dracula and other vampire films. The studio had actually informed Browning that they wanted Dracula to attack only female characters because of the sexual subtext. The female vampires, however, have a limited role in the movie when compared to the novel, avoiding the overt sexual nature of these characters altogether.

The characters of Mina and Lucy do not have a great deal of depth or any kind of backstory presented, but the minimalist approach is still effective. The women are young and pretty and after meeting the Count share a brief scene where they giggle about his charismatic appearance and eccentric manner. Lucy is slightly more offbeat and, therefore, expendable within the narrative. She is attacked first, and we do not see her as a vampire but are aware only via the newspaper account and Mina's reference. Mina, however, is more the ingénue. While she is sophisticated enough to recognize aristocracy—coming from wealth and not being unfamiliar with such characters—her manner exudes greater innocence and, being engaged, the more romantic character. She would likely be most relatable to female moviegoers at the time.

Special effects were limited at this time, so Dracula's transformation into a bat is never presented on-screen as it would be years later. Along with the close-ups, this early talkie uses long periods of silence and no music in the background and incorporates intertitles to enhance the narrative. This adds to the eeriness of the film. Browning was more comfortable with silent movies than he ever would be with talkies (he made only a few), but his use of silent film methods in *Dracula* works well with the material. The performances are, in some ways, beholden to stage acting, where broader gestures are necessary for patrons in the back row, while others employ the florid movements of silent movie acting. Lugosi, however, who anchors the entire film, responds well to the intimacy of the movie camera, with subtle gestures and an economy of movement. His bursts of bigger movement (response to the mirror, to a crucifix, and so on) are sudden and jarring, keeping with the effectiveness of his performance.

Sometimes the filmmaking limitations are evident. In a transition shot of the schooner taking Dracula and Renfield to London, there are stock shots of a crew manning a ship through harsh waters from the 1927 Universal silent feature *The Storm Breaker*. Because silent movies are projected at 18 frames per second, when this footage is included in a sound film projected at 24 frames per second, the movements are faster and jerkier.

The performances are generally good. Along with the previously mentioned Dwight Frye, the work offered by Helen Chandler as Mina and David Manners as her fiancé are competent, as is Frances Dade as

Lucy. Both Edward Van Sloane as Van Helsing and Herman Bunston as Seward had been in the play with Lugosi and were hired along with him for the movie version. Bette Davis was actually among those considered for the Mina role, but Junior Laemmle didn't feel she exhibited as much appeal as Chandler. Manners and Chandler appeared in a few other films together. Chandler had a difficult life filled with substance abuse, being committed to a sanitarium, and disfigurement in a fire. Manners lived to the ripe old age of 97, and when asked in later years about *Dracula*, he would sheepishly admit he never had actually seen the movie for which he was most known.

A month prior to the film's premiere, the January 1931 magazine *Silver Screen* did a full-page spread on Bela Lugosi with the headline "Is He the Second Chaney?" The article stated,

> His name is Bela Lugosi. Like the beloved Lon, he is a man of mystery and a master of makeup. He is working in movies at Universal, where Lon Chaney worked, being directed by Tod Browning, the man who directed nearly all of Lon's greatest pictures. His great role, *Dracula*, is that of an "undead" vampire who lives on the blood of humans, a part, that had he lived, would inevitably have gone to Chaney. Only in appearance does he differ. He is six feet one in height, with the dreamy, strange face of a mystic. Lon is gone but his art lives after him. May Lugosi be worthy of following in the path he made so thoroughly his own.[1]

Dracula appeared at the Roxy in New York on February 12, 1931, and sold over 50,000 tickets within the first 48 hours. The film was released nationwide a couple of days later. In a February 13 *New York Times* review, Mordaunt Hall stated, "[*Dracula*] is a production that evidently had the desired effect upon many in the audience yesterday afternoon, for there was a general outburst of applause when Dr. Van Helsing produced a little cross that caused the dreaded Dracula to fling his cloak over his head and make himself scarce."[2] A few days later, *Variety* reported, "It is difficult to think of anybody who could quite match the performance in the vampire part of Bela Lugosi, even to the faint flavor of foreign speech that fits so neatly."[3]

Lugosi's performance is indeed made more effective by his accent, as it lends an exotic air to the character that simultaneously makes him appear more charming and threatening. Of course, that's also part of the reason why he became typecast as a villain and found it much harder to get other work than even someone like Boris Karloff.

One element of *Dracula* that we are unable to see today is Edward Van Sloane's appearance at the end of the movie. He addresses the audience thusly:

> Just a moment, ladies and gentlemen! A word before you go. We hope the memories of Dracula and Renfield won't give you bad dreams, so just a word of reassurance. When you get home tonight and the lights have been turned out and you are afraid to look behind the curtains—and you dread to see a face appear at the window—why, just pull yourself together and remember that after all, there are such things as vampires!

This epilogue was removed, as were some scenes, when *Dracula* was re-released in 1936. However, although the excised scenes were later restored, Van Sloane's epilogue remains lost.

Dracula was an enormous success for Universal, profiting by over $700,000 at a time when admission tickets were around 10 to 25 cents. This was at a time when the studio was in bad financial shape, having lost over $2 million in revenue by 1930. The success of *Dracula* helped keep them afloat, so Junior Laemmle announced immediate plans for more horror movies. Universal then planned to do a film based on Mary Shelley's book *Frankenstein*.

With its dark imagery, foggy surroundings, expansive shots, tight close-ups, affected dialogue, broad acting, periods of silence, and slow movement, *Dracula* continues to be a quintessential example of horror in early American sound cinema. Bela Lugosi's interpretation remains the definitive representation of the character. Even schoolchildren who have never seen the movie or are not aware of Lugosi will likely "pretend" to be Dracula by mimicking his delivery and stock lines like "I vant to drink your blood!" while hiding their face with an imaginary cape—a prop used to further emphasize the character's aristocracy.

At the same time this movie was being shot, a simultaneous Spanish-language version of *Dracula* was being filmed at night on the same sets. This was a practice that producer Paul Kohner had suggested to Carl Laemmle, convincing him it would expand the market to Spanish-speaking audiences. The Spanish version of *Dracula*, starring Carlos Villarias (Carlos Villar) as Conde Drácula and Lupita Tovar as Eva Seward, was considered a lost film for decades until a print was discovered in the 1970s and subsequently restored. It appears on many DVDs of *Dracula* as a special feature, sometimes also including an interview with Ms. Tovar, who lived past 100. Ms. Tovar, who lived to be 106, was married to producer Kohner.

As the Universale Studios production team enjoyed the profits of this successful experiment, they realized that audiences liked to be frightened. Their early reports about being in production with *Frankenstein* generated a great deal of publicity and interest. This time, the central character is an actual monster, created by various dead bodies, a legend that most audiences knew due to the popularity of Mary Shelley's nineteenth-century novel.

Because of his success in *Dracula*, Universal wanted Lugosi to appear in *Frankenstein* as well. However, Lugosi did not like the idea of his voice not being used and wanted to instead play Dr. Frankenstein, stating, "I was a star in my own country and I refuse to be a scarecrow here."[4] Lugosi eventually turned the role down. Dwight Frye, however, accepted the part of Ygor, while Edward Van Sloane also signed on for a role, beginning what would turn out to be a 20-year career in movies. For the monster, the studio hired freelance actor Boris Karloff, whose career dated back to silent films. The movie would make him a star, and he and Lugosi would remain rivals for the remainder of their careers, even while costarring in future projects.

2

FRANKENSTEIN

(1931)

Director: James Whale.
Screenplay: Garrett Fort and Francis Faragoh; based on John Balderston's adaptation of the novel by Mary Wollstonecraft Shelley.
Producer: Carl Laemmle Jr. *Cinematography:* Arthur Edeson. *Art Direction:* Charles D. Hall.
Cast: Colin Clive (Dr. Henry Frankenstein), Boris Karloff (the monster), Mae Clarke (Elizabeth), John Boles (Victor), Edward Van Sloan (Dr. Waldman), Dwight Frye (Fritz, the dwarf), Frederick Kerr (Baron Frankenstein), Marilyn Harris (Maria), Lionel Belmore (the burgomaster), Francis Ford (Hans), Michael Mark (Ludwig), Cecil Reynolds (Waldman's secretary), Carmencita and Seesel Johnson (little girls), Pauline Moore, Arletta Duncan (bridesmaids), Paul Panzer, Soledad Jimenez, Margaret Mann (mourners).
Released: November 21, 1931.
Running Time: 70 minutes.
Availability: DVD (Universal Home Video).

The box office success and critical acclaim of *Dracula* led to the production and release of *Frankenstein* within the same year, 1931. And as great as *Dracula* had been, *Frankenstein* was even better. All of its methods—narrative and cinematic—set the tone and became the blueprint for the horror movie genre.

The early stages of preproduction were fraught with conflict. At the center was a script by Robert Florey, who was also hired to direct, and actor Bela Lugosi, who had scored with *Dracula*. Lugosi wanted to play Dr. Frankenstein, but the studio insisted he be cast as the monster. Lugosi balked at playing a role where he does not speak but agreed to begin creating the makeup for the monster. The makeup Lugosi devised was not pleasing the studio, while Florey's script presented the monster as a soulless killer without any substance.

Universal had recently acquired the services of director James Whale, who began his career directing stage plays in England, which eventually led him to success as a Broadway director. In 1930, studios were looking for stage directors due to their experience with dialogue. Whale directed the low-budget independent production *Journey's End* (1930) based on a play and in which actor Colin Clive repeated his stage role. This film became a worldwide success, so Whale headed to Hollywood amid offers from several studios. Universal signed him to a five-year contract, and his first film for the studio, *Waterloo Bridge* (1931), was a success with both critics and moviegoers. Carl Laemmle Jr. then allowed Whale to choose any property on the studio's roster, and Whale chose *Frankenstein*. Robert Florey was taken off the project, and Whale was now in charge of casting, arranged to have the screenplay completely rewritten, and began casting the film.

Bela Lugosi was already unhappy about playing the role, but it is unclear as to whether he left the project or was taken off once Whale was put in charge. Some studies believe this to have been detrimental to Lugosi's career. However, even though this was not a role he wanted to play, he likely had no misgivings. Lugosi was a working actor and appeared in the Charlie Chan mystery *The Black Camel* (1931) and the Joe E. Brown comedy *Broad Minded* (1931). Both Florey and Lugosi would return to Universal to do *Murders in the Rue Morgue* (1932).

Just as *Dracula* was based on a play that was adapted from a novel, so was the movie version of *Frankenstein*. James Whale discovered that while Mary Shelley's novel was in the public domain, the film rights to a stage adaptation by Margaret "Peggy" Webling had been purchased by Universal. Webling's play was produced for the stage by Hamilton Deane, who had also adapted *Dracula* from a novel into a play. The American stage adaptation was rewritten by John L. Balderson. One of the most notable aspects of Webling's stage adaptation was that it gave the monster the name Frankenstein, like its creator. Shelley's novel was considered too long and complicated to adapt to the screen, the monster eventually evolving to having a mate, speaking articulately, and wrestling with his own demons. The play, however, truncated the narrative and was more direct and easy to adapt to the still-new sound medium.

James Whale chose Colin Clive, whom he had worked with on *Journey's End*, to play Dr. Frankenstein. He was impressed with the performance of actress Mae Clarke when he worked with her on *Waterloo Bridge* and cast her as Elizabeth. The studio wanted Bette Davis, but Whale wisely believed she would not register as effectively in the role.

Whale then set out to find an actor to play the monster, settling on Boris Karloff, a busy character actor who had been in films since 1919. Karloff had created something of a niche playing unsavory characters in such films as *Young Donovan's Kid* (1931), in which he played the cocaine-addicted Cokey Joe, as well as *Five Star Final* (1931), in which he is part of a journalist team whose sensational stories destroy lives. Whale was fascinated by the tension Karloff could exude as an actor and believed that even behind the monster makeup, he could offer what the part needed to be successful. Karloff was fascinated by the challenge and accepted the role. Karloff would later recall,

> I was having lunch and director James Whale sent either the first assistant or maybe it was his secretary over to me, and asked me to join him for a cup of coffee after lunch, which I did. He asked me if I would make a test for him tomorrow. "What for?" I asked. "For a damned awful monster!" he said. Of course, I was delighted, because it meant another job, if I was able to land it. Actually that's all it meant to me. At the same time I felt rather hurt, because at the time I had on very good straight makeup and my best suit, and he wanted to test me for a monster! Whale and I both saw the character as an innocent one. Within the heavy restrictions of my make-up, I tried to play it that way. This was a pathetic creature who, like us all, had neither the will nor the say in his creation, and certainly did not wish upon itself the hideous image which automatically terrified humans it tried to befriend. The most heartrending aspect of the creature's life, for us, was his ultimate desertion by his creator. It was as though man, in his blundering, searching attempts to prove himself, was to find himself deserted by his God.[1]

Makeup artist Jack Pierce is responsible for creating the iconic makeup for the monster. Collaborating with Karloff, it was Pierce who designed the rectangular shape of the head with the flat top, the protruding brow, and the electrodes on either side of the monster's neck, while Karloff removed his partial dental plate, causing part of his face to indent. Pierce used pale green greasepaint for the makeup on the monster's hands and face, as that photographed properly in black and white. Pierce's vision of the Frankenstein monster has since become the most noted representation of the character.

Trade ad for Frankenstein.

James Whale's approach to the direction of *Frankenstein* extended beyond the influence of German expressionist films. He screened *The Cabinet of Dr. Calligari*, *The Golem*, and *Metropolis* as part of preparation during preproduction on *Frankenstein*, and this style does help inform the visual brilliance of the film. Rather than use German cinematographer Karl Freund, who had shot *Dracula*, Whale hired Arthur Edeson, whose work as a cameraman dated back to the early narrative cinema of 1914. Edeson was American born but quickly became one of the most innovative cameramen in film. He expanded German expressionism to feature a greater sense of realism. He came up with the idea of camouflaging microphones in exterior shots, resulting in the film *In Old Arizona* (1929), the first talkie to be shot outside of a soundstage. His experiments with special effects for *The Lost World* (1925) continue to be the blueprint for what has been done since.

The film opens with actor Edward Van Sloane coming out and addressing the audience:

How do you do? Mr. Carl Laemmle feels it would be a little unkind to present this picture without just a friendly word of warning: We are about to unfold the story of Frankenstein, a man of science who sought to create a man after his own image without reckoning upon God. It is one of the strangest tales ever told. It deals with the two great mysteries of creation; life and death. I think it will thrill you. It may shock you. It might even horrify you. So, if any of you feel that you do not care to subject your nerves to such a strain, now's your chance to uh, well,—we warned you!!

The picture then fades into an opening scene with Dr. Frankenstein and his hunchbacked assistant Fritz waiting for a funeral to end so that they can exhume the freshly buried corpse. Frankenstein intends to reanimate dead tissue with electrodes and reactivate the corpse's life with a new brain, which Fritz is assigned to steal from the laboratory of a local medical university. When he clumsily drops the contents containing the "normal" brain, he must then steal an "abnormal" one and bring it back to Frankenstein. The doctor's plan is to utilize the best features of various dead bodies he has accumulated and stitch together his own living being.

Dwight Frye, who had played Renfield in *Dracula*, plays Fritz here, a character who does not appear in the novel. In the play, he is a mute character, but he speaks here. It is his wide-eyed face that is the first eerie thing in *Frankenstein*. Whale pans over the dark images of funeral mourners crying over an open grave and rests on the area where Fritz and the doctor are hiding and waiting for the services to end and the burial to take place. Whale rests the camera on his subjects, keeping the action within the frame but surrounding both Fritz and the doctor with appropriate negative space as they collect dead bodies. Fritz is reluctant to climb up a hanged corpse and cut him down, but the doctor persuades him by stating the dead can't hurt anyone—a bit of ominous foreshadowing while also revealing that Frankenstein intends to make a harmless creature, not a monster.

Frankenstein's fiancée Elizabeth, his colleague Dr. Waldman, and his friend Victor are concerned about the doctor's ideas and go to the castle where he is conducting his experiments with Fritz's assistance. It is a stormy night, and Frankenstein plans to use the lightning to charge the electrodes he has inserted on either side of his creation's neck. The arrival of Elizabeth, Waldman, and Victor results in their watching Frankenstein work. While he wants to be left alone, the storm means he must at least allow them shelter.

James Whale's method of filming these scenes is visually arresting. The interior shots of the castle, built on a Universale Studios soundstage, are majestic with their high ceilings and expansive laboratory setting. Editing from close-ups of a determined, tireless Frankenstein focused on his experiment as the necessary storm rages, to medium two-shots of Fritz and Frankenstein, then back to a further shot with greater negative space framing the actors. Frankenstein is surrounded by large, imposing equipment over which he has full command. This command is to be extended to the re-creation of human life. Whale has Edeson pan the camera between sets rather than cut away, keeping the rhythm of the scene flowing.

When the visitors enter, the darkness of the laboratory area is emphasized. Even though a storm rages, the outside looks brighter than the inside as Elizabeth, Henry, and Waldman enter. Frankenstein excitedly tells them that his experiment is almost completed. Elizabeth states, "I understand, and I believe in you, but I cannot leave you tonight." However, Victor accuses Frankenstein of being crazy. Whale cuts to a chilling close-up of Frankenstein's face as he says, "Crazy am I? We'll see if I am crazy or not." While Frankenstein does not hide what he is doing, when Waldman approaches the covered corpse that is planned for reanimation, he is told by both Fritz and Frankenstein to get away from their work. "That body is not dead," Frankenstein said. "It has never lived. I created it from bodies I have taken from graves, from the gallows." Waldman is then allowed to inspect the body, but it is not revealed to the viewer.

Whale keeps light on the work that Frankenstein and Fritz are doing while surrounding them with darkness. We see the platform on which the body lies rise up to the roof far above. The violent lightning hits the electrodes. The body is lowered. The hand begins to move. Actor Clive received immortality for Frankenstein's ecstatic reaction, shouting, "It's alive. IT'S ALIVE!" repeatedly and with more volume and passion each time. Revealing his true nature, Frankenstein then proudly announces, "Now I know how it feels to be God."

In many subsequent stories about "mad scientists" attempting to create life, the idea is to create a monster for the creator's personal use. Frankenstein wants to achieve with science the level of a God-like creation of life. He has no intention of creating evil. He believes he has used a "perfectly good brain" until Waldman reveals that the only brain taken from the laboratory was "an abnormal brain." This version of the creation of Frankenstein's monster is the most commonly used in other adaptations, even though, again, it's vastly different from the original novel.

The film is nearly half over before we first see Frankenstein's creation. It is the brain that makes him a monster, along with his freakish appearance. Whale brilliantly makes the audience wait, and then when the creature is first shown, it is from the back. It slowly turns around to reveal its face. There is a close-up of the head and shoulders, then a deeper close-up of just the head. In the seconds that this image is on-screen, first-time moviegoers reportedly screamed and ran from the theater. Its impact remains as late as the twenty-first century.

The monster aspect of Frankenstein's creation is a misunderstanding. There is a softness in the creature's eyes, his hands outstretched to reach out to his master. When the monster is distracted by sunlight coming from high above, it reaches to the heavens, trying to grasp the light. Fritz loudly enters and torments the creature with a burning torch, which frightens him. The tiny, ugly hunchback enjoys his own level of God-like control and continues to whip and torment the creature until Frankenstein hears screams and finds his assistant hanged. The monster is now out of control.

In another iconic scene, the escaped monster happens to spot a little girl throwing flowers into a pond and watching them float. Her innocence makes her unafraid of the monster despite his appearance. He approaches her gently, allows her to take his hand, and delights in the activity of throwing the flowers. When they run out of flowers, the monster throws the little girl in the water, expecting her to float. She does not, so he wanders off. This characterizes him as evil despite his not having that intention. In contrast to the scenes in the laboratory, this scene is shot in bright sunlight.

While the scene with the little girl ends with her horrific death, it begins very peacefully, and the monster exhibits a certain pathos in his response to the child and the activity. The creature audibly moans in delight when throwing the flowers. His confusion when the child does not float, slapping the water as if it would help her rise up, all present a confused creature whose mental abnormality results in unwitting reactions that cause harm. He is forced to comprehend mortality and quickly escapes the situation.

The monster's sympathetic side is one of the reasons why this film so successful. It's obvious to the audience that he doesn't mean to be bad, but the characters in the movie see only a hideous creature and instantly judge him on his appearance. Rather than merely being a monster who goes around hurting people, everything Frankenstein's monster does is either out of confusion or accidental, giving an added layer of depth and tragedy to the character.

In another particularly striking image, we see the little girl's father walking through town with her drowned corpse in his arms. His face is ashen, stunned as he walks robotically through a gaggle of celebrants for Frankenstein's wedding to Elizabeth. Musicians, dancers, and other partygoers each stop what they are doing as he walks past with the child's wet, limp body in his arms. It remains another of the film's most impactful images.

The film climaxes with townspeople chasing the creature for killing the child. The monster scoops up Frankenstein and carries him to an abandoned windmill, pursued by the villagers. Once in the castle, he attacks his master, who struggles free and plummets to the ground but survives. The windmill is set on fire, and the monster is destroyed. Whale cuts quickly between medium shots of the villagers setting fire to the structure, long shots of the burning, and shots of a screaming monster trying to escape the rising flames. The creature is caught in the floorboards and burns with the windmill. The film shows Frankenstein lying in bed recovering, Elizabeth at his side, realizing his power got away from his control.

This was not the first screen version of Mary Shelley's novel. There is one infamous effort that dates back to 1910, made by the Edison company. It was considered lost until a print was revealed in the 1970s to be in the collection of Milwaukee, Wisconsin, film collector Alois Dettlaff. He had a safety print made from the fading nitrate and issued a DVD release of 1,000 copies. Other screen versions of the story include *Life without a Soul* (1915) and *The Italian Master of Frankenstein* (1920), but neither was nearly as significant as this 1931 Universal feature.

Jack Pierce's groundbreaking vision as makeup artist was quite a chore for actor Karloff. It took hours to apply each day and included 30-pound boots and steel struts on the actor's legs to help create his walk. Karloff was said to have lost 20 pounds during the six-week shoot. He found the scene where the monster carries Frankenstein to be especially difficult, and a sympathetic Colin Clive suggested they use a dummy. However, director Whale insisted on authenticity, and Karloff did many takes carrying Clive and would years later state that he suffered back problems for the rest of his

Karloff and Marilyn Harris.

life as a result. And for all his hard work, Boris Karloff does not ever receive screen credit in the opening of the film. He is billed simply as a question mark in an attempt to maintain an air of mystery surrounding the monster. He is named in the closing credits.

Along with Karloff's performance, Colin Clive's Dr. Frankenstein also set the bar not only for future interpretations of that specific character but also for the mad scientist type in general. Clive's combinations of madness and euphoria, of pensive reflection and determined activity, all blend to create a complex and fascinating character.

The special effects utilized during the scene where Frankenstein re-animates the monster were created by Kenneth Strickfaden. Because they were so successful, these effects were used in every other Universal film that featured the Frankenstein monster. Some studies claim that Strick-faden used an actual Tesla coil built by Tesla himself.

When discussing this movie in later years, Karloff would often point to the scene between the monster and the little girl as his favorite sequence, and it remains an iconic scene in American cinema. Marilyn Harris, who played the child, told Richard Lamparski that she never feared the monster while shooting the movie and that Boris Karloff was very kind to her, stating, "He had such warmth and gentleness about him."[2] She recalled for author Gregory William Mank,

I first saw Boris Karloff on the Universal lot before we got in our limos to go on location to the lake. Nobody wanted to ride in the car with "the Monster" so I went over and took his hand. "I'll ride with you," I said. Boris Karloff was a very sweet, wonderful man and I just loved him. We seemed to have a rapport together, and it was like magic.[3]

Marilyn also stated,

James Whale was very very sweet, very nice. I never saw the script, he just told me what the scene was about and what my lines were. They had rowboats in a semi-circle outside of camera range in case I got caught in the undergrowth in the water, so I was fully protected.

The actress was drawn to Karloff's and Whale's kindness because her mother was emotionally and physically abusive. Harris told Mank,

I would go on an interview for a part, and if I didn't get it, I'd get a beating. When my baby teeth fell out, I got beaten for that because I couldn't work until the teeth came back. It was a very horrid childhood.

She also recalled for Lamparski that she was unsettled about doing a retake where the monster throws her into the water, so James Whale told her that if she would do a second take, he would give her anything she wanted. She asked for one dozen hard-boiled eggs, which was her favorite snack:

Actually, he gave me two dozen. My mother was furious I hadn't asked for something like a bicycle. I loved hard boiled eggs and at home I was only allowed one. She always had me on a diet.

The scene of the monster throwing the child into the water caused screams and gasps from first-time audiences. Some contemporary theater reports indicated grown men were audibly weeping.

Frankenstein was made for $250,000. It opened in New York City at the Mayfair Theater on December 4, 1931, and grossed $53,000 in one week. It ended up making a total of $12 million, which would be the equivalent of over $170 million in 2016. And as impressed as the critics were with *Dracula*, Mordaunt Hall of the *New York Times* stated, "*Dracula* is tame" by comparison.[4] In Canada, however, the film was met with some resistance by a censorship board, and in order to avoid cutting the film, the studio offered this disclaimer:

The story of Frankenstein is pure fiction. It was written by the wife of the famous English poet Percy B. Shelley on a challenge from him and Lord Byron as to who would write the most fantastic tale. Like *A Trip to Mars* by Jules

Verne and other imaginative books, it delves into the physically impossible. For almost a hundred years this story has furnished entertainment for countless people, and, though no moral is intended, it might tend to show what would happen to man if he delved into something beyond his ken.[5]

Years later, when the film was re-released, the production code was in place, and thus several scenes were cut. Colin Clive's line "Now I know what it's like to be God" was replaced by noise over the sound track. The scene where the monster reaches for the little girl is where that scene ends. The actual throwing of the child into the water was removed. Unfortunately, the cuts were made on the film's original negative, so they remained well into the TV age and were not restored until the 1980s, when the missing scenes were found in the collection of the British National Archives.

Frankenstein lives on as one of the great cinematic achievements in American film as well as one of the most influential. And Universale Studios continued to realize that the horror genre was their most profitable. Plans were made for another production, this time from a story by Nina Wilcox Putnam and Richard Schayer, with no literary antecedent. Boris Karloff was again hired to play the title role. The movie was called *The Mummy*.

3

THE MUMMY

(1932)

Director: Karl Freund.
Screenplay: John Balderston. Based on a story by Nina Wilcox Putnam and
   Richard Schayer.
Cinematography: Charles Stumar. *Editing:* Milton Carruth. *Art Direction:* Willy
   Pogany.
Cast: Boris Karloff (Imhotep/Ardath Bey), Zita Johann (Helen Grosvenor/
   Princess Anck-es-en-Amon), David Manners (Frank Whemple),
   Edward Van Sloan (Professor Muller), A. S. Byron (Sir Joseph
   Whemple), Bramwell Fletcher (Norton), Noble Johnson (the Nubian),
   Kathryn Byron (Frau Miller), Leonard Mudie (Professor Pearson),
   James Carney (Pharaoh).
Released: December 22, 1932.
Running Time: 73 minutes.
Availability: DVD (Universal Home Video).

For Universal's next horror film, Junior Laemmle recalled the 1922 excava-
tion of King Tut's tomb and asked veteran short-story writer Nina Wilcox
Putnam and Universal story editor Richard Schayer to find a literary source
from which they could create a screenplay. They found no literature but did
create a nine-page treatment about Cagliostro, a 3,000-year-old magician
who remains alive by injecting himself with nitrates. Putnam developed this
into a screenplay titled *Cagliostro: The King of the Dead* about "a 3000 year
old who appears 35 and preys on the souls of beautiful women. He has the
power to create and to destroy."[1]

Junior Laemmle liked the idea but wanted the film to have a monster. He assigned John L. Balderston to rewrite Putnam's screenplay. Balderston had scored with his stage version of *Dracula* on which the Universal movie was based and wrote the story adaptation for *Frankenstein*. Balderston had also covered the Tut event for the *New York World* back when he was a reporter. It is Balderston who set the film in Egypt and named the central character Imhotep, an ancient Egyptian mummy.

Karl Freund, the German-born cinematographer on *Dracula*, was hired to direct the film, which was now titled *The Mummy*. Boris Karloff was hired for the title role, and actress Zita Johann was cast as a reincarnated princess. Jack Pierce once again designed the makeup, while the supporting cast was rounded out with the return of Edward Van Sloan and David Manners, both of whom worked with Freund on *Dracula*. Arthur Byron, a veteran stage actor from a theatrical family, was also cast in what would be only his second movie appearance, although he was already 60 years old.

The story deals with Imhotep, an ancient Egyptian priest whose mummy is found during a 1921 expedition led by Joseph Whemple. Noting that the viscera was not removed, they realize he had been mum-

Boris Karloff as the Mummy.

mified alive. Whemple's assistant goes against strict orders and reads aloud from a scroll that revives Imhotep, who frightens the assistant into madness and gets away with the scroll. The film then moves to 10 years later, and Imhotep is now living as Ardath Bey, an Egyptian scholar. He visits Whemple's son Frank and his partner Professor Pearson, who are just concluding a disappointing expedition where they netted little of any use. Bey tells them where they can find the tomb of the ancient Egyptian princess Ankh-es-en-amon. Whemple summons his father to Egypt to be there for the discovery.

Once the tomb is found, Imhotep says words over the remains and attracts the incarnate of the princess, Helen Grosvenor. She is under his spell, but her feelings clash with her current life, where she is under the care of a Dr. Muller, who works with Joseph Whemple to understand the connection between her and Ardath Bey. Muller soon realizes Bey is the incarnate of Imhotep. During a flashback sequence, we are shown that Imhotep was mummified and buried alive for attempting to resurrect his forbidden lover. He now wants to kill Helen, mummify her, and then resurrect her to be with him forever. She prays to the goddess Isis, who destroys Imhotep and allows Helen to live in the modern world.

The Mummy might have been a new screenplay with no literary source, but it was not the first motion picture to explore the idea. As far back as 1911, the Thanhouser corporation shot a one-reel film that was marketed as a novelty where, according to publicity, "the mummy pops out alive from her coffin." A few other films from the silent era also explored the same idea. But it was this film that made the greatest impact.

While both *Dracula* and, especially, *Frankenstein* had been innovative in their aesthetic presentation of an evil central character who preyed on others, *The Mummy* appears to be a cinematic pastiche of what had worked in those two movies. Freund bases his directorial decisions on what Browning or Whale had done in the previous films, and the original screenplay features many ideas that can be found in *Dracula* or *Frankenstein*.

One of the earliest scenes, as the initial plot is being introduced, features the assistant going against orders and curiously investigating what is written on the ancient scroll. Distracted by his focus on the task at hand, he does not see the mummified Imhotep slowly opening his eyes. Freund shoots this in close-up, then cutting back to the assistant as the Mummy's hand reaches into the frame and slowly drags the scroll away. The assistant screams, then dissolves into hysterical laughter as Imhotep escapes. His reaction is similar to the mad giggling of Renfield in *Dracula*.

Makeup artist Jack Pierce created the mummy makeup as he had *Dracula* and the monster in *Frankenstein*. And although Karloff's appearance in full mummy makeup is the most iconic image in the film, he appears this way only in the opening scene. For the remainder of the movie, he is the more humanlike Ardath Bey. The shot of the Mummy coming to life was the first scene Karloff shot. He reported to the set at 11 a.m. and was in the makeup chair for a full eight hours. At 7 p.m., he went to shoot his scenes, which lasted well into the early hours of the morning. It was another two hours removing the makeup after his work was done, resulting in the actor being on the set for nearly 24 full hours. In Mark Vieira's book *Hollywood Horror: From Gothic to Cosmic*, Karloff is quoted as later recalling this to be "the most trying ordeal" he'd experienced in his long film career.[2]

Karloff gives another outstanding performance here that, as he had in *Frankenstein*, creates a complex monster who is more than just a creature out for destruction. His facial expressions alone help humanize Imhotep. Karloff conveys all of the proper nuance and emotion with his usual economy of movement, and this adds layers of depth to the Imhotep character. There is a palpable tension every time the character enters any scene. His impact is forceful, while his demeanor is very measured. It really is a truly remarkable bit of acting.

Karl Freund's direction was obviously inspired by ideas from *Dracula* and *Frankenstein*, especially since Freund is said to have directed much of the former due to Tod Browning's leaving the set for long periods of time and his lack of interest stemming from Lon Chaney's death during preproduction. Freund used Hungarian cinematographer Charles Stumar, who had shot Universal's *The Hunchback of Notre Dame* (1923) and responded well to Freund's instructions. There are many close-ups of Karloff's face in order to offer a striking, unsettling image. The most effective, of course, is the initial one, in which Karloff is in full makeup. Freund begins with a long shot and cuts to a close-up. Imhotep's ability to mesmerize Helen has throwbacks to *Dracula*. As he had for Lugosi in *Dracula*, Freund uses pencil flashlights on the eyes of the Karloff close-ups to enhance the effect.

While *The Mummy* is not the landmark cinematic achievement that *Frankenstein* had been, it is still an excellent film with a strong story and great ideas. When Imhotep stops Whemple from his attempt at burning the scroll, director Freund shows him visualizing this act in a dark room, gazing in a pool of water. We see him clenching his fist, and then Freund cuts to Whemple clutching his heart and trying to maintain consciousness. The cross-cutting from each image has a most effective rhythm, building its emotional impact until Whemple succumbs to Imhotep's power. One of Imhotep's minions then retrieves the scroll and delivers it. This is later attempted on the younger Whemple, but he survives and subsequently attempts to rescue Helen, whose prayers cause Isis to destroy Imhotep.

The destruction of Imhotep is impressive with its early use of manipulating graphics: Imhotep's face devolves into a shriveled, hardened image that shatters. Along with his prowess with camera work, Freund was brilliant with special effects, and for a 1932 film, this transition is most impressive.

Freund's visuals continue to be striking throughout the film, with nicely framed long shots dollying into medium shots; complete fade-outs after every scene; effective uses of darks, lights, and grays; and the same economy of movement that had helped make *Dracula* so effective. Once again, music is used sparingly, many of the scenes benefiting from the eeriness of absolute silence. However, in the scene featuring Whemple's heart attack, background music is effectively used, building to a rising crescendo and enhancing the building tension of the scene.

Perhaps due to its having been directed by a top-level cinematographer, *The Mummy* is as visually stunning as *Dracula* or *Frankenstein* despite not being the better film. The atmosphere of this film is simultaneously creepy and beautiful, and it helps elevate the film to a more artistic level than what would eventually become the standard horror movie.

Although it had no specific literary source, there are elements of the story that can be traced to H. Rider Haggard's *She*, which contains a reincarnation love story.

Since appearing in *Frankenstein*, Boris Karloff had scored in Universal's nonmonster horror film *The Old Dark House* and successfully appeared in *The Mask of Fu Manchu* for MGM. He was slated for Universal's proposed movie version of H. G. Wells's *The Invisible Man*, but Karloff's reaction to the role and a salary dispute caused that project to be shelved in June 1932, after which the actor was cast in *The Mummy*. *The Invisible Man* would be resurrected about a year later and put back into production with Claude Rains in the title role.

The Mummy was a box office success both in the United States and abroad (it was especially popular in England). Its success resulted in Junior Laemmle continuing his interest in producing horror movies with a monster theme. The *New York Times* stated in its review,

> Mr. Karloff acts with the restraint natural to a man whose face is hidden behind synthetic wrinkles. Zita Johann and David Manners make a properly disturbed pair of lovers, and Arthur Byron has little to do but look startled as the leader of the expedition. The photography is superior to the dialogue.[3]

Even over 80 years later, the superior visuals over the dialogue is evident. This is especially emphasized by the review in the December 1932 issue of *American Cinematographer*, a magazine that examined cinema as per the visuals:

> We hope that every producer in Hollywood will see this picture, and learn what a great cinematographer can do as a director. For *The Mummy* is not like the average directorial debut: Freund exhibits a sure touch with a mastery of his medium that many a well-established director might envy. He tells his story effectively, intelligently, and artistically. Moreover, he reveals something which is all too lacking of late—especially in pictures of this type: dramatic good taste. He has not overstressed any element, either of horror or anything else, he has made the most of all the eerie, spine-chilling elements provided in the story. Both dramatically and cinematically, Freund's touch is that of a master of his art. He has guided his players in presenting deft, positive characterizations with the minimum of effort, and in the minimum of footage. His cinematic treatment could not be improved upon; there are no superfluous scenes, nor angles, nor any superfluous movement of the camera.

American Cinematographer also gave praise to Charles Stumar, the actual cinematographer on this movie:

> Charles Stumar's photography is of an equally high order, and evidences the possibilities latent in the cooperation of a great cinematographer-director and an outstanding cinematographer. *The Mummy* shows two fine artists working together with perfect understanding. Photographically, the picture is excellent; it is probably the best work that Stumar has done in some time. Many of the sequences require unusual effect lightings, which he has handled with unusual skill.

The Mummy is not as well written as *Dracula* or *Frankenstein*, and despite a good cast, David Manners as the younger Whemple and Zita Johann as Helen are the only actors who offer significant support. Byron, as the older Whemple, has little impact, and Edward Van Sloan is given the thankless role of Dr. Muller.

Other studies indicate a young Katharine Hepburn was briefly considered for the role of Helen before Zita Johann was cast. While it is interesting to speculate how an actress like Hepburn might have approached the role of Helen, Zita Johann's performance is among the best in the film. Unfortunately, Johann did not get along well with director Freund. Many of her scenes in the flashback sequence (including several examples of her various reincarnations over the centuries) were cut, which is why actor

Henry Victor is listed in the cast as a Saxon warrior but does not appear in the released film. Stills of these cut sequences and a shooting script containing them do survive.

Boris Karloff was now enjoying a lofty status as the heir apparent to Lon Chaney, something that had been considered for Bela Lugosi after *Dracula*. But while Lugosi did a nice job in Universal's *Murders in the Rue Morgue* and Paramount's *Island of Lost Souls*, the actor spent the majority of 1932 in low-budget movies for poverty-row studios. *White Zombie* and *The Death Kiss* are considered quite good today, but at the time of their release they were dismissed by critics. The budget for *White Zombie* was less than a third of the budget for *The Mummy*. Karloff's more noted appearances in *The Old Dark House* and *The Mask of Fu Manchu* resulted in greater recognition. Of course now, decades later, both Lugosi and Karloff enjoy the same iconic status as Chaney—and deservedly so.

The Mummy is a visual triumph, another excellent entry into the monster movie subgenre, and a real success for Boris Karloff as an actor. He continued to find his niche in horror and suspense movies, and his career continued to progress in this direction. As 1933 approached, Karloff returned to his native England to star in *The Ghoul*, which would be his only film that year.

Bela Lugosi would be a bit busier than Boris Karloff, appearing in everything from the serial *The Whispering Shadow* for Mascot pictures to a role in an ensemble comedy for Paramount, *The International House*, which also featured W. C. Fields, George Burns, and Gracie Allen. In 1934, Boris Karloff and Bela Lugosi would team up for Universal's *The Black Cat*, which would be the first of several nonmonster horror films the two would do together. Universal, meanwhile, would next embark on a movie version of H. G. Wells's story *The Invisible Man*, with James Whale once again directing and a newcomer to movies, Claude Rains, in the title role.

THE INVISIBLE MAN

(1933)

Director: James Whale
Screenplay: R. C. Sherriff, based on a novel by H. G. Wells.
Producer: Carl Laemmle Jr. *Cinematography:* Arthur Edeson. *Editing:* Ted J.
    Kent. *Art Direction:* Charles D. Hall. *Music:* Heinz Roemheld.
Cast: Claude Rains (Jack Griffin/the Invisible Man), Gloria Stuart (Flora
    Cranley), William Harrigan (Dr. Kemp), Henry Travers (Dr. Cranley),
    Una O'Connor (Jenny Hall), Forrester Harvey (Herbert Hall),
    Holmes Herbert (police chief), E. E. Clive (Constable Jaffers), Dudley
    Digges (detective), Harry Stubbs (Inspector Bird), Donald Stuart
    (Inspector Lane), Merle Tottenham (Millie), Robert Adair (Detective
    Thompson), Bob Reeves (Detective Hogan), Dwight Frye (reporter),
    John Carradine (informer), Walter Brennan (man with bicycle), John
    Merivale (newsboy), Mary Gordon (screaming woman), Leo White
    (man calling for the police) Tom Ricketts (farmer), Kathryn Sheldon
    (orphanage worker), Paul Kruger and Jack Montgomery (constables),
    Tiny Jones (woman in pub).
Released: November 13, 1933.
Running Time: 71 minutes.
Availability: DVD (Universal Home Video).

After the success of *Dracula* and *Frankenstein*, Junior Laemmle wanted to mine literature once again and produce a film version of H. G. Wells's novel *The Invisible Man*. Wells, living at the time, was intrigued with the idea of Universal filming his 1897 novel and supported the project. It was to star Boris Karloff in the title role and be directed by Cyril Gardner.

Production was to begin in the summer of 1932, but a series of difficulties disrupted these plans. There were several rewrites of the script, none of them developing into something the producer found satisfactory. Preston Sturges was one of the writers involved with these early treatments, as was Phillip Wylie. In the end, only R. C. Sherriff was credited for the screenplay. Sherriff had come to America from England to write this screenplay, but when he arrived at the studio, he found there was no copy of the Wells novel he was adapting. He had to buy one himself at a bookstore.

The biggest blow to the production was when Boris Karloff left the project due to Junior Laemmle's repeated attempts to reduce his contracted salary (some sources claim it was Karloff's reluctance to play a role where he is covered up and only his voice is heard). Karloff was placed into *The Mummy*, and plans to film *The Invisible Man* were shelved in June 1932.

When the project was reactivated a year later, James Whale was hired to direct. Whale wanted actor Claude Rains in the title role. Whale knew the British-born Rains as one of the finest actors on the London stage, but other than a small part in the silent *Build Thy House* (1920), he had made no movies. Rains was also a noted acting teacher, instructing such students as John Gielgud and Lawrence Olivier. Claude Rains had a very unique approach to teaching diction. For example, if a student had a problem with stuttering, Rains had him or her sing the lines, even in their conversations. An offbeat idea but reportedly an effective one.

Junior Laemmle did not want to hire Rains for the title role in his next horror production, fearing an actor unknown to American moviegoers would hamper box office success. Whale then suggested Colin Clive, who had scored in *Frankenstein*. Junior Laemmle agreed and didn't realize this was a ploy on Whale's part. Clive was set to do a film in his native England but agreed to postpone that production if his friend James Whale needed him for this one. Whale explained wanting Rains and encouraged Clive to take the role in England, which he did. Laemmle finally agreed to use Rains for the role.

Ironically, the stage-trained Rains looked like a bad idea at first. He failed his first screen test miserably. He would often recall in his later years how bad it was. Whale still hired him, mostly because of his distinctive voice, which was important for a role in a movie such as this. In order to prepare for the role, Whale assigned Rains to watch as many Hollywood movies as he could prior to shooting. Once production commenced, Claude Rains was ready to tackle the role.

Claude Rains as the Invisible Man.

The plot of the film deals with a stranger whose face is wrapped in cloth arriving at an inn on a snowy night. Dark goggles hide his eyes. He asks for a room and demands complete privacy. However, when he is behind on his rent and also acting erratically and mixing chemicals in his room, the proprietors ask him to leave. He responds by shoving one of the proprietors down the stairs. When a police constable and several villagers come to help, he frightens them away by removing his clothing and revealing his invisibility. This allows him to escape.

The opening scenes, while scary in some ways, are also very comical. Unlike the previous monster films, this one opens with the central character entering among the lower classes, whose cockney accents and fluttery gestures offer a comic element to the proceedings. Forrester Harvey and Una O'Connor are the proprietors who are both intrigued and unsettled by the mysterious stranger, as are the patrons in their pub. O'Connor reacts in an over-the-top comical manner to the Invisible Man's actions, screaming and carrying on with reckless abandon. Once invisible, the man moves about the cop and the villagers in his room, pushing them down, throwing things in their way, and bopping them in the head. Once outside, he throws the hat of a man into a pond, steals a bicycle and rides it a few yards, and breaks windows. The entire time, he laughs maniacally, offering both a creepy and a playful accent to his activities.

The viewer is, at this point, unaware of who this man is. This backstory is revealed in the next scene. But during the opening sequences, there are cutaways to scenes involving a Dr. Cranley, who is presented as having been the man's employer and whose daughter, Flora, is the man's fiancée. The scenes involving the doctor are more serious, attempting to scientifically explain that the man might have been experimenting with a very dangerous chemical called monocane. Giving scientific reasoning for the proceedings helps anchor the film and does not allow the comical sequences to shift the attitude of the film.

By now, the film reveals that the invisible man is Dr. Jack Griffin, who has indeed used the dangerous monocane, which has allowed him to make himself invisible. His problem is the inability to find his way back. In order to maintain some level of sanity as this condition causes him to slowly descend into madness, he engages in seemingly playful activities that come off as comical but conclude with violence.

Griffin finds his way to the home of his other colleague, Dr. Kemp, who is forced to drive to the inn so that Griffin can retrieve his notebooks. He comes on a meeting with police and villagers and disrupts it by spraying the chief with ink and throwing debris at the frightened villagers. But it also suddenly gets serious when the scene concludes with murder. Once back in Kemp's car, the invisible man explains, "I killed a stupid little policeman, smashed his head in."

A desperate Kemp phones Cranley, seeking his help, but Cranley will not come until morning. Cranley promises his daughter they will work to help Griffin return to visibility but will not let his daughter see him until he is well ("right now he is mad"). Kemp, still desperate, calls the police and tells them the invisible man is in his home.

But it is Cranley who shows up, with Flora. Griffin is pleasant with Flora, and when the police do arrive, he is protective of her. Angered, he tells Kemp he plans to kill him the next night "even if you hide in the darkest cave on earth." Griffin then goes on a murderous spree, alternating between playful mischief (clad only in visible pants, he skips after a fleeing, screaming woman as he sings "here we go gathering nuts in May") to real terror (he causes the crash of a train, killing all on board). The police offer a £2,000 reward for his capture.

A decision is made by the detective in charge of capturing Griffin. He plans to use Griffin's threat to Dr. Kemp as a means of capturing him. Kemp is dressed in a police uniform and drives his car away from his house. However, the invisible Griffin is present as Kemp puts on his disguise and stows away in the car's backseat. He ties Kemp up, puts him in the vehicle, takes it out of gear, and allows it to coast over a cliff and crash into an explosive blaze.

It is when Griffin seeks shelter from the cold in a barn that he is identified and eventually captured. A farmer walks into his barn, hears snoring, and sees movement in the hay with which Griffin covered himself for warmth. The farmer alerts police, who burn down the barn, forcing the invisible Griffin out into the snow. His footprints in the snow reveal his location, and he is shot. As he dies in the hospital, he says good-bye to Flora. As he fades into death, his invisible fades to visibility, and the film fades out to conclude.

The Invisible Man is noted for being closer to the original source novel than either *Dracula* or *Frankenstein* had been. This is essentially true, but there are some key differences. The book is set in the nineteenth century, while the movie is set in then contemporary times. In the novel, Griffin is a mysterious loner, with no friends and certainly no fiancée. He is already insane when he becomes invisible, and he does not descend into madness as a result of it. And Dr. Kemp survives in the novel, his life saved by those who kill Griffin. However, overall, these are trifling quibbles, and the movie was close enough to the original book that it pleased its author.

James Whale's direction once again takes advantage of the set design with expansive long shots of the doctor's palatial home while also using close-ups to rest on Griffin's revealing himself as invisible under his various wrappings. He does an excellent job with camera placement, using lower-angle shots to exhibit authority, higher-angle shots to present victimization, and some artful overhead and dolly shots that keep the narrative brisk and aesthetically satisfying. He once again benefits from Arthur Edeson's cinematography, as he had with *Frankenstein*.

But the real star of *The Invisible Man* is the special effects team of John P. Fulton, John J. Mescall, and Frank D. Williams. They used wires when items were moved by the fully invisible Griffin. However, when he was partially clothed or disrobing, Claude Rains was shot in a black velvet suit against a black velvet background. This shot was combined with another shot of the area of the set where the scene took place. By using a complex matte process that combined images and controlled the areas being exposed, the effect was successful.

The Invisible Man follows essentially the same format as *Frankenstein*, with a man defying conventional science with his experiments and daring to flirt with ideas with the potential for danger and a monster being created and causing destruction and eventually being destroyed. This formula would soon settle into a niche for nearly all subsequent monster movie narratives.

With all its entertainment value and aesthetic significance, there are several aspects of *The Invisible Man* that have caused viewers to have misgivings. Perhaps the most noted one is at the conclusion, when Griffin comes out of the barn and his footprints in the snow are not of bare feet. They are shaped as if he is wearing shoes. Some studies claim that even when this pre-code movie was made, bare feet would give the illusion of nudity too forcefully. Also, the naked Invisible Man is cavorting in the cold winter climate for some time, killing Kemp and playfully scaring the villagers. Wouldn't these cold conditions affect him more completely? It has been argued that his invisibility would deaden much of the cold effect, while other arguments insist he should not feel cold at all, just as he would not cast a shadow. The elements go through him. There is something absurd about discussing logical elements to a sci-fi movie about a man becoming invisible, but these have been part of the discussion about this movie since its initial release.

Claude Rains offers a brilliant performance despite being limited by not being seen. Even the shots of a heavily wrapped Griffin were sometimes a double (who was shorter than the actor) because Rains was claustrophobic. Still, with his distinctive voice, he was able to convey shrill madness (his maniacal laughter) and deadly threats (his voice deepens to a terrifying growl whenever he makes threats). The character is very complex, fluctuating from vulnerable pleading when he is about to be thrown out of his room at the inn to remorseless destruction as he kills for the mere sake of acting out. As he lies dying, his body revealed to viewers for the first time, he admits, "I meddled in things that man must leave alone."

There are several noted actors supporting Rains, including the comical histrionics of Una O'Connor, whose performance is said to have particularly pleased H. G. Wells. Henry Travers, noted for playing Clarence the angel in *It's a Wonderful Life*, is Dr. Cranley, while his daughter Flora is portrayed by Gloria Stuart, whose performance in *Titanic* (1997) was nominated for an Oscar 65 years later. She lived to be 100 years old. Dwight Frye enjoys an offbeat role as an ordinary reporter, while future Oscar winner Walter Brennan has a small part as the man whose bicycle is stolen by Griffin.

The Invisible Man was shot for $328,000 and made a substantial profit, as it was the studio's most successful horror film since *Frankenstein*. In the trade magazine *Motion Picture Herald*, there is a section called "What the Motion Picture Did for Me" in which exhibitors report on how films went over in their theaters. Comments on *The Invisible Man* included the following:

There is comedy and suspense and it keeps your audience entertained every minute. One of the most different pictures ever made. It will please and make them wonder.

Critics agreed, with Mordaunt Hall of the *New York Times* indicating on November 18, 1933, that

this eerie tale evidently afforded a Roman holiday for the camera aces. Photographic magic abounds in the production, the work being even more startling than was that of Douglas Fairbanks's old picture "The Thief of Bagdad." The story makes such superb cinematic material that one wonders that Hollywood did not film it sooner. Now that it has been done, it is a remarkable achievement. Although various incidents may be spine-chilling, it is a subject with a quota of well-turned comedy.

The combination of thrills and laughs was effective and would later help to inform movies in which comedy became a more significant factor—not only the Abbott and Costello movies but also later sequels to this film, especially *The Invisible Woman* (1940), which boasts a cast of actors ranging from John Barrymore to Shemp Howard. One of the main reasons *The Invisible Man* holds up well today is because of its humorous element, which helps to offset the truly creepy or the scientifically serious aspect of the story.

The success of *The Invisible Man* caused the horror productions to continue at Universale Studios, but there were no monster movies in all of 1934. Their horror movie offering was *The Black Cat* starring Boris Karloff and costarring, for the first time, Bela Lugosi. They would subsequently work together in several more movies.

However, the following year, Universal decided to film the portion of Mary Shelley's novel *Frankenstein* that was left out of their initial movie version. Boris Karloff, Dwight Frye, Colin Clive, and Una O'Connor were among those hired to be in the cast. James Whale was slated as director from another script adaptation cowritten by John Balderston. Junior Laemmle stated that he wanted them to produce a film that surpassed even its predecessor. They did.

THE BRIDE OF FRANKENSTEIN

(1935)

Director: James Whale.
Screenplay: John L. Balderston, William Hurlbut.
Producers: Carl Laemmle Jr., James Whale. *Cinematography:* John Mescall. *Film Editing:* Ted Kent. *Art Direction:* Charles D. Hall. *Music:* Franz Waxman.
Cast: Boris Karloff (the monster), Colin Clive (Dr. Henry Frankenstein), Valerie Hobson (Elizabeth Frankenstein), Elsa Lanchester (Mary Shelley/the monster's mate), Ernest Thesiger (Dr. Pretorius), Dwight Frye (Karl), Gavin Gordon (Lord Byron), Douglas Walton (Percy Bysshe Shelley), Una O'Connor (Minnie), E. E. Clive (burgomaster), Lucien Prival (Butler), Reginald Barlow (Hans), Mary Gordon (Hans's wife), O. P. Heggie (blind hermit), J. Gunnis Davis (Uncle Glutz), Sarah Schwartz (Marta), Tempe Pigott (Auntie Glotz), Neil Fitzgerald (Eddie), Dwight Frye (Karl), Joan Woodbury (queen), Peter Shaw (devil), Pop Byron (king), Kansas DeForrest (ballerina), Maurice Black (Gypsy), Elspeth Dudgeon (Gypsy's mother), Helen Jerome Eddy (Gypsy's wife), Josephine McKim (mermaid), John Carradine (hunter at cottage), Walter Brennan, Mary Stewart (neighbors), Marilyn Harris (little girl), Brenda Fowler (mother), Billy Barty (baby), Frank Benson, Mae Bruce, Grace Cunard, John George, Helen Gibson, Edward Peil Sr., Anders Van Haden (villagers).
Released: April 19, 1935.
Running Time: 75 minutes.
Availability: DVD (Universal Home Video).

Universal wanted to film the rest of Mary Shelley's book, as *Bride of Fran-kenstein*, as early as 1932 due to the immense popularity of *Frankenstein*. There were a number of script problems that caused a series of delays. Robert Florey wrote a treatment that was rejected. Tom Reed offered a treatment that was accepted and then a full screenplay. James Whale did not like this script, nor did he accept one offered by L. G. Blochman and Philip MacDonald. Whale then assigned John L. Balderston, who had worked on the previous film. Balderston recalled that the Shelley novel fea-tured Dr. Frankenstein creating a mate for his monster but never bringing it to life. Whale liked Balderston's ideas better but was still not completely satisfied. The addition of William J. Hurlbut and Edward Pearson to alter Balderston's screenplay resulted in the final script that was eventually used.

In January 1935, the studio was ready to film a sequel. The production code had been passed in 1934, limiting a lot of the creative freedoms the earlier film enjoyed, but the film turned out to be even greater than its brilliant predecessor.

Boris Karloff was back as the Frankenstein monster, this time billed before the title but only by his last name. His status had grown to where his last name was all that was necessary. His mate was billed by a ques-

Boris Karloff and Elsa Lanchester in *Bride of Frankenstein*.

tion mark (but received billing for her alternate role as Mary Shelley in the film's prologue). James Whale was not interested in directing but was eventually persuaded to do so. He agreed to take the job only if he was given full creative control. Junior Laemmle did not want Colin Clive to repeat his role as Dr. Frankenstein. Clive had developed an alcohol problem in the past few years and had been deemed unreliable by the studio. Whale, however, insisted on Clive for the role. Mae Clarke could not return as Elizabeth due to illness (although not a serious one, as she would live another 57 years), so 17-year-old Valerie Hobson was hired for the role. The cast was dotted with such familiar faces as Dwight Frye as yet another assistant (this time to Pretorius) and a cameo by Marilyn Harris, the ill-fated Little Maria in *Frankenstein*.

Unlike a spoken prologue as presented in *Frankenstein*, the opening scene in *The Bride of Frankenstein* features Elsa Lanchester portraying Mary Shelley, who, after being praised for her story by her husband and Lord Byron, chooses to tell them "the rest of the story." The scene then fades to where the movie *Frankenstein* ended and takes up from where that story left off. While Edward Van Sloan's cryptic warnings in the *Frankenstein* prologue set the tone, the opening skit in *The Bride of Frankenstein* introduces the origin of its creative process.

Director James Whale then offers an establishing shot showing the burned windmill where the villagers are cheering the alleged demise of the monster while mourning the apparent death of Dr. Frankenstein from the injuries he sustained at the hands of his creation. The father of little Maria, who drowned when the monster threw her into a pond, wants to actually see the creature's burnt remains. He enters the ruins and falls into a flooded pit where the monster, who has survived, strangles him. His wife, who went in after him, is thrown into the pit of water by the monster, and she drowns as her daughter had.

At this point, we realize the monster has now evolved from confused and well meaning, whose violence was accidental, into an angry and dangerous creature. This was initially evident at the end of *Frankenstein* when the monster turned on Dr. Frankenstein in a frustrated and angry response to being chased by villagers with burning torches. When in *Frankenstein* the monster threw little Maria into the water, he expected her to float like the flowers had. When he did the same to her mother in this movie, it was deliberate. When the monster emerges from the ruins, he is first seen by Minnie, an elderly villager, who shrieks and flees (the part is played by Una O'Connor, who notably offered noisy comedy relief in *The Invisible Man*). She yells throughout the village that the monster has survived and is at large, but she is ignored. Meanwhile, the monster has indeed moved on and is roaming the village.

Dr. Frankenstein's body is returned to his fiancée Elizabeth, who discovers he is, in fact, alive. She nurses him back to health, and while Frankenstein realizes his creation was a failure in that it turned out to be dangerous and deadly, he still plans to continue investigating the secrets of life and immortality. He is visited by his mentor, Dr. Pretorius, who shows Frankenstein several miniature people he has created (a king, a queen, an archbishop, a ballerina, a mermaid, and a devil). Pretorius wants to team up with Frankenstein and create a female creature as a mate for the monster. Henry refuses, believing he needs further study before again investigating this process.

Meanwhile, the monster is caught, chained to an ersatz crucifix, but when he is left alone, his strength allows him to escape. The film then focuses on the monster's exploits, showing that despite his bitterness at how he's been treated by the villagers, there remains an inherent goodness. He sees an innocent maiden drowning and saves her. However, her screams alert nearby hunters who spy the monster and shoot at him, forcing him to run away.

The act of drowning appears to be a common theme and is used as a way to determine the complexity of the monster. With little Maria in the previous movie, the monster is confused and innocent despite the tragedy. With her mother, he is angry and deliberate. With this maiden, his role is changed to protector and rescuer, perhaps the Maria incident having allowed him to realize the danger of humans in bodies of water. The scene where the monster saves the woman is a key moment that shows how he is evolving and tapping more deeply into his inherent human characteristics. He learned from his mistake the first time around and applies his new knowledge to this situation.

It is also important to note the monster's appearance in this movie. Makeup expert Jack Pierce decided to show the effects of the fire on the monster. His hair has been singed, and there is less of it. There are burns on his face. As the film progresses, Pierce shows the hair slowly growing back and the burns gradually healing into scars. This visual progression is subtle but adds greater nuance to the character.

The film continues to stay with the monster as he disrupts a Gypsy camp. Hungry, he reaches for the meat that had been cooking over the campfire but burns his hand, furthering his frightened response to fire and adding to the wounds on his body. In pain, he is distracted by the sound of a violin and follows it to the cabin of a blind hermit. It is at this point that the film more deeply explores the creature and adds far more depth to the character.

The concept of the monster's ability to learn is already being investigated at this point. He learns that people can be evil and try to hurt him. He realizes fire hurts. He realizes water kills these people. And he appears to be able to discern the innocent (the Gypsy girl drowning in the water) from the dangerous (Maria's father coming into the ruins). However, on arriving at the cabin where the blind hermit lives, the cautious, growling creature is as soothed by the hermit's gentle voice as he had been by his violin's music. He is led into the cabin, offered food and drink, and patiently taught how fire can be good and can be used for positive things like cooking the food we eat.

The scene fades into a few weeks later, showing that the monster has sought comfortable refuge in the cabin of the blind man, who has helped heal his burn wounds, fed him, given him drink, and entertained him with his violin. He has also taught him manners and how to communicate verbally. Studies have indicated that director Whale and the screenwriters studied the vocabulary of 10-year-old children to determine how many words the monster would use as his ability to speak increased. The monster can identify food, drink, good, and bad and responds with his limited vocabulary well enough to where the blind man is able to hold some semblance of a conversation with him. The creature is happy and no longer dangerous. He has relaxed.

The scenes between the monster and the hermit have a real poignancy but also effectively explore areas of the creature's potential, making Dr. Frankenstein's concept and execution even more impressive. These scenes show the monster capable of settling into a domestic existence with the hermit and never venturing far from his secluded cabin, remaining safe from the dangers he'd encountered. All of this is disrupted when two hunters arrive at the cabin to ask for directions, see the monster, and start shooting at it. The monster flees, the cabin is set on fire, and the hunters lead the blind hermit away. The monster is again alone but now with the ability to verbally communicate and to more accurately understand his surroundings.

Meanwhile, Henry Frankenstein has married Elizabeth and expresses no interest in creating another creature, while Pretorius has insisted they do so and continues with preparations, hiring two ex-convicts to help him steal a body from its crypt. Pretorius is alone in the crypt when he is approached by the monster, who lurks there. The monster sees that Pretorius is not intimidated; admits, when asked, that he does realize who Frankenstein is; and states, "I love dead. Hate the living." His experiences have caused him to conclude that even a nice situation like he had with the blind man will end badly in the world of the living. However, the monster is intrigued when told of plans to create a woman friend for him. He agrees to kidnap Elizabeth but not harm her in order to force Frankenstein to agree to the experiment.

There are two particularly impressive scenes here. The first is when Pretorius confronts Frankenstein with the monster, who communicates verbally with his creator, insisting he make him a mate. The monster does not address Frankenstein as "master." He does not perceive him as rescuing him from death but holds some contempt toward the doctor for stealing him from that level of peace and into a life of turmoil.

The other scene involves Frankenstein actually working on the project once being forced to agree to do so. Once assured Elizabeth is safe and would be safely returned on completion of the experiment, Frankenstein loses himself in his work. He is now focused, determined, and every bit as engaged as he had been with the creation of the monster. When success is achieved, he again yells an ecstatic, "It's alive!" Pretorius proclaims, "The bride of Frankenstein!"

The complexity and depth of the monster is explored once more as the bandages are removed from this new creation and a woman emerges. She glances around quickly. She sees the monster approach her, smiling and gently holding out his hands. She screams. A released Elizabeth comes to the laboratory, banging on the door, and is let in. She rushes to Frankenstein as the monster tries once again to engage with his new mate. She continues to respond with fear. "She hate me," the monster sadly states, "she hate me like all the others." He then grabs a lever that he realizes will blow up the lab and destroy everyone. He orders Frankenstein and Elizabeth to flee to safety but insists Pretorius stay. "We belong dead," he says, as he pulls the level and the explosion destroys the laboratory and tower.

Boris Karloff objected to the idea of the monster speaking, even though in Shelley's book he becomes quite articulate, while in the films he is limited to the vocabulary of a 10-year-old. Karloff felt that the creature was more effective conveying his emotion with nonverbal communication. However, one of the reasons *The Bride of Frankenstein* is such a superior film is that it allows the monster to progress, bringing out the inherent human qualities that were within him. The blind man, who cannot see that he is a frightening creature, merely responds to his grunts and growls as if he were a mute. The hermit bonds with one who he believes is also afflicted. His desire for company teaches the monster the word "friend" before any other word. Karloff felt the concept of the monster speaking destroyed the character. In fact, his performance as the monster struggling to articulate is among the finest of his career. It was also the most grueling, even more so than *Frankenstein* had been. Karloff had to wear a rubber suit under his already cumbersome monster costume when shooting scenes in the cold water of the windmill ruins. Air got into the suit and expanded as he entered the water on the very first day of filming. Also during the production, he fell and broke his hip.

Karloff wasn't the only actor who was injured. Colin Clive broke his leg in an accident before shooting began, which is why he is seated or bedridden during some of the earlier scenes.

Some sources claim Claude Rains was originally slated to play Pretorius, but by the time filming was ready to begin, he had committed to another project. Other sources indicate Bela Lugosi was considered. Still others insist that nobody other than Ernest Thesiger, who had worked with James Whale on the British stage, was sought for the role. Thesiger truly makes the character his own, alternating between evil stares and wicked cackling that made the character truly dark and frightening but never to the point where his support of the leading players overshadowed them.

The score by Franz Waxman replaces the largely silent sound track of the earlier *Frankenstein*. Whale had met Waxman at a party and hired him to score the film. Waxman created themes for the monster, the bride, and Pretorius. The score was conducted by Constantin Bakaleinikoff, who recorded it during a nine-hour session with 22 musicians.

Kenneth Strickfaden was again hired to create the laboratory equipment, using many of the ideas that were so successful in *Frankenstein*. John P. Fulton and David S. Horsely were responsible for the effects used to create the miniature characters collected in jars, used to introduce Pretorius's experiments with creating life. This scene is another example of how innovative, groundbreaking visual effects had been something of a constant in Universal monster movies even when considering the technology available as early as the 1930s.

Filming began on January 2, 1935, but went 10 days beyond its scheduled 36-day production schedule because Whale shut down the film for as many days until actor O. P. Heggie was available to play the blind hermit. The 58-year-old Heggie was a longtime stage actor in his native Australia and came to Hollywood during the silent era. *Bride of Frankenstein* was among his most notable roles, as was his performance in John Ford's *The Prisoner of Shark Island*, which was released only weeks after his death in February 1936.

Whale originally had produced an ending where Dr. Frankenstein is killed while fleeing the explosion but went back and filmed a successful escape. However, if you look closely, you can see Clive in the lab as the castle is collapsing.

The Bride of Frankenstein went $100,000 over budget but was still a moneymaker and was well received by critics. *Variety* stated,

> [It is] one of those rare instances where none can review it, or talk about it, without mentioning the cameraman, art director, and score composer in the same breath as the actors and director.

Variety also praised the cast, writing that

> Karloff manages to invest the character with some subtleties of emotion that are surprisingly real and touching. . . . Thesiger as Dr Pretorious [is] a diabolic characterization if ever there was one. . . . Lanchester handles two assignments, being first in a preamble as author Mary Shelley and then the created woman. In latter assignment she impresses quite highly.[1]

Audiences responded favorably as well. In the *Motion Picture Herald*'s section "What the Picture Did for Me," where theater owners wrote in to indicate how films went over in their establishments, an exhibitor from Idaho offered some effective ideas for promotional activities:

> We made a lot of money with this picture. In fact, I think it now holds the box office record for Friday and Saturday this year. It has some wonderful opportunities to make money and we took advantage of them and made a cleanup. Everyone within a hundred miles were talking about the picture. We started advertising about three weeks in advance of the show and when we opened on Friday night the house was filled in 15 minutes. Large crowds were standing in line for the second show which was the first sellout I have had in months. The picture itself is good and enjoyed by the large crowd.

There was a problem with the censors. Since making *Frankenstein* three years earlier, Hollywood movies had now came under a production code in which there were tighter restrictions on movie content. The Hays office, which oversaw each production, objected to any comparisons Frankenstein might make between himself and God, wanted the number of murders in the film reduced, and felt the dress Elsa Lanchester wore in her scenes as Mary Shelley showed too much of her breasts. Even after the film was approved, there were other countries that objected to various scenes. Swedish censors insisted on so many edits that Universale Studios withdrew the film from release in that country.

Elsa Lanchester's staid, attractive appearance in the prologue makes her later role as the new female creature at the conclusion of the movie even more jarring. While the characters are completely unrelated in the narrative, Lanchester's performance as Frankenstein's new creation appears crazed and jittery and communicates with hisses and screams. Her reaction to the monster—and the tears in his eyes in response—is one of the more emotionally stirring scenes in the horror genre. While the mate appears for only a few minutes at the end of this movie, her impact has resulted in an enduring legacy.

As popular and acclaimed *The Bride of Frankenstein* was during its own time, its reputation grew continually from the 1950s on. Magazines like *Famous Monsters of Filmland*, celebrating the Universal horror genre, always singled it out as the studio's masterpiece. This movie feels like a culmination of all the elements Whale explored in his previous horror films. *Frankenstein* had been a very serious tale. This movie is also very serious and creepy at times (due in large part to the outstanding cinematography that makes it all the more moody), but it also employs some of the dark humor Whale used in *The Invisible Man*. Not that *The Bride of Frankenstein* is funny, but it does offer scenes containing an underlying wit that adds another dimension.

The Bride of Frankenstein always finds a place in the various top 100 movies lists found in various magazines, having been voted in by myriad critics. The movie was added to the National Film Registry as being "culturally, historically or aesthetically significant" in 1998.

For its next monster movie, Universal chose to explore the story of the werewolf. This next movie could be considered something of a dry run, as a better film regarding the same character would be produced years later. But although the studio would enjoy greater success with this character a few years later in *The Wolf Man*, the studio's next effort and the first featuring this monster was *Werewolf of London*.

6

WEREWOLF OF LONDON

(1935)

Director: Stuart Walker.
Screenplay: John Colton, based on a story by Robert Harris, adapted by
   Harris, Harvey Gates, and Edmund Pearson.
Cinematography: Charles Stumar. *Editing:* Russell Schoengarth, Milton
   Carruth. *Art Direction:* Albert D'Agostino. *Music:* Karl Hajos.
Cast: Henry Hull (Glendon), Warner Oland (Yogami), Valerie Hobson (Lisa),
   Lester Matthews (Paul Ames), Lawrence Grant (Forsythe), Spring
   Byington (Ettie Coombes), Clark Williams (Renwick), J. M. Kerrigan
   (Hawkins), Charlotte Granville (Lady Forsythe), Ethel Griffies (Mrs.
   Whack), Zeffie Tilbury (Mrs. Moncaster), Jeanne Barlett (Daisy),
   Reginald Barlow (Timothy), Herbert Evans (detective), Jefferey Hassel
   (Alf), Maude Leslie (Mrs. Charteris), Joseph North (Plimpton), Harry
   Stubbs (Jenkins), Helena Grant (mother), Noel Kennedy (boy), Beal
   Wong, Wong Chung (coolies).
Released: May 13, 1935.
Running Time: 75 minutes.
Availability: DVD (Universal Home Video).

Werewolf of London, Universal's first foray into the story of a man who suf-
fers from something called lycanthropy, where he changes into a werewolf
on a full moon, is decidedly inferior to their later effort, *The Wolf Man*
(1941). As a result, this film comes off as disappointing when watching it
with the knowledge of the later movie. However, if we take it in the context
of its time, being the first film to offer this story, it is quite effective under
its own terms.

Henry Hull as the Werewolf of London.

The story deals with English botanist Dr. Glendon, who is attacked by a creature while searching for an elusive species of flower called the mariphasa. The beast that attacks him is identified as a werewolf. A doctor named Yogami tells Glendon that because he has been bitten by a werewolf, he has now become one. However, the elusive flower sample that Glendon brought back to London from Tibet is noted to be an antidote that works on a temporary basis.

The way Glendon begins to discover the truth of Yogami's claims is when he sees his hand start to evolve and grow fur under the moon lamp in his laboratory. A blossom from the mariphasa halts the transformation. It is then revealed that Yogami is also a werewolf and breaks into Glendon's lab, stealing the remaining mariphasa flowers, except for one that has not yet bloomed and thus is not yet effective. As a result, Glendon transforms into a werewolf on the full moon and kills a young girl. The next day, he is remorseful because he remembers what he's done and realizes he is powerless against the desire to do so when the werewolf curse is in full effect.

When the third flower blooms, Glendon catches Yogami trying to steal it and realizes it is he who was the werewolf that attacked him in Tibet, giving him this curse. Because the werewolf seeks to destroy what he loves most, Glendon goes to the home of his fiancée. He has her cornered but is killed by Colonel Forsythe of Scotland Yard, and as he lies dying he thanks the colonel for ending his torment. Once he dies, he returns to his human form.

The makeup that Jack Pierce designed for the werewolf originally resembled the beastly quality that would later be utilized by Lon Chaney Jr. for *The Wolf Man*. However, actor Henry Hull, who played Glendon, objected to the makeup being so animalistic and wanted it to seem more humanlike so that his face would be recognized by the other characters as per the narrative. Pierce refused to alter his original vision, so Hull went to Junior Laemmle, who agreed with the actor and ordered the change. Hull further humanized the character by having him don a hat and scarf as he left on one of his bloodthirsty killing sprees. However, the howls used on the sound track were more realistic than what would be presented in the later film, said to be a combination of actor Hull's own voice and that of an actual timberwolf.

The lesser makeup can be considered as being more effective for a character like this, who can venture out among people with less chance of being noticed but who isn't any less deadly. Perhaps Hull felt he was able to give a more expressive performance without as much makeup. His anguish at his condition and the terrible things he's done is more evident in his face.

Director Stuart Walker helmed only a dozen movies in his career, of which *Werewolf of London* is second to last. He had none of the vision or stylistic grace of either Tod Browning or James Whale and certainly did not have the cinematic vision of Karl Freund. Charles Stumar, cinematographer on *The Mummy*, had been inspired by Freund and mirrored his approach. Despite some nicely framed shots and a few isolated scenes that are more striking (such as one of the werewolf's victim seeing his reflection in her makeup mirror as he approaches from behind), Walker's direction did little more than functionally tell the story. Stumar would shoot one more film before dying in a plane crash in the summer of 1935, only six months after *Werewolf of London* completed shooting in February of that year.

The film is slow moving with some dull stretches, and despite having essentially the same running time as the previous Universal monster movies, it appears to run much longer. However, this does not mean *Werewolf of London* is a complete misfire. Hull was a good actor and does a nice job in the role, and he benefits from strong support by Warner Oland as Yogami. Bela Lugosi was originally requested for this role, but he was involved with shooting *Mark of the Vampire* at MGM. However, Hull is more a competent journeyman than he was the sort of actor who defined the role as Chaney would six years later. In his book *The Pleasure and Pain of Horror Movies*, author Bartlomiej Paszylk stated,

The person most blamed for the movie's lack of success is Henry Hull, and although he plays his role with confidence, it is true that his character is neither as sympathetic as nor as memorable as those created by Bela Lugosi, Boris Karloff, or Lon Chaney Jr. in Universal's more famous monster movies. But even with the main character being a bit of a bore, there's enough good acting in *Werewolf of London* to keep us interested in what's happening onscreen.[1]

The veteran Oland, at this time, was already established as Chinese detective Charlie Chan in a popular film series at Fox studios (Boris Karloff had appeared in one of the best entries, *Charlie Chan at the Opera*, the year before *Werewolf of London* was filmed). Oland adds a measured amount of mystery to the role, at once warning Glendon, then revealing himself as also afflicted and having been responsible for the other doctor's condition. Some of the most effective scenes feature Oland's pensive reaction to Yogami hearing (or reading) the news of Glendon's exploits as the werewolf. It appears Yogami is no more able to control his desperate need to steal the flower antidote than Glendon is to commit violent murder. His supporting role may be the best performance in the movie.

Elizabeth Risdon as Lisa, Glendon's fiancée, and Lester Matthews as the cad Paul Ames who has designs on her, are uniformly lifeless in their roles until their initial confrontation with the werewolf where Paul manages to rescue Lisa by hitting the creature with a clublike tree branch. This is when Paul recognizes that Glendon was the werewolf—the scene behind actor Hull's reasoning that the makeup not be too obscuring.

The special effects used to show Glendon's transformation are effective when one realizes the limitations of a 1935 film with a budget of under $200,000. The director usually shoots the initial changes to Glendon's face, then pans down to show the transformation of his hands, before panning up to reveal his face has fully transformed. Within its context, it is effective enough.

One of the most effective aspects of the Pierce makeup that was retained was the beast's underbite. This is a particularly scary part of his ensemble in that it causes the viewer to conclude that unlike the upper fangs of Count Dracula that pierce the arteries so he can suck blood, these sharp lower teeth would effectively tear apart the hapless victims in a most vicious and painful manner.

There are some comic scenes with the two fluttery spinsters played by Ethel Griffies and Zeffie Tilbury in an attempt to break up the seriousness of the story, but comic relief is not what *Werewolf of London* needs. It would have benefited more from a truly standout performance by its star, and Hull's competence is limited by his lacking the charisma to pull that off. He was not at the level of Boris Karloff, Bela Lugosi, or Claude Rains.

Still, *Werewolf of London* was a box office success and pleased critics. Frank S. Nugent of the *New York Times* stated,

> Designed solely to amaze and horrify, the film goes about its task with commendable thoroughness, sparing no grisly detail and springing from scene to scene with even greater ease than that oft attributed to the daring young aerialist. Granting that the central idea has been used before, the picture still rates the attention of action-and-horror enthusiasts.[2]

The magazine *Silver Screen* offered this capsule review in its June 1935 issue:

> Weird and thrilling. An expertly handled tale of the fantastic type which fascinates even while it horrifies.[3]

Exhibitors in the "What the Picture Did for Me" section of the *Motion Picture Herald* reported enthusiastically,

> A howling success. This bested *Frankenstein* here. Hull is perfect. A good picture of the *Dr Jeckyl and Mr Hyde* type.

At around the same time *Werewolf of London* was being shot, James Whale was filming *The Bride of Frankenstein*. According to Gregory William Mank's book *Karloff and Lugosi*, Henry Hull was receiving $2,750 per week for *Werewolf of London*, while Boris Karloff was receiving $2,500 per week for *The Bride of Frankenstein*. Mank also stated that the studio paid Hull's agent $82.50 per week and an additional fee of $1,375 to compensate Hull for any trick shots. Warner Oland, meanwhile, received $12,000 for his supporting role. It is intriguing that Karloff would be paid less than Hull since Boris had already established himself as "the next Lon Chaney," while Hull was an actor whose credentials were, as stated, competent but not a standout.

Publicity ideas for *Werewolf of London* were quite clever. Jack Fink, manager of the Capitol theater in Miami, Florida, advertised for a courageous woman to sit alone through a midnight performance of *Werewolf of London* in a dark theater with no other seat occupied. She was then to relate her reactions after the screening. The contest received no takers.

Werewolf of London has something of a legacy in more contemporary folklore due to the late Warren Zevon's popular song "Werewolves of London" from his 1978 album *Excitable Boy*. However, it is Lon Chaney Jr. whom Zevon carefully identifies in the lyrics, not Henry Hull.

Despite it not holding up as well as the previous Universal monster movies have, the studio was happy with the success of *Werewolf of London* with both critics and at the box office and continued to flourish in the horror genre. Theaters clamored for the films so intensely that at one point the Rialto in New York sued the Roxy, contesting its right to show *Bride of Frankenstein*. The Rialto dropped its claim only after securing exclusive rights to distribute *Werewolf of London*. The popularity also caused trouble in some cities. Theaters in Kansas City were forbidden to show *Werewolf of London* to children under age 12. City censor Guy Holmes indicated he was influenced by protests he received from women, indicating that juvenile attendance had been above average for *Bride of Frankenstein*.[4]

Universal wanted to next revisit the story of Dracula by making a sequel based on Bram Stoker's short story *Dracula's Guest*. However, negotiations with Stoker's widow revealed that she wanted to have more creative control over a film version, while Bela Lugosi was demanding a rather large salary to play the role. This plan was therefore scrapped, and John Balderston was hired to write a new screenplay based on the original character that was itself in the public domain and not subject to any negotiation with Stoker's widow. The result was *Dracula's Daughter*, a remarkably effective sequel.

7

DRACULA'S DAUGHTER

(1936)

Director: Lambert Hillyer.
Screenplay: Garrett Fort; *Story:* Charles Belden, John L. Balderston, R. C.
Sherriff, Kurt Neumann, Finley Peter Dunne, Bram Stoker.
Producers: E. M. Asher, Harry Zehner. *Cinematography:* George Robinson.
Film Editing: Milton Carruth. *Art Direction:* Albert D'Agostino. *Music:*
Heinz Roemheld.
Cast: Gloria Holden (Countess Marya Zaleska/Dracula's daughter), Otto
Kruger (Jeffrey Garth), Marguerite Churchill (Janet), Edward van
Sloan (Von Helsing), Gilbert Emery (Sir Basil Humphrey), Irving
Pichel (Sandor), Halliwell Hobbes (Hawkins), Billy Bevan (Albert),
E. E. Clive (Sergeant Wilkes), Hedda Hopper (Lady Esme Hammond),
Claud Allister (Sir Aubrey), Nan Grey (Lili), Edgar Norton (Hobbs),
Fred Walton (Dr. Beemish), Agnes Anderson (Elena), Gordon Hart
(Mr. Graham), John Blood (Bobby), David Dunbar (Motor Bobby),
Eily Malyon (Miss Peabody), Vernon Steele (Squires), Douglas Wood
(Dr. Townsend).
Released: May 11, 1936.
Running Time: 71 minutes.
Availability: DVD (Universal Home Video).

Universal was not the first studio to consider doing a sequel to *Dracula*.
In 1933, David O. Selznick planned to produce one for Metro-Goldwyn-
Mayer (MGM). MGM optioned Bram Stoker's short story *Dracula's Guest*,
which had been published two years after Stoker's death. The author's
widow was paid $500 for the property, and John Balderston was hired to
write the treatment. Balderston felt his scripts for *Dracula*, *Frankenstein*,

and *The Mummy* for Universal did not adhere well enough to his original vision once filmed. He was hoping the opportunity with this property, titled *Dracula's Daughter*, would be closer to his more macabre tastes. He wanted to feature the title character wickedly enjoying torturing her victims.

MGM had already attempted to match Universal in the horror department, hiring Boris Karloff to star with Myrna Loy in *The Mask of Fu Manchu* (1932) and Tod Browning to direct the notorious *Freaks* (1932). While both of these films have emerged as cult favorites over the past many decades, they did not please critics or moviegoers at the time of their initial release. Thus, MGM passed on the *Dracula's Daughter* property, and Selznick took the idea to Universal. Junior Laemmle liked the idea and hired screenwriter R. C. Sherriff to write a screenplay based on Balderston's treatment. However, because Selznick was still working for MGM, he was billed here as Oliver Jeffries.

James Whale was hired to direct the film, but he expressed little interest in helming yet another horror movie. During preproduction, Whale added homoerotic material to Sherriff's screenplay, which the censors rejected, so the studio replaced him as director with A. Edward Sutherland, while Garrett Fort and Finley Peter Dunne were asked to rewrite the script once again. Whale then went on to direct the musical *Show Boat* (1936). Bela Lugosi was hired to reprise his role as Count Dracula in the early portion of the movie, while the romantic leads were given to actors Cesar Romero and Jane Wyatt. And while early publicity indicated both Colin Clive and Boris Karloff would appear in the movie, neither does.

Sutherland was a curious choice as director, as his forte had essentially been comedies. such as the W. C. Fields films *It's the Old Army Game* (1926), *International House* (1933), and *Mississippi* (1935). His only real qualification for directing a film like *Dracula's Daughter* was his having helmed *Murders in the Zoo* (1933) for Paramount. Delays in production resulted in Romero and Wyatt being replaced by Otto Krueger and Marguerite Churchill. Edward Sutherland became disgruntled with the constant delays in production and left the project (taking a guaranteed payment of $20,000) and went to Paramount to direct another W. C. Fields feature, *Poppy* (1936). Lugosi also left the project, signing a permission waiver to allow the studio to use a wax figure of his likeness as Count Dracula in a coffin during the film's opening scene. Some studies claim that Lugosi secured a payment of $4,000 while waiting for production to begin, which was twice as much as he'd received for *Dracula*. Sutherland was replaced as director by Lambert Hillyer, who'd just finished successfully helming *The Invisible Ray*, which remains one of the better Lugosi–Karloff team-ups.

The finished script resulted in something of a landmark in the narrative progression of the vampire in cinema. The title character does not want to be a vampire, does not like to kill, feels remorse after being compelled to do so, and seeks a cure. These elements would find their way into subsequent vampire dramas and would be used as effectively for *The Wolf Man* five years later. Shooting finally began on February 4, 1936, and concluded on March 10, running seven days over its production schedule's allotted time and over budget by $50,000. Because the delays caused the budget to escalate, *Dracula's Daughter* does not have the special effects noted in previous Universal monster movies. It is a straight, no-frills horror melodrama.

Gloria Holden as Dracula's daughter.

Dracula's Daughter picks up where *Dracula* left off. Professor Von Helsing is taken to Scotland Yard by police after they find him in a tomb along with a corpse in a coffin with a stake through it. Von Helsing admits to having driven the stake through the heart of Count Dracula to destroy him. He also claims Dracula has been dead for 500 years; thus, he cannot be charged with murder. He secures the help of a former student, Dr. Garth.

There is no prologue and no backstory, but the film does take place immediately where *Dracula* had ended and picks up the story from that point. Edward Van Sloane is back as Von Helsing, exuding a calm presence amidst the more passionate questioning of arriving police who discover the corpse with the stake through his heart and a confessing suspect. Despite his careful explanation, Von Helsing is dismissed as preposterous by Scotland Yard's Sir Basil Humphrey, and he hopes Dr. Garth will be able to sort things out.

Dracula's Daughter utilizes comedy much more so in its early scenes than the previous monsters have. Silent screen comedian Billy Bevan and character comedian Halliwell Hobbes are two fluttery guards at the morgue who act as something of an ersatz comedy team in their reaction to the presence of the coffins containing the remains of the notorious Count Dracula. Countess Marya Zaleska spiriting the remains of the count away makes for some silly comic reaction from Bevan and Hobbes, with Bevan becoming a victim in the end. This tragic conclusion to the dose of comic relief allows the movie to transition to melodrama for its duration.

Whereas in previous horror films any comic relief was organic to the narrative, the lighthearted tone of these scenes seems out of place in this movie. There really isn't any comedy to be found in the rest of the film, so having such a silly opening sequence doesn't work.

The lighthearted manner in which Dr. Garth is first introduced is also much different than the subsequent seriousness of the drama, but it fits comfortably within the movie's narrative parameters. Garth is with Janet, a wealthy socialite, and preparing to go on a fox hunt when he receives word that Von Helsing needs him. He must immediately leave a party of privileged sorts in order to fly to the "real world" from which these wealthy types seclude themselves and deal with the seriousness of murder. This opening shows both Garth and Janet as aloof, amusing, and engaging in some mock bickering with witty repartee. Their manner is attractive despite their privileged status, and their introductory scene successfully establishes each character and his or her relationship.

During Garth's first meeting with Von Helsing, the professor explains the same story about vampires to the doctor as he had to Scotland Yard.

While Garth also dismisses the idea of vampires, he believes there is an underlying theme to how Von Helsing feels. The professor had been the doctor's mentor, so it is believed his brilliant mind must be suffering from a psychological disruption that can be uncovered and treated.

Countess Zaleska and her servant, Sandor, burn Count Dracula's remains in an effort to destroy her own vampirism. It is not effective. She meets Dr. Garth at a society party and responds to his background in psychiatry, hoping he can help her cope with the psychological conflict she endures from her acts as a vampire, believing he may be able to help thwart Dracula's power over her from beyond the grave. Garth suggests she confront her fears, not realizing specifically what they are, as her explanation is vague.

It is worth noting that, unlike other vampires, the countess tries to get rid of her powers using not supernatural means but rather her own willpower, adding another layer of sympathy to her character. She's the first sympathetic vampire character and, arguably, the most sympathetic of all the Universal monsters up to this point.

There are several nice touches while showing the countess settling into the society party's trappings. She listens with a bored indifference to the various partygoers and their shallow interpretation of the murders that have taken place. She is absorbed by Garth's more learned, open-minded approach. She has an abrupt, unsettling reaction when mirrors are mentioned. She delivers the line "I never drink . . . wine" in homage to Lugosi and *Dracula*. It is important to note that this party is also where the countess meets Janet, and there is some measure of jealousy over her relationship with Garth.

Sandor meets Lili, a troubled young woman, and convinces her to come to a studio where an artist would like to use her as a model. Believing she is to be painted, Lili meets the countess, who asks her to remove her top. Lili is comfortable with revealing herself, but when the countess begins to mesmerize her with a ring that hypnotizes her victims and approaches the woman, Lili's protests are for naught. She does survive the ordeal but dies in a hospital as Dr. Garth attempts to discover, through hypnosis, exactly what happened.

There is always an underlying romantic element to many vampire characters, mostly due to Bela Lugosi's approach to the role of Count Dracula. The countess exhibits that sort of quality in her dealings with Garth, but they come forth even more in her response to Lili. She shows her the ring on her finger that causes her to be hypnotized. Although under the power of the countess, Lili's will is strong, and she protests in fear as the countess is shown approaching her. It is a terrifying scene, nicely directed by Lambert Hillyer, who never reveals the actual murder on-screen but presents everything by its approach and aftermath. The attraction—and the sensuality—between the two women is palpable without being blatant. The entire scene is subtly brilliant.

When Garth confronts a terrorized Lili in the hospital, his hypnosis results in her offering enough detail to allow the doctor to realize that there may be more to what Von Helsing claims than he had previously believed. His next confrontation with the countess reveals even more, especially when she expresses her desire that he go away with her, as she has finally concluded that a cure from her vampirism is not possible. Science is not powerful enough to combat the supernatural control Dracula has over her from beyond his grave.

When Garth refuses to go away with the countess, she schemes to place him under her power and secure him as an eternal mate against his will. This causes a negative reaction from her servant, Sandor, who had been promised the eternal life she is now planning to give to Garth.

The countess lures Garth to her castle in Transylvania by kidnapping Janet. However, the conflict with Sandor puts Garth in further danger. Garth arrives at the castle and agrees to sacrifice his life for Janet's safety, but Sandor kills the countess with an arrow through the heart. He attempts to also murder Garth but is shot to death by police, who arrive with Von Helsing after Scotland Yard had been alerted to the fact that the doctor was headed to the Transylvanian castle. Janet is rescued, and the body of the countess is found dead. An officer exclaims, "She's beautiful!" Von Helsing concludes the film by stating, "She was beautiful when she died 100 years ago."

Despite limited experience directing horror movies, Hillyer does a good job of framing the action and telling the story. For, when Garth enters the Transylvanian castle, his image is small, surrounded by vast negative space and appearing powerless in this environment. At one point, the countess says to him, "You're not in London anymore. You're in my castle."

While Cloria Holden remains striking and captivating as the countess, she did not want to play the role and was unhappy throughout the production. The aloofness and indifference her character often exudes is said to stem from her own disdain for having to appear in what she considered a dismissible movie. It works effectively with her role and enhances her performance. Holden would go on to appear in 40 movies, working with such stars as Clark Gable, Spencer Tracy, Errol Flynn, Mickey Rooney, and Cary Grant. She left movies in the 1950s but lived to be 87 years old, dying in 1991. When fans would approach for an autograph and mention *Dracula's Daughter*, she was alleged to have stated, "Oh, that awful thing."[1]

Critics and audiences liked *Dracula's Daughter*, but their reactions were conflicting. While the *New York World-Telegram* noticed in its review that the countess was "giving the eye to sweet young girls" and recommended adults only,[2] the review in the *New York Times* said, "Don't forget to bring the kiddies."[3] The *Motion Picture Herald* stated,

> A picture of creeps and chills, this production bases its bid for entertainment and commercial success upon the unusual and potent appearance of terror and thrill situations. A worthy sequel to the shuddery *Dracula*, memory of which is still vivid, it is built of eerie and weird material, which, quite smartly, is more spine tingling in character than terror inspiring. Here the fiend is a woman, played with skillful understanding and conviction by Gloria Holden. A haunting melodrama, naturally having a romantic and some little comedy counterpart, the picture is nevertheless the story of a dead thing—a companion of the evil one—a fatal woman who was a demon at night as she satisfied her lust for blood. Thus the picture is loaded with a spine-chilling character that has proved its capability to thrill in a strange way and amuse in equal style.[4]

The review in the *Motion Picture Herald* concluded by stating that the screening was previewed in the studio projection room and that the audience was composed almost entirely of newspaper critics "who accepted the picture with enthusiasm."

Dracula's Daughter was profitable, earning back more than its costs. Several more horror productions were therefore being planned. Unfortunately, these plans were thwarted. *Dracula's Daughter* ended what is now known as the first wave of monster movies from Universale Studios. Despite the films' profitability, Junior Laemmle's excesses on other studio productions resulted in less satisfying results at the box office. The Laemmles considered selling the studio and were looking at various offers in 1935. In November of that year, they reached a negotiation with J. Cheever Cowdin of the Standard Capital Corporation. In a deal arranged by producer Charles R. Rogers, Junior Laemmle borrowed $1 million from Cowdin against ownership of the studio. When the note became due as production on *Dracula's Daughter* was concluding, the studio was unable to pay, so Cowdin took over ownership of the studio in March 1936, replacing Junior Laemmle with Charles Rogers as production supervisor. Charles Rogers did not like horror movies and canceled all productions planned after *Dracula's Daughter*.

On taking over the studio, Charles Rogers took several drastic cost-cutting measures and hired producer Joe Pasternak to produce musicals and comedies. Rogers focused most of his attention on Deanna Durbin, who had just been dropped by MGM in favor of Judy Garland. The first Durbin musical, *Three Smart Girls*, was released at the end of 1936 and turned an enormous profit. It would also go on to be nominated for an Academy Award for Best Picture. With its focus on musicals and comedies, Charles Rogers hoped that Universale Studios would no longer be known as "the monster movie studio." However, the 1937–1938 season was a financial disaster for Universal, the movies with Deanna Durbin saving the studio from folding completely.

By 1938, Rogers was replaced as studio production head by Cliff Work. Work looked over the studio's schedule and decided to keep only the successful Durbin musicals planned as further productions. He also hired W. C. Fields to make films at Universal. Fields, who'd been plagued by illness, had just been dropped by his longtime studio Paramount. His recent radio appearances with ventriloquist Edgar Bergen and dummy Charlie McCarthy were very popular with listeners, so a film was planned with Fields and Bergen. It went on to be a big success.

Cliff Work also looked into the studio's past records to see what films had enjoyed good profits in the past and noticed the success of the monster movies but could not determine if the resulting box office receipts would be enough to earn a profit. Then in April 1938, a theater in Los Angeles that had been losing money decided to run a festival of older movies, as they cost far less to rent. They scheduled a triple feature with *Dracula*, *Frankenstein*, and the RKO feature *King Kong* (1933). The films were extremely profitable, broke attendance records, and inspired other theaters to run older horror movies as weekend special matinees.

Cliff Work felt that the success of these revivals indicated it was worthwhile producing another horror feature. Both Boris Karloff and Bela Lugosi were available, and makeup man Jack Pierce was still at the studio, so Work okayed production to begin on a new sequel to *Frankenstein*. He even considered shooting the movie in color, and some test footage was shot, but that was determined to be a bit too expensive.

James Whale, although currently in a career slump, did not accept Work's offer to direct the film, not wanting to make any more horror movies. Work then hired studio director Rowland Lee to helm the feature, from a screenplay by Wyllis Cooper, who had no screenwriting experience and was known primarily for writing the radio mystery program *Lights Out*. Lee and Cooper redefined a lot of the familiar elements of the story and characters. And another Universal monster movie was in production.

8

SON OF FRANKENSTEIN

(1939)

Producer/Director: Rowland V. Lee.
Screenplay: Wyllis Cooper, based on the novel *Frankenstein* by Mary Shelley.
Cinematography: George Robinson. *Editing:* Ted Kent. *Art Direction:* Jack
  Otterson. *Music:* Frank Skinner.
Cast: Basil Rathbone (Baron Wolf von Frankenstein), Boris Karloff (the
  monster), Bela Lugosi (Ygor), Lionel Atwill (Inspector Krogh), Josephine
  Hutchinson (Elsa von Frankenstein), Donnie Dunagan (Peter von
  Frankenstein), Emma Dunn (Amelia), Edgar Norton (Thomas Benson),
  Perry Ivins (Fritz), Lawrence Grant (burgomaster), Lionel Belmore
  (Lang), Michael Mark (Ewald Neumüller), Caroline Frances Cooke (Mrs.
  Neumüller), Clarence Wilson (Dr. Berger), Dwight Frye (villager), Ward
  Bond, Harry Cording (gendarmes), Gustav von Seyffertitz, Lorimar
  Johnston, Tom Ricketts, Ed Cassidy, Russ Powell (burghers).
Released: January 13, 1939.
Running Time: 99 minutes.
Availability: DVD (Universal Home Video).

As indicated in the previous chapter, after Junior Laemmle lost control of
Universale Studios due to his excesses and Charles Rogers became production manager, all planned horror productions were canceled. However,
despite cost-cutting measures and a profitable new star in Deanna Durbin,
the studio had little box office success during the 1937–1938 season. Rogers was replaced as production manager by Cliff Work. At about that time,
older Universal horror films were enjoying revival popularity in theaters, so
Work arranged to have another *Frankenstein* project activated.

Son of Frankenstein had been planned to be filmed shortly after *Dracula's Daughter*, but the project was shelved when Charles Rogers took over the studio. When Cliff Work reactivated it, he placed Rowland Lee in charge. Original plans had Peter Lorre cast in the title role, but Lee instead chose Basil Rathbone, with whom he had worked on *Love from a Stranger* (1937). Boris Karloff was available to play the monster, and Bela Lugosi was attached to the project. Since Lugosi was at a point in his career where he needed work, he agreed to a rather paltry $500-per-week salary. Lee felt the actor was worth much more, so he and scriptwriter Wyllis Cooper created the role of Ygor, based on the other assistants in previous Frankenstein movies, giving him steady work throughout the production and more weekly $500 paychecks. Ygor did not appear in the original screenplay submitted by Cooper. It was added, at Lee's insistence, once production began.

Since radio writer Cooper had no real experience as a screenwriter, revisions would keep occurring throughout production. Some scenes would be written the very day they were filmed. This also helped keep the Ygor character active in the narrative and allowed Lugosi more work. Lugosi would remain forever indebted to Rowland Lee for his kindness. In return, Lugosi delivered one of the finest acting performances of his long career.

Son of Frankenstein begins with Baron Wolfgang von Frankenstein, along with his wife and son, relocating to the family castle. He wants to restore the family name and his father's legacy despite a suspicious and sometimes hostile reaction from the villagers. He is befriended by Inspector Krough, who lost his arm to the monster years earlier and now has an artificial one.

While exploring the castle, Wolf von Frankenstein meets Ygor, who had been hanged for grave robbing but lived. His neck was severely broken and is now deformed and immobile. Ygor takes Frankenstein to a secluded area of the castle where the remains of Wolf's father and grandfather are entombed and where he also finds the monster, alive. The monster needs to be revived and his energy restored. Frankenstein decides to do this, with Ygor's help, believing it will help to restore his father's name.

Once the monster is revived, he responds only to Ygor's commands. Frankenstein does not want the monster to leave the castle, but Ygor uses him to destroy the men on the jury who sentenced his hanging. Frankenstein shoots and kills Ygor, so the monster kidnaps Wolf's son. However, the monster cannot bring himself to kill the boy. Frankenstein and Inspector Keough go after the monster, who tears out the inspector's false arm during a struggle. Frankenstein then knocks the monster into a molten sulfur pit, destroying him, and rescues his son.

Boris Karloff, Bela Lugosi, Basil Rathbone.

Rowland Lee's approach to the material is as atmospheric as James Whale's had been but in a much different manner. His sets are not as dark but are much bleaker. While the dinner sequences in previous films were set in wealthy, ornate dining areas, similar scenes in *Son of Frankenstein* are in a very barren area framed by shadows. There are crooked staircases and slanted angles, and the simple mise-en-scène calls attention to few of the objects in the frame. The influence of German expressionism is clearly evident.

The presentation of the monster is also altered from his most recent appearance. In *Bride of Frankenstein*, the monster was gradually learning greater coping skills and becoming gradually more articulate. In *Son of Frankenstein*, he is once again mute. He again communicates with growls and grunts. The scene in which the monster approaches Frankenstein from behind and places his hand on the baron's shoulder provides a very striking image. It is followed by the creature's carefully feeling Frankenstein's face, first planning to strangle him, then stopping himself and backing away. When the monster sees his reflection in a mirror, he reacts with a combination of fear and disgust. He drags Frankenstein in front of the mirror and looks at the comparison. As Gregory William Mank puts it in his book *Karloff and Lugosi*, "Sadly humiliated by his horrific appearance . . . groaning dismally at the reflected awful truth. This touch of bizarre 'monster vanity' is worthy of James Whale—a clever scene played by Karloff with all his magic."[1]

Despite the veiled compassion that had been presented in *Bride of Frankenstein*, here the monster is capable of cold-blooded murder as he destroys the various jurors, one by one, while under Ygor's control. The ways the various murders are presented are interesting in their cinematic variation. One is staged completely in shadows on the wall, showing the monster approaching the seated victim from behind, the startled reaction, and then the violence.

The most noted compassion from the monster occurs when he discovers the dead body of Ygor, whom he chose as his master. He responds with an agonized scream, and this leads to his vengeful kidnapping of Franken-stein's child. The monster then displays too much compassion to kill the child, as he had so easily murdered the others. The parallel to the accidental killing of little Maria in the first *Frankenstein* is evident. The final confron-tation, with Baron Frankenstein swinging by a rope and kicking the monster into a molten pit, is perhaps the most violent and spectacular ending to any of the Universal monster movies up to this time.

Basil Rathbone was not a fan of horror movies but wanted to play the role. Usually portraying villains, Rathbone enjoyed having the opportunity to play what was considered the "good guy" in the story. Rathbone has great command of the role, fluctuating from controlled security to frustrated anguish. He does not flirt with madness like Colin Clive had done, but the scene where he is confronted by Keough while playing darts shows him in a more emotionally uninhibited state. However, he does not present the conflicting emotions, the curiosity, and the need of man to be as God in the way his predecessor had.

Frankenstein's quest here is to make the monster "well" in order to vin-dicate his father's name and legacy. However, once Ygor is in control of the creature, any further experimentation is halted. Ygor growls, "He is well enough for me. You no touch him again!"

Universal was hardly finished with Basil Rathbone. Making an impact as Sherlock Holmes in two 20th Century Fox features—*The Hound of the Baskervilles* and *The Adventures of Sherlock Holmes*—a Holmes series was launched at Universal in 1942 with Rathbone playing the character (op-posite Nigel Bruce as Watson) for a dozen more movies. It is the Sherlock Holmes character for which Basil Rathbone is best known today.

Lionel Atwill does a superb job as Inspector Keough and would soon be a regular in Universal's horror productions. Atwill brilliantly registers greater knowledge of what Frankenstein is hiding as more and more clues come forth, especially the murders. His confrontations with Frankenstein grow in intensity.

Bela Lugosi turns in what some consider to be the finest performance of his career. Ygor has none of the aristocratic class of Count Dracula. He is a shaggy, dirty, deformed, snarling derelict. Lugosi's complete command of the role, using the intensity of his eyes under the heavy makeup, is one of the strongest elements of the entire production. When Ygor stands over the monster and growls to Frankenstein, "He's my friend. He does things for me," it is one of the most chilling moments in the movie.

This was the last time Boris Karloff would portray the Frankenstein monster in a movie (he would don the makeup for a celebrity baseball game in 1940 and again for a 1962 episode of TV's *Route 66*). Along with the previously mentioned scenes, he is especially good when, in close-up, he conveys both anguish and anger at the murder of Ygor. His kidnapping of the child shows the youngster going along willingly with the monster, being the same innocent, trusting soul as little Maria had been in *Frankenstein*. As the monster lifts the child to drop him into the lava, his inability to toss yet another child to his death consumes him. The final confrontation is very effectively filmed, showing the screaming monster falling to his death, followed by a medium shot of his smoldering in the molten pit. Karloff would later state, "There was not much left in the character of the monster to be developed; we had reached his limits."[2]

Donnie Dunagan, who appears as the child Peter Frankenstein, recalled that Boris Karloff was a delightful man who was in a great mood during filming because his wife was about to have a baby, his firstborn. When Karloff, in full makeup, was alerted on the set that his wife gave birth to a baby daughter on November 21, 1939, the actor burst into tears and headed to the hospital in full makeup. It was also Karloff's fifty-first birthday. Fortunately, his arrival was met with celebration rather than fear. Hospital staff realized it was new father Boris Karloff despite his showing up as the Frankenstein monster. The next day, he was given a cake on the set by Basil Rathbone and Bela Lugosi (Lugosi himself was a new father). Dunagan told Gregory Mank,

> Mr. K was a trip. He was a real dude—gentle , strong, treated my mom like a queen, was very friendly and a fun guy with me. He had a good sense of humor. He'd walk around with me, hold my hand. The costume hurt him a lot. You could see the agony in his face as you watched him trying to get into a sitting position. I can remember vaguely asking him about it, but he wasn't a wimp.[3]

In the role of Mrs. Frankenstein, Josephine Hutchinson, playing the same sort of ingénue that Elizabeth had been in the earlier *Frankenstein* films, had trouble with her lines and found the lack of a complete script to be a difficult challenge. Still, she does well in her role, adding the new dimension of protective mother to the character traits for the Frankenstein wife. Living 94 years, the actress was, like many others, always bemused that in her long career it is the horror movie she did that she'd be asked about most in her later years.

The idea to film *Son of Frankenstein* in Technicolor was a fairly grandiose idea for Cliff Work, who was trying to bring Universal out of its financial slump. It was far better to retain black and white, especially with Lee's dark and rather artistic images born of German expressionism. There are reports of Technicolor test footage that no longer survives, but documentaries have offered Boris Karloff's color home movie footage from the set, including him, as the monster, playfully sticking his tongue out at the camera.

While the earlier *Frankenstein* films were noted for using less music, *Son of Frankenstein* benefits greatly by Frank Skinner's rousing, dramatic score. Skinner would score many of the Universal monster movies hereafter. His distinctive approach to scoring the 200-odd films on which he worked netted him five Academy Award nominations during his career.

The Universal brass was not pleased with Rowland Lee going over budget on the film with such indulgent measures as lengthening Bela Lugosi's role and increasing his salary. The budget was the most expensive of the *Frankenstein* movies thus far, coming in at over $400,000. Production went so far beyond its projected end date that the actors had to work around the clock during the last couple of days so the film could be finished in time for its planned release date. Shooting finally concluded at 1:15 a.m., early on the morning of January 5, 1939. It was released eight days later.

The studio's misgivings about the budget ended when *Son of Frankenstein* turned out to be the most profitable horror movie the studio ever produced, grossing over $900,000. Moviegoers, recently reminded of the past monster movies with the re-release of the original *Frankenstein* playing in various theaters over the past year, clamored to see a new production. The powerhouse cast of Rathbone, Karloff, and Lugosi generated even further interest. That *Son of Frankenstein* was on par with the other *Frankenstein* films caused word of mouth to further increase box office success.

Critics, for the most part, were also impressed, welcoming back the horror films and their monsters with affection. *Variety* called it

well mounted, nicely directed, and includes cast of capable artists. Karloff has his monster in former groove as the big and powerful brute who crushes and smashes victims. Bela Lugosi is the mad cripple who guides the monster on murder forays. Lionel Atwill is prominent as village inspector of police.[4]

However, the stodgy *New York Times* turned its nose up at the entire horror genre, stating,

> No use beating around the razzberry bush: if Universal's *Son of Frankenstein* isn't the silliest picture ever made, it's a sequel to the silliest picture ever made, which is even sillier. But its silliness is deliberate—a very shrewd silliness, perpetrated by a good director in the best traditions of cinematic horror, so that even while you laugh at its nonsense you may be struck with the notion that perhaps that's as good a way of enjoying oneself at a movie as any. It must have been all the actors themselves could do, in this day and age, to keep straight faces—always excepting poor Boris Karloff, of course, who couldn't laugh through all that make-up even if he tried.[5]

The public disagreed. *Son of Frankenstein* was one of the key reasons why 1939 turned out to be, up to then, the biggest moneymaking year in Universal studio's history.

Studio production manager Cliff Work was pleased with the success of *Son of Frankenstein* and gave the order to put more horror movies back into production. However, he no longer wanted to deal with indulgent filmmakers like Rowland Lee, who would go over budget and so far past their shooting schedule that the film had to scramble in postproduction to meet its slated release date. Work decided to allow sequels to past monster movies like *The Invisible Man*, *The Mummy*, and *Dracula*, along with more *Frankenstein* films. He would assign stock directors to helm these movies and reduce their budget to the B-movie level. This ensured a larger profit for the studio, which was now operating in the black for the first time in years.

Universal recently acquired the services of German director Joseph Otto Mandel, who had given Fritz Lang his start in films, hiring him as a screenwriter. Mandel fled Nazi Germany and began directing American movies under the name Joe May, taken from his wife's stage name, Mia May. May was very dictatorial on the set, did not bother formally learning the English language, and was not well liked by actors. Cliff Work hired May to helm a sequel to *The Invisible Man* titled *The Invisible Man Returns* from a story May wrote with Curt Siodmak and Lester Cole.

THE INVISIBLE MAN RETURNS

(1940)

Director: Joe May.
Screenplay: Curt Siodmak and Joe May, from a story by Siodmak and May, based on the character created by H. G. Wells.
Producers: Cliff Work and Ken Goldsmith. *Cinematography:* Milton R. Krasner. *Film Editing:* Frank Gross. *Art Direction:* Jack Otterson. *Music:* Hans J. Salter, Frank Skinner.
Cast: Sir Cedric Harwicke (Richard Cobb), Vincent Price (Geoffrey Radcliffe), John Sutton (Dr. Frank Griffin), Nan Grey (Helen Manson), Cecil Kellaway (Inspector Sampson), Alan Napier (Willie Spears), Forrester Harvey (Ben Jenkins), Billy Bevan (Jim), Rex Evans (Briggs), Mary Gordon (Cookie), David Thursby (Bob), Harry Stubbs (Tewsbury), Matthew Boulton, Ed Brady, Frank Hill, Cyril Thornton (policemen), Tom Coleman, Chet Brandenberg, Kit Guard, Bobbie Hale, George Hyde, Ellis Irving, Dick Johnstone, George Lloyd, George Kirby, Jack Lowe, Robert Robinson, Denis Tankard (miners).
Released: January 12, 1940.
Running Time: 81 minutes.
Availability: DVD (Universal Home Video).

Although this was produced to be a sequel to *The Invisible Man*, it has only a tangential connection in that John Sutton plays Dr. Frank Griffin, the brother of Jack Griffin, the real name of the title character in the previous movie. It is Frank who repeats his brother's experiment of turning a man invisible.

The man he chooses to help turn invisible is Sir Geoffrey Radcliffe, who is in prison and about to be executed for murdering his brother

Michael. Dr. Griffin believes that Geoffrey is innocent, so he injects him with the invisibility drug, allowing him to escape and bring the true killer to justice. He must do so before the invisibility serum drives him insane as it had Jack Griffin.

Having Jack Griffin's brother as one of the supporting characters in the narrative is the only thing that makes *The Invisible Man Returns* a sequel. Otherwise, it is just another saga about someone using the ability to turn invisible. Unlike Jack Griffin, however, Radcliffe is not attempting to do so for grandiose reasoning. He is using it as a desperate measure in order to clear his name, realizing the possible consequences of doing so.

Scotland Yard's Inspector Sampson, who remembers Jack Griffin's exploits, has suspicions about Dr. Griffin, knowing that he and Radcliffe are friends. He visits Dr. Griffin and discusses his brother's serum, indicating he realizes that the ability to create it still exists. Radcliffe, meanwhile, is suspicious of Willie Spears, who had been one of the key witnesses at his trial. Spears was recently promoted in the Radcliffe family's coal mining company by Radcliffe's cousin Richard Cobb, who took over the family coal mine on Radcliffe's imprisonment. To further complicate matters, Cobb also has designs on Helen, Radcliffe's girl.

Radcliffe confronts Spears by stowing away in his car. Taking advantage of his invisibility, he tampers with the engine. When Spears lifts the hood to investigate, Radcliffe closes it on his hand. Using his voice, Radcliffe claims to be his own ghost, and a terrified Spears begs for pity. "Did you have any pity for me, Mr. Spears?" Eventually, Spears is frightened into confessing

Nan Grey, Vincent Price, Harry Stubbs, Forrester Harvey.

that Cobb is the killer of Radcliffe's brother, weeping uncontrollably until he realizes the spirit has left him. Spears runs to seek shelter but is again confronted by Radcliffe, who knocks him out and ties him up.

Unlike similar scenes in *The Invisible Man* that reveal a wicked playfulness in Jack Griffin that was by no means comedic, this sequence is performed in a much more comical fashion. The previous movie would be amusing when the invisible Griffin stole a bicycle, and the image of it going down the street without a rider would confuse onlookers. But in this scene, Radcliffe toys with Spears, who reacts with comical double takes, looking around to see where his nemesis might be. Director Joe May darts the camera about to offer a visual for Spears's reaction, and the bouncy background music responds to Willie's reaction as well. It is all done comically, even when a blubbering Spears confesses all he knows.

Radcliffe finds Cobb trying to entice Helen and reveals himself with his voice just as he had with Spears, only Cobb does not react comically; rather, he is both shocked and frightened (Helen already knowing Radcliffe's plan to use their mutual friend's ability to turn him invisible). Radcliffe tells Cobb to write a confession and reveals to Helen that Cobb tried to "get rid of both of us by killing Michael and implicating me." Cobb wildly shoots his gun, hoping to hit Radcliffe, and runs from the room, running into Inspector Sampson, who puts him into protective custody. The inspector then has police go after Radcliffe with fog machines in an attempt to reveal his image.

The revealing of the Invisible Man's image in this movie is one thing that is superior to its predecessor. Special effects in 1940 were somewhat better than they had been in 1933 when *The Invisible Man* was filmed. Thus, a scene in which Radcliffe quickly walks past Sampson and his image is briefly visible in the smoke from the inspector's pipe is an impressive visual.

Radcliffe cunningly outsmarts the police with their fog machines by capturing one and taking his clothes. Clad in a gas mask and full body covering, he blends in with the other police and escapes. Radcliffe finds Cobb and takes him to where he has Willie Spears tied up, standing on a chair with a noose around his neck. After they enter, Spears again implicates Cobb, who kicks over the chair on which Willie is standing, and shuts out the lights. He flees from the building toward the coal mine, with Radcliffe in pursuit and the police pursuing them both. Caught on a coal car rising up on a grid, Cobb is fatally injured as the cart dumps its contents onto the ground far below and confesses to the murder as he lies dying. Radcliffe, having been shot in the fracas, escapes, dons a scarecrow's clothing, and makes his way to Dr. Griffin. A blood transfusion and an antidote is found to end his invisibility, allowing Griffin to perform necessary surgery.

Vincent Price, playing Radcliffe, is not seen on-screen until the final moments when the serum wears off as he lies injured. While he does not descend into madness, he does gradually embrace the power the invisibility allows him, especially after his successful confrontations and gathering the necessary information. His bellowing laughter as he playfully toys with Willie Spears and his emotional outburst while dining with Helen and Dr. Griffin during his determined attempts to bring Cobb to justice are effective in spite of Price being limited only to his voice. While Price would eventually become one of the true greats of horror cinema, this early appearance is comparatively inauspicious.

Even though *The Invisible Man Returns* belongs in this study as being part of the Universale Studios monster cycle, it does not really play as a horror movie at all. It comes off as a rather light drama with comic touches about a man attempting to clear his name, using the power of invisibility to do so. Part of the suspense of *The Invisible Man Returns* is Radcliffe's hurriedly trying to solve his case before the serum makes him insane while at the same time Dr. Griffin searches for an effective antidote before that happens. During the course of Radcliffe's investigation, Griffin continues to take samples of Radcliffe's blood. At one point, Griffin breaks down after repeated attempts to find an antidote have failed. Vincent Price's quiet, sinister, threatening voice as he holds a gun on Cobb, murmuring, "Nobody can help you now," might be the only truly chilling portion of the movie. On its own terms, *The Invisible Man Returns* is an amusing trifle but nowhere near the aesthetic brilliance of the previous monster movies, including its own predecessor.

The supporting cast is good, with actors like Sir Cedric Hardwicke as Cobb, Alan Napier as Willie Spears, Cecil Kellaway as Inspector Sampson, and Nan Grey as Helen turning in solid, competent performances. Napier, best known as Alfred, the Wayne butler on the 1960s TV series *Batman*, is especially fun in his over-the-top comic portrayal.

Critics noticed that *The Invisible Man's Return* was much more light-hearted than its predecessor, the *New York Times* stating,

> *The Invisible Man Returns* is a mite on the ghostly side, too, although neither so horrendous nor so humorous as the first one was. Blame that on time and *Topper*, which have given us several other peeks at the unseen. Somehow we were not as astonished as once we were when a man unrolled a bandage from his head and revealed no head, or when he shucked off his clothes and became nothing but a nothing, or when he went for a stroll in the woods and all we could see were twigs snapping back and underbrush being trampled. This camera hocus-pocus still has its fascination, of course, for fantasy has

been fascinating since Melies made his *Trip to the Moon*, but the script is annoyingly unoriginal. Special effects are even more effective when novelty is not confined to camera technique.[1]

Variety noted,

> Picture is a high spot in special effects and trick photography. John Fulton and his staff, also responsible for the same work in the first Invisible Man, provide some amazing scenes and eerie situations.[2]

The reviews paying attention to the special effects over the screenplay or performances is quite accurate, as it is these Oscar-nominated effects, by John P. Fulton, Bernard B. Brown, and William Hedgcock, that are the most effective elements of the production. A scene where Radcliffe walks by Inspector Sampson and his image is quickly revealed in the detective's pipe smoke as he goes by is just one of the impressive special effects moments in the movie. The score by Frank Skinner is also very effective. Director Joe May does have a few interesting ideas outside of the effects. His establishing shots often show a clock, reminding us that both Radcliffe and Griffin are working against time. His uses of darkness and light and the way the camera pans to follow a character we cannot see also help to enhance the movie's visuals. However, May's reputation for being dictatorial and his refusing to learn the English language made working with him difficult during the making of this movie. Vincent Price would later recall,

> He was very difficult, mainly because he didn't speak English. He would try to give me direction and I'd say, "For God's sake, Joe, tell me in German, because I can get along better with you in German than I can in English." I don't think anyone in the cast ever understood a word he said![3]

The Invisible Man Returns is nowhere near the cinematic level of its predecessor, but this certainly did not hurt its box office. Audiences seemed to enjoy the lighter approach to the material, and the movie was a big hit. *The Invisible Man Returns* was made for less than $300,000 and grossed over $800,000 at the box office. As a result, Universal went right to work on another variation of the H. G. Wells creation, this time with a gender variation and playing it for straight comedy. *The Invisible Woman* went into production right away. And at the same time, Universal decided to revisit the Mummy series with *The Mummy's Hand*. Both films were in production at the same time.

⑩

THE MUMMY'S HAND

(1940)

Director: Christy Cabanne.
Screenplay: Griffin Jay and Maxwell Shane, from a story by Griffin Jay.
Producer: Ben Pivar. *Cinematography:* Elwood Bredell. *Editing:* Phillip Cahn. *Art Direction:* Jack Otterson. *Music:* Hans J. Salter, Frank Skinner.
Cast: Dick Foran (Steve Banning), Peggy Moran (Marta Solvani), Wallace Ford (Babe Jenson), Eduardo Ciannelli (high priest), George Zucco (Professor Andoheb), Cecil Kellaway (Solvani), Charles Trowbridge (Dr. Petrie), Tom Tyler (Kharis), Sig Arno (beggar), Leon Belasco (Ali), Frank Lackteen, Murdock MacQuarrie (temple priests), Boris Karloff, James Crane (archive footage).
Released: September 20, 1940.
Running Time: 67 minutes.
Availability: DVD (Universal Home Video).

Universale Studios' return to producing monster movies continued to be successful with *The Mummy's Hand*. However, it was virtually impossible to not make a profit on this movie, as its budget was a paltry $80,000. This is very low, even for 1940. Despite the meager budget, *The Mummy's Hand* succeeds as an effectively creepy B movie.

The film opens with a veritable explanation of what happened in the 1932 movie *The Mummy*, truncating and simplifying its narrative while renaming the central character Kharis. When showing his crime of wanting to bring the Princess Ananka back to life, they add an element: his crime is identified as stealing sacred tana leaves. It is for that reason that he has his tongue cut out and is mummified and buried alive. The tana leaves are

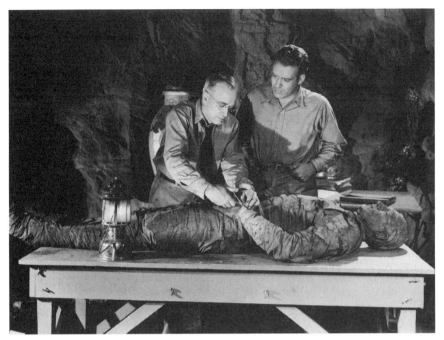

Charles Trowbridge, Dick Foran, and the Mummy (Tom Tyler).

buried with him and continue to be the key to Kharis's later existence. This creature is kept alive by administering the brew of three tana leaves during a full moon. This opening is very effective, blending stock footage with scenes newly shot for this specific film. It sets up the narrative parameters effectively before changing scenes and introducing the other characters.

The lighter element of *The Invisible Man Returns* had been effective enough to add a humorous touch to this film. Steve Banning and Babe Jenson are two wisecracking archaeologists, with Dick Foran playing Banning, the more serious-oriented one, and Wallace Ford as Jenson, more of a sidckick who engages in things like card tricks and smart patter. Both Foran and Ford were established actors who played supporting roles in A movies and leading roles in B movies. They have a solid screen presence, are likable and amusing, and fit the proceedings nicely.

Banning finds a broken vase at a Cairo bazaar and believes it to be an ancient relic that contains the key to Ananka's tomb among its hieroglyphics. They receive the support of Dr. Petrie, head of the Egyptian museum; receive funding from Solvani, a magician they meet in a bar; and plan to set out on an expedition. However, Andoheb, a museum employee, warns the magician's daughter, Marta, and claims that Banning and Jenson are frauds. This results in the magician and his daughter going along on the expedition.

The film's structure is a bit unlike the previous horror films. While it contains the serious story and the lighthearted humorous element, it also interrupts the narrative for a fight scene that doesn't have a great deal of discernible motivation. The fight is brief and involves punches, broken bottles, and broken chairs before Banning, Jenson, and Solvani go out the window.

Once the expedition is under way, the use of stock footage for transitions is more evident, but they mix well with newly shot scenes. One of the most effective is their discovery of Kharis's tomb. The camera pans darkly over the group as they remove the top of the casket, and as it focuses on the mummified remains, the music swells to a crescendo. Earlier films of the 1930s effectively used silence. But by now, even the low-budget films took advantage of the background musical score.

The film transitions from the light comedy and narrative drama to horror when Dr. Petrie is confronted alone in the Mummy's tomb by Andoheb, who gives Kharis the serum from tana leaves and brings him to life. The wakened Mummy kills Petrie and leaves through a secret passage with Andoheb.

Kharis later moves through the camp, killing Ali, the expedition's overseer; attacking Solvani; and kidnapping Marta. Banning and Jenson go after Kharis to rescue Marta. Meanwhile, Andoheb finds himself compulsively attracted to her and plans to inject her and himself with the fluid of tana leaves so they can be immortal together. This particular plot element is a bit bemusing. While it appears that Andoheb's attraction to Marta is supposed to parallel Kharis and Ananka, it comes out of nowhere. There isn't even a minor setup to indicate any such feelings toward her. Suddenly, he is in love with her and wants to retain her eternally.

Jenson finds Andoheb and shoots him when he refuses to tell where Marta is. Meanwhile, Banning finds Marta but is confronted by Kharis. Banning's bullets are ineffective as the Mummy approaches him, and the creature is too powerful to fight. Instead, the urn of tana fluid is shot, splattering its contents to the floor. Kharis lies on the floor and tries to lap it up but is destroyed when Banning breaks a fiery brazier over the Mummy, causing it to go up in flames. The film ends when the expedition returns to America with the Mummy of Ananka.

While *The Mummy's Hand* is an entertaining low-budget horror movie, it is filled with the sort of plot holes and misconceptions that require one to realize that fun is more important than logic. First, Kharis is considered the bad guy. Yet all he did is commit a crime for the sake of pure love. For that, he is buried alive and later resurrected by one who commits him to do evil. Meanwhile, the good guys are essentially grave robbers for profit who swindle a magician into financing their expedition. But somehow it all comes off efficaciously due to good direction, strong performances, a brisk narrative, and a great score by H. J. Salter.

The makeup by Universal monster master Jack Pierce is once again quite brilliant. The dried tissue, darkened face, and blackened eyes offer a horrifying image. While actor Tom Tyler, who played Kharis, would undertake the grueling makeup process for close-ups, in other shots he wore a rubber mask. In tighter shots, his eyes and mouth were blackened frame by frame to create the more frightening image.

Tom Tyler specialized in western films throughout his career. He appears in such classics as *Stagecoach* (1939) and *The Westerner* (1940) and appeared in a series of Three Mesquiteers westerns at Republic Pictures studios as the character Stony Brooke. His appearance as Kharis is something of a career aberration. But his scary, shuffling approach more accurately defines how we perceive the Mummy in horror movies of this period than Karloff's interpretation, so this career aberration remains impactful.

Director Christy Cabanne had little background in horror movies and directed few films in the genre during his long career. By the time he directed *The Mummy's Hand*, he had been an active filmmaker for nearly 30 years, dating back to the earliest days of silent cinema. His veteran talents are evident in scenes like when Kharis is shown, in shadow, approaching the tent—filmed every bit as effectively as similar scenes in *Dracula*.

According to an article in the June 1, 1940, issue of *Showmen's Trade Review*,

> The top role in Universal's forthcoming mystery thriller *The Mummy's Hand* is slated for Peter Lorre if his present commitments permit. The picture will be directed by Christy Cabanne, who is at present lining up the rest of the cast.

However, Lorre was still filming *Stranger on the Third Floor* at RKO, in which he had the lead, and the same studio committed him to next appear with bandleader Kay Kyser in *You'll Find Out*, along with Boris Karloff and Bela Lugosi. Thus, he does not appear in *The Mummy's Hand*.

Critics recognized *The Mummy's Hand* as a B movie that would play in a double feature but were generally impressed. Some pointed out the inherent humor, while others responded more to the somber tone of the proceedings. The stodgy *New York Times* was dismissive, as it often was for Universal's monster movies. Its critic Bosley Crowther stated,

It's the usual mumbo-jumbo of secret tombs in crumbling temples and sala-cious old high priests guarding them against the incursions of an archaeologi-cal expedition, led this time by Dick Foran, Peggy Moran and Wallace Ford. While the scientists busily explore dank passageways and decipher weird hieroglyphics on tombs and chests, jackals howl outside, the native work-gangs mutiny and the Mummy is always just around the corner. Once or twice Miss Moran makes a grimace—as if she had caught an unpleasant odor—and screams. Otherwise every one seems remarkably casual. If they don't seem to worry, why should we? Frightening or funny, take your choice.[1]

This did not hurt the box office, especially for such a low-budget movie. Perhaps part of the reason that this specific film had such a low budget was because of how much was being spent on the simultaneously shot *The Invisible Woman*. The special effects in that movie expanded that budget to over three times the amount of this one. *The Mummy's Hand* was very profitable, taking in anywhere from $10,000 to $20,000 at theaters where it appeared. Recouping its $80,000 was quite easy, and a substantial profit to help offset the special effects costs of *The Invisible Woman* made the studio very happy.

However, despite this low budget and its comfortable B-level status, *The Mummy's Hand* might be the most compelling and entertaining of all the Mummy movies subsequent to the 1932 original. Later films would be entertaining but not quite as stirring and absorbing as this one despite the limited budget and previously mentioned cinematic flaws. The Mummy series was originally intended to feature high-level sequels like *The Bride of Frankenstein* and *Dracula's Daughter*. But when Charles Rogers halted production on all horror movies, these ideas were jettisoned. Then when Cliff Work took over and restarted the horror productions, they were oper-ating on lesser budgets and different concepts. And still, within its B-level status, *The Mummy's Hand* remains compelling and entertaining decades later. Perhaps this is something of a testament to period B movies as it is to the capabilities of the Universal team under tight budget restrictions.

While *The Invisible Woman*, which was released soon afterward, is also part of the Universal monsters cycle, like the other sequel to *The Invisible Man*, it is hardly a textbook example of a horror movie. In fact, the humor that lightened up *The Mummy's Hand* was the focal point of *The Invisible Woman*, even to the point of having Shemp Howard in the supporting cast.

THE INVISIBLE WOMAN

(1940)

Director: A. Edward Sutherland.
Screenplay: Robert Lees, Fred Rinaldo, Gertrude Purcell, from a story by
    Curt Siodmak and Joe May.
Producers: Cliff Work, Burt Kelly. *Cinematography:* Elwood Bredell. *Editing:*
    Frank Gross. Art *Direction:* Jack Otterson. *Music:* Frank Skinner.
Cast: Virginia Bruce (Kitty), John Barrymore (Professor Gibbs), John
    Howard (Richard Russell), Charlie Ruggles (George), Oskar
    Homolka (Blackie), Edward Brophy (Bill), Donald MacBride
    (Foghorn), Margaret Hamilton (Mrs. Jackson), Shemp Howard
    (Frankie), Anne Nagel (Jean), Kathryn Adams (Peggy), Maria Montez
    (Marie), Charles Lane (Growley), Mary Gordon (Mrs. Bates),
    Thurston Hall (Hudson), Eddie Conrad Hernandez), Kitty O'Neill
    (Mrs. Patten), Kay Leslie (model), Sarah Edwards, Kay Linaker
    (showroom buyers), Harry C. Bradley (want ad clerk).
Released: December 27, 1940.
Running Time: 72 minutes.
Availability: DVD (Universal Home Video).

While shooting the low-budget *The Mummy's Hand*, Universal spent a bit more on special effects for *The Invisible Woman*, which was shot around the same time and released three months later. However, while *The Invisible Woman* is often a delightful and amusing B movie, it is not a horror film. It deals with the concept of invisibility and is considered part of the Invisible Man series, but it plays as a straight comedy.

The story for the previous *The Invisible Man Returns* had been written by Curt Siodmak and Joe May, so Cliff Work asked them to submit another variation on H. G. Wells's concept. The story that Siodmak and May created was a more serious horror picture about a mad scientist turning a woman invisible, and, unlike a man, her response is to cattily get even with others. The story was turned over to Robert Lees and Fred Rinaldo, who specialized in comedy and had an affinity for slapstick. Gertrude Purcell, who had contributed to the screenplay for the popular western comedy *Destry Rides Again* (1939), was hired to help add a woman's perspective to the script due to its having a female title character. Finally, the director hired is A. Edward Sutherland, who also specialized in comedy, having directed silent comedies with Wallace Beery and Raymond Hatton as well as W. C. Fields in several films, including *Mississippi* (1935) and *Poppy* (1936), along with having helmed the Laurel and Hardy feature *The Flying Deuces* (1939). *The Invisible Woman* may have been a more serious story as envisioned by Siodmak and May, but after rewrites by Lees and Rinaldo and with Sutherland at the helm, the result is a lightweight comedy.

John Barrymore responds to an apparition known as the Invisible Woman.

The story deals with an eccentric professor being funded by a wealthy lawyer. He has had little success with his experiments until he comes up with a way to make people invisible. He puts an ad in the paper for subjects, and it is answered by Kitty Carol. Kitty is a dress model who has to deal with a bitter, overbearing boss. She isn't happy with life and is intrigued by the scientist's ad. The experiment is successful, and she goes to get even with her sadistic employer. He is so spooked by the invisible image in his office that he changes his ways and becomes accommodating and friendly.

In a tangential subplot, a group of bumbling gangsters steal the machine that causes invisibility, but they can't figure out how it works. They kidnap Kitty, no longer invisible, and force the scientist to show them how to work the device. She finds that drinking straight alcohol restores her invisibility, so she vanishes again and defeats the gang. The movie concludes with Kitty, now married with children, showing that her invisibility has become hereditary, as one of her children vanishes when rubbed with alcohol. The film also has a romantic element (between Kitty and the wealthy lawyer, to whom she is married by the end of the movie), but it has little impact on the overall structure of the film.

As with *The Invisible Man Returns*, the special effects in *The Invisible Woman* by John P. Fulton are quite impressive, garnering him another Oscar nomination. The script has amusing dialogue and a good amount of slapstick, deftly handled by the cast and director Sutherland. It plays effectively as a pleasantly diverting B comedy. Unlike *Frankenstein* or *Dracula* or even *The Invisible Man*, this movie does not have the same aesthetic level and works only when not taken seriously.

The classically trained John Barrymore enjoyed relaxing in unpretentious comedy roles and chews the scenery with gusto as Professor Gibbs, the scientist. Charlie Ruggles is delightfully stuffy and sarcastic as wealthy lawyer Richard Russell's brother. John Howard is a handsome, anchoring presence as Russell. And, in the title role, Virginia Bruce is attractive and appropriately wisecracking. Margaret Sullivan was originally slated for the role of Kitty but balked at appearing in the film and was suspended by the studio. That is when Miss Bruce was hired.

The supporting cast lends a great deal to the amusement of this feature. The gangsters who steal the machine are played by comedy veterans like Donald MacBride, Edward Brophy, and Shemp Howard (a few years before he would rejoin the Three Stooges in 1946). Oscar Homolka, as their blustery leader, maintains the same comic presence.

Some of the comedy is positively silly. An experiment gone wrong causes the deep voice of gangster Foghorn to become shrill and high pitched.

When the nervous butler is told to call the airport, he hollers "Airport!" before doing a double take and heading to the phone. But this sort of absurdity fits the movie nicely. The climax with her invisible presence slapping, bopping, and tripping the gangsters is pure outrageous slapstick and competently entertaining. The humor coming from Kitty's invisibility works best toward the beginning of the film. Kitty using her invisibility to get revenge on her former boss adds a feminist element to the proceedings that was not explored further.

At the time of its release, *The Invisible Woman* was considered a bit risqué. The idea that the woman is naked while invisible is used for comedy, but the very idea of such a thing in a 1940s movie caused misgivings among more conservative moviegoers. They also reacted to a scene where models are changing into other sets of clothes backstage at a showing. Although there was nothing revealing about any of these scenes, the production code was quite strict in 1940.

Critics were generally dismissive of *The Invisible Woman*. They did not connect it to any sort of series or to the Universal horror output. They approached it simply as a silly comedy. Theodore Strauss of the *New York Times* offered a rather backhanded complimentary review on January 9, 1941, stating,

Perhaps the maddest jape to have arrived hereabouts recently is *The Invisible Woman*. It is silly, banal and repetitious; it is essentially a two-reel comedy with elephantiasis and full of the trick disappearances and materializations that seemed new when *Topper* first came out. The script is as creaky as a two-wheeled cart and were it not for the fact that John Barrymore is taking a ride in it we hate to think what *The Invisible Woman* might have turned out to be. But Mr. Barrymore takes to this trash as if he were to the manner born. He gives a performance that lampoons all actors, but especially his brother Lionel, who would be perfectly within his rights to sue John as an impostor and a plagiarist. As a crafty old scientist, full of formulas for making people invisible, he gives a ludicrous portrait of dementia. He is arch and gleeful by turns; he gropes with his hands, he blows in his cheeks and makes mirthful clucking sounds. As usual, there are the infatuation between a young Romeo and a lady he has never seen, bottles and cocktail glasses floating through air and puffs of smoke coming from a point in space. There is also the glamorous, if invisible, nonentity known as Virginia Bruce, who has perhaps the most thankless assignment since Constance Bennett in *Topper*. There is the butler who faints on cue, otherwise Charles Ruggles. But it is Mr. Barrymore who so scandalously accents a preposterous affair that it becomes amusing as a lampoon on itself. At least we like to believe that Mr. Barrymore's wink meant that there was more nonsense in *The Invisible Woman* than met the eye.

The Invisible Woman was well received by moviegoers and made money for the studio. Despite the effects driving up the film's budget to nearly $300,000, quite a large sum when compared to the $80,000 for The Mummy's Hand, the investment was worthwhile. The success of The Mummy's Hand helped offset these costs, and The Invisible Woman made nearly $700,000 at the box office.

The year 1940 was a fairly transitional one for Universal. By the time The Invisible Woman was released in December, the studio had acquired the services of a burlesque comedy team that had scored in the Broadway show The Streets of Paris a few years earlier. Bud Abbott and Lou Costello had become a hit on Broadway and on radio, so they were added as a comic afterthought to the musical One Night in the Tropics, which starred Allan Jones, Nancy Kelly, and Robert Cummings. Abbott and Costello easily stole the film from its stars and were such a sensation that some theaters were citing them on marquees as the leads of the film. This caused the studio to focus more on producing their comedies, and thus, during 1941, the duo would have four hit movies in the theaters: Buck Privates, In the Navy, Hold That Ghost, and Keep 'Em Flying. This is significant not only because it put into perspective where Universal was by 1940 but also because the comedy and horror franchises would be blended together before the end of the decade.

The monster movies would continue, as they proved to be consistent moneymakers for the studio and enjoyed a strong legacy. The next film in the monster series was not a sequel. Curt Siodmak, who had been contributing stories for the studio's horror films, penned a complete screenplay for a movie based on the concept of the werewolf, as shown in Werewolf of London (1935). The Wolf Man would star Lon Chaney Jr., whose father had been one of the studio's biggest stars during the silent era. It would also be the finest Universal monster movie since Bride of Frankenstein.

12

THE WOLF MAN

(1941)

Director: George Waggner.
Screenplay: Curt Siodmak.
Producers: Jack J. Gross, George Waggner. *Cinematography:* Joseph A.
    Valentine. *Film Editing:* Ted Kent. *Art Direction:* Jack Otterson. *Music:*
    Charles Previn, Hans J. Salter, Frank Skinner.
Cast: Lon Chaney Jr. (Larry Talbot), Claude Rains (Sir John Talbot), Evelyn
    Ankers (Gwen) Warren William (Dr. Lloyd), Ralph Bellamy (Colonel
    Paul Montford), Patric Knowles (Frank Andrews), Bela Lugosi (Bela),
    Maria Ouspenskaya (Maleva), J. M. Kerrigan (Conliffe), Fay Helm
    (Jenny), Doris Lloyd (Mrs. Williams), Forrester Harvey (Twiddle),
    Harry Cording (Wykes), Leyland Hodgson (Kendall), Connie Leon
    (Mrs. Wykes), Ottola Nesmith (Mrs. Bally), Ernie Tanton (Phillips),
    Harry Stubbs (Reverend Norman), Tom Stevenson (grave digger),
    Jessie Arnold (Gypsy), La Riana (dancer), Anne Sterling (Gypsy girl),
    Caroline Francis Cooke, Margaret Fealy (women), Gibson Gowland,
    Olaf Hytten, Monte O'Grady (villagers), Eric Wilton (chauffeur).
Released: December 12, 1941.
Running Time: 70 minutes.
Availability: DVD (Universal Home Video).

The Wolf Man extended beyond the werewolf ideas featured in *Werewolf of London* and explored deeper issues within the character and his response to becoming a monster. An original screenplay by Curt Siodmak that had no real basis in literature, *The Wolf Man* is, in every way, as great a cinematic classic as *Dracula, Frankenstein,* or *The Bride of Frankenstein.* It helped define the career of Lon Chaney Jr., the son of the silent screen horror master, even though the younger Chaney had achieved critical acclaim for playing Lennie in the 1939 screen version of John Steinbeck's *Of Mice and Men*. Chaney would remain with Universal for several years, revisiting the Wolf Man character and also doing other iconic monster roles.

Not only does this film benefit from an original script and a strong leading man, but the cast is also rounded out by Bela Lugosi, Claude Rains, Maria Ouspenskaya, Ralph Bellamy, Warren William, Patrick Knowles, and Evelyn Ankers. Each offers somewhere near their best work despite how much or little footage is dedicated to their respective characters.

The plot of *The Wolf Man* features Larry Talbot, a man of privilege and breeding, returning to his Wales home on learning of his brother's death. He has been absent for 18 years, effectively making it on his own, but now he has returned to reconcile with his father. Little is spent detailing Larry's reasons for leaving and his lack of contact with the family, but his father exhibits patience and understanding, more glad to be reconciled with his only surviving son than upset that he'd been away without contact for so long. Alluding to a younger interest in astronomy, Larry enjoys looking out of a telescope in his old room. He notices a pretty lady working at a nearby antique shop and makes an effort to go introduce himself to her.

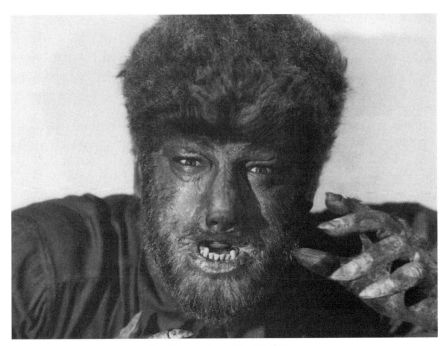

Lon Chaney Jr. as the Wolf Man.

The narrative does an effective job of introducing the Larry Talbot character. It establishes his independence and his ability to make it on his own away from the wealth and privilege to which he's accustomed but also presents him as a good man, one who believes in honesty and hard work. He is a big man with an imposing presence and an easy manner. When he introduces himself to Gwen, the pretty lady at the antique shop, he has no problem admitting he initially saw her through a telescope. She is more amused by him than unsettled by this indication. As a friendly icebreaker, Talbot purchases a walking stick with a silver head of a wolf as its handle and continues to flirt with Gwen even after she reveals she has a boyfriend.

It is the walking stick that causes Talbot to first learn about the existence of werewolves. Gwen tells him that the walking stick's handle represents a legend where a man turns into a wolf and kills others against his will, returning to his mortal self the next day with nothing but vague, haunting memories of his murderous deeds. She recites a poem that goes with the legend:

> Even a man who is pure in heart,
> And says his prayers by night.
> May become a wolf when the wolf bane blooms,
> And the autumn moon is bright.

Talbot's manner is steady when he makes a date with Gwen but discovers on picking her up that they are to be joined by her friend Jenny. Chaney, the actor, plays this beautifully—displaying disappointment and shrugging acceptance at the same time as he willingly escorts both girls to an outdoor festival where Gypsies have set up camp.

Jenny goes into a tent to have her fortune read. The fortune-teller sees a pentagram in her hand (revealing her to be a werewolf's next victim) and orders her to leave. Jenny becomes very frightened and runs out of the tent. Larry and Gwen hear her screams and run to her aid. Larry sees her being attacked by a wolf. He goes to her rescue, beating the wolf to death with the silver tip of his walking stick.

Bela Lugosi plays the fortune-teller and, with only a few minutes of screen time, turns in one of the strongest performances of the entire film. He is at first attractively mysterious as if to be in character as a quintessential Gypsy fortune-teller, making extra money with what Jenny and friends respond to as an amusing exhibit. The shot of the pentagram is accentuated by a sudden "bang" in the musical background as the camera cuts to Lugosi's face, displaying both concern and terror. When his manner abruptly changes and he leaps to his feet ordering Jenny to leave immediately, the frail girl screams in fright and leaves quickly. The music swells throughout this scene, further enhancing the drama. We realize that the fortune-teller is a werewolf, and his ordering the woman away is an attempt to save her from what he is about to become.

The director makes a good choice in showing Talbot beating the wolf who is attacking Jenny through a tree from a medium shot. Talbot frantically beats downward with his walking stick, but the tree does not allow us to see the beast being beaten. There are a few quick edits to Talbot wrestling with the animal, the close shots focusing on his wild eyes as he subdues the beast from further damaging its victim. He flails again with his stick, his arm slowing down from fatigue. The music, the editing, and the camera all structure this very pivotal scene brilliantly, while Chaney's focused reactions giving a heroic strength to his character.

It is important to note that when Bela turns into a werewolf, it is not in the form of a wolf man. He emerges as an actual wolf, an animal that looks like any other wolf, so Talbot does not see any semblance of a human form; he simply sees an animal. He is bitten in the chest when he wrestles with the beast but otherwise escapes unharmed. He is brought home by Gwen, with the help of Maleva, an old Gypsy lady, who is later revealed to be the fortune-teller's mother. Talbot is put to bed after announcing he attempted to save Jenny from a wolf attack. The police run to the scene and discover Jenny's dead body and, nearby, the fortune-teller, who has returned to human form. He is barefoot and had been bludgeoned to death. Larry's walking stick is found nearby.

The next day, the police, a doctor, and Larry's father confront him with the walking stick, which he identifies as his own. When they explain it appears to have been used to kill the fortune-teller, Larry is bewildered. He did not see the wolf transform back to a man. He saw only a wolf. In a later meeting with Maleva, the curse of the werewolf is explained. She states that whoever is bitten by a werewolf and survives will become one. She further states that the only way to kill a werewolf is with a silver bullet, a silver knife, or a stick with a silver handle (like Larry's walking stick). Larry tries to be dismissive of this as malarkey, but a visit to the morgue where the fortune-teller lies in state; the angry barking of an otherwise friendly dog; and the family doctor's gentle patronizing, which seems to deem him insane, all combine to make him increasingly more unsettled.

Larry has been established as a relaxed, friendly individual who sought life as a working man who understood machines, electronics, and other matters. Something psychological that baffles science simply bewilders him. Because he is shown as very social, his gregarious nature is thwarted by the lust to kill that overtakes him. This is finally borne out when we are shown Talbot's first transformation. He twitches and itches, feeling hairs growing on his arms and chest. He removes a sock and finds his leg and foot covered with hair. A shot of his feet shows a slow transformation into appendages that seem more like back paws. The camera follows these paws into the woods before panning up and revealing the whole werewolf. Larry, the Wolf Man, makes his first kill. It is a grave digger in the churchyard. When he awakens the next morning, a fully clothed, barefoot Larry Talbot finds himself lying on his back in bed, a window open with animal tracks leading up to his feet. He wipes them away.

The trajectory of the Wolf Man is much different than the other noted Universal monsters. The Frankenstein monster responded to stimuli. Count Dracula was a vampire who remained so, even when associating with others. The Invisible Man had a quest for power. But Larry Talbot is a victim who was bitten while trying to rescue a young woman. He did not gamble with danger in a quest for power; rather, he tried to help someone who was being attacked.

Talbot becomes gradually more emotionally unstable until he finally accepts his curse and believes he must leave the area and attempt to sort it out. When he goes to see Gwen to tell her he is leaving the area, he sees a pentagram in the palm of her hand. He frantically warns her to stay away.

Larry's father tries to convince him that all he needs is proper psychiatric care. He ties Larry to a chair near a window so he can watch a hunting party that plans to kill the wolf they believe is roaming about and attacking villagers. The father, part of this group, wants Larry to witness this in hopes that it will cure him from believing he is somehow responsible. Larry insists that his father take the walking stick with the silver handle.

Larry transforms into a werewolf and breaks from his bonds. He goes into the woods and finds Gwen, attacking her. Larry's father comes to her rescue and bludgeons the Wolf Man. Once he has killed the beast, he looks in horror as it slowly reverts back to Larry. By the time the others in the hunting party arrive, they conclude that the wolf attacked Gwen, that Larry came to her rescue, and that he was killed in the confusion. Mr. Talbot, however, realizes he killed his own son. The film concludes on that note.

While the basic legend of the werewolf was old, Curt Siodmak's script defined it for all subsequent portrayals. Even the poem was his creation, and in later years the writer would laugh at how people believed it was actual folklore. It would be repeated in some subsequent Universal movies featuring the Wolf Man character. This film does not use the full-moon angle, however. In subsequent movies, it is a full moon that causes Talbot's transformation. Here it is merely at night as the wolf bane blooms. In actual folklore, a curse from making a pact with the devil resulted in becoming a werewolf. The transformation could happen day or night, and werewolves could be killed in standard ways that could kill anything mortal.

Most of the werewolf tale was original to this movie. Some could be found in the earlier *Werewolf of London*, but a person becoming a werewolf from a bite, a silver weapon being necessary to kill a werewolf, the mark of the pentagram, and so on were the creation of screenwriter Siodmak.

The Wolf Man was also the title of a 1924 John Gilbert melodrama in which he plays a mild-mannered man who becomes a beast (figuratively so) when he drinks to excess. While there is no indication the concept of this earlier movie inspired this film, Siodmak's script did not call for a physical transformation at all. The script is ambiguous as to whether such a transformation takes place or whether it is simply within the mind of the character. Siodmak did not indicate that a Wolf Man creature would ever actually appear on-screen. The script was revised when the studio reasoned that an actual monster on-screen made the movie better. An early draft of the script also presents Larry not as Talbot's son but as a working-class engineer who comes to the Talbot castle to repair Sir John Talbot's telescope.

Boris Karloff was originally considered for the title role, but he was busy with other projects. Bela Lugosi actively campaigned for the part, but it ended up going to Lon Chaney Jr. Curt Siodmak told Keith Alan Deutsch for *Black Mask Magazine*,

> Lon Chaney Jr. was a friend of mine. I never met senior. Lon was a very patient man and a pro. You know it took almost 6 hours to put the Wolfman's mask on his face, the claws, the hair, and two hours to take it all off. He could eat only liquid food through a straw when he wore that mask. Jack Pierce, the famous make-up man, devised the Wolfman's mask.[1]

The makeup Lon Chaney uses for the character was Jack Pierce's original idea for Henry Hull in *Werewolf of London*. Hull's insistence on lesser makeup so he could exhibit nuanced facial expressions (and his character within the narrative could be recognized) resulted in his not fully agreeing to Pierce's vision.

Siodmak was already established at Universal as a screenwriter when producer/director George Waggner hired him to write the screenplay. He told Dennis Fischer,

> George Waggner said to me, "We have a title called *The Wolf Man*. It comes from Boris Karloff, but Boris has no time to do it, he is working on another pic-

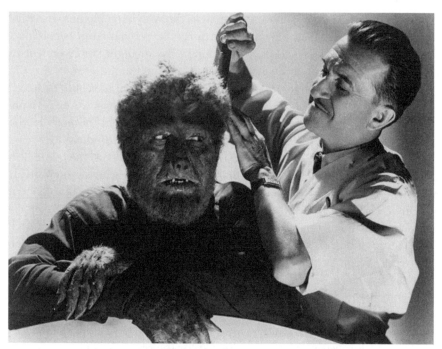

Jack Pierce applies the Wolf Man makeup to Lon Chaney Jr.

ture. So, we have Lon Chaney, Madame Ouspenskaya, Warren William, Ralph Bellamy, and Claude Rains. The budget is $180,000 and we start in ten weeks." In seven weeks I gave George the screenplay. I made $3000 on that job.[2]

The film's cast is especially impressive. Aside from Chaney and Lugosi, Claude Rains was cast as Sir John Talbot. Removing himself completely from his title role performance in *The Invisible Man*, Rains must now portray the concerned patriarch who observes the madness his performance exhibited in the earlier movie. The look on his face as he realizes he has just killed his son is one of the most striking images in the entire film.

Madam Maria Ouspenskaya was a noted acting teacher whose role as the Gypsy lady Maleva gave her something of a legendary status as an actress despite past accomplishments with the Moscow Art Theater and her cofounding the School of Dramatic Arts in New York City. Familiar faces like Warren William, Ralph Bellamy, and Patric Knowles round out the cast nicely.

Evelyn Ankers, who played Gwen, did not get along well with her costars. Coming to Universal from Fox, she was at the studio only a week before being cast in *Hold That Ghost* (1941) with Abbott and Costello. The comedy team enjoyed having an active set with practical jokes and pie throwing to keep up the comedy spirit between scenes. Ankers was, as described by her husband, actor Richard Denning, "this almost 'stuffy' English girl." She spent most of the movie standing with her back to the wall, avoiding pie throwing and the comedians' penchant for tickling her, which, according to Denning, "didn't go over too well."[3] She then was placed in the Dead End Kids feature *Hit the Road* (1941). Ankers recalled in a later interview,

> On one occasion after a day's shooting I thought I was the last one to leave but on my way out I bumped into Dead End Kid Huntz Hall (acne and all). He put his arms around me and tried to force me to kiss him. I responded as my daddy taught me to—I let him have it with my knee right between his legs.[4]

By the time she did *The Wolf Man*, she had learned how to rise above her disdain for the actors she didn't like and get the job done. Her performance is quite good, and she agreed to pose in publicity shots with Lon Chaney Jr. She and Chaney would work together frequently on subsequent films, even though they never got along well.

One particularly difficult scene for Ankers to perform in *The Wolf Man* was the scene in which the monster attacks her. She was overcome by the

Evelyn Ankers and Lon Chaney Jr. joke around in a publicity shot.

fog produced by machines for the atmosphere of the scene and fainted on the set without anyone noticing. She told Doug McClelland, "It would have been a short career if they hadn't tripped over me."

But the worst situation on the set was a planned scene with a trained bear. Ankers recalled,

> The bear decided he wanted to know me better. The next thing I knew, Lon took off as did everybody else. I turned, wondering what the commotion was all about and where my leading man had gone, and saw the bear coming after me. I never ran so fast in all my life. With the bear coming close behind me, I shot up a ladder into the rafters, where an electrician grabbed my hand and pulled me on top of his platform. He then blinded the bear with a hot floodlight. The trainer finally caught up with the animal, retrieved his chain, reprimanded him, and gradually got him back down onto the stage.[5]

The footage with the bear that was filmed was not used, although some shots can be found in one of the movie's trailers.

Director George Waggner does an excellent job with his choice of shots, use of editing, and framing of each scene. Waggner's other work does not reveal him to be the sort of consistent stylist that a James Whale or Tod Browning had been. He was, in fact, a journeyman director who worked competently in several genres, mostly westerns, without making a real impact (he had previously directed Chaney in the movie *Man Made Monster*). *The Wolf Man* might be indicative of his best work. Waggner would later helm many TV episodes, including seven in *The Man from U.N.C.L.E.* series and 10 for *Batman*. Other than *The Wolf Man*, Waggner may be best known for writing and directing the John Wayne feature *The Fighting Kentuckian* (1949), which featured a solo supporting appearance by Oliver Hardy of Laurel and Hardy fame.

The film's score, by musical director Charles Previn, plays loud and soft, swirling behind the action and settling behind the dramatic scenes. It accents rather than overcomes and is highly effective. For example, it plays furiously behind Sir John bludgeoning the Wolf Man at the end of the movie but quiets for the last two blows, leaving only the sound of the walking stick pounding the creature. This is another one of the most powerful moments in the movie.

A great deal happens in the movie's 70-minute running time, and not a second is wasted. All the performances by the capable cast are outstanding, and each scene is staged most effectively. On its $180,000 budget, *The Wolf Man* was another box office success for the studio during a year when the newly hired Abbott and Costello climbed to the top spot among movie moneymakers. Universal was now rising to the level of a major studio again and on the strength of B horror movies and a couple of burlesque comics. *The Wolf Man* was the highest-grossing film of the year at the prestigious Rialto theater in New York, breaking a box office record.

Trade ad for *The Wolf Man.*

Lon Chaney Jr. proved he could live up to his late father's success in horror films, sharing his dad's ability to portray a wild beast as well as a tortured, sensitive soul. During his subsequent tenure at Universal, Chaney would play nearly every noted monster character (or a variation thereof) and star in a series of Inner Sanctum Mysteries that were popular B movies for the studio.

Chaney's impressive work in *The Wolf Man* resulted in his being cast as the Frankenstein monster in a planned production titled *The Ghost of Frankenstein*. Boris Karloff was no longer interested in the role, believing he had taken it as far as he could. But the studio was not about to abandon the profitable *Frankenstein* series. Along with Chaney, three actors from *The Wolf Man* would be hired to act in *The Ghost of Frankenstein*, including Evelyn Ankers, once again as leading lady; Bela Lugosi reviving his role of Ygor; and Ralph Bellamy. It began shooting only three days after production wrapped up on *The Wolf Man*.

13

THE GHOST OF FRANKENSTEIN

(1942)

Director: Erle C. Kenton.
Screenplay: W. Scott Darling, from a story by Eric Taylor.
Producer: George Waggner. *Cinematography:* Milton Krasner. *Film Editing:* Ted Kent. *Art Direction:* Jack Otterson. *Music:* Hans J. Salter.
Cast: Lon Chaney Jr. (the monster), Sir Cedric Hardwicke (Ludwig Frankenstein), Ralph Bellamy (Erik Ernst), Lionel Atwill (Doctor Bohmer), Bela Lugosi (Ygor), Evelyn Ankers (Elsa Frankenstein), Janet Ann Gallow (Cloestine), Barton Yarborough (Kettering), Doris Lloyd (Martha), Leyland Hodgson (chief constable), Olaf Hytten (Hussman), Holmes Herbert (magistrate), Harry Cording (Frone), Brandon Hurst (Hans), Julius Tannen (Sektal), Janet Warren (goose girl), William Irving (bully).
Released: March 13, 1942.
Running Time: 67 minutes.
Availability: DVD (Universal Home Video).

Continuing the *Frankenstein* saga was the studio's plan after *Son of Frankenstein* became such a hit at the box office. However, beginning with *The Ghost of Frankenstein*, the series continued as B movies with lower budgets and a few production shortcuts. A studio director like Erle C. Kenton was given the assignment rather than a stylist like James Whale. The script was put together by Scott Darling, who based his ideas on the screening of past films as well as the original story by Eric Taylor, who had worked on previous Universal horror films *The Black Cat* and *Black Friday*. Kenton, whose forte was comedy (he started with Mack Sennett during the silent era), simply followed an established pattern. It was basically a case of "we need another Frankenstein picture, guys, put one together."

Cost-cutting measures included utilizing the score written for *The Wolf Man* as the music, throwing in a few moments of stock footage, and making use of the available sets on the studio lot. The actors hired were under contract for the studio and had some background in the genre. Lon Chaney Jr., Evelyn Ankers, Ralph Bellamy, and Bela Lugosi were all working on *The Wolf Man* when they were hired to appear in *The Ghost of Frankenstein*.

However, despite its B-movie trappings, the talents of the screenwriter, the director, and the cast result in *The Ghost of Frankenstein* being a very succinct, entertaining film that effectively continues the progression of the series. Chaney, the first actor to take the role of the monster after Karloff refused to continue playing it, gives his own interpretation. The studio wisely kept Jack Pierce's makeup ideas, realizing any such change might seem jarring to moviegoers.

The Ghost of Frankenstein picks up where *Son of Frankenstein* leaves off, continuing the seamless narrative from movie to movie. *The Ghost of Frankenstein* opens with the Frankenstein residents believing they are under a curse because of the village's name. Cooler heads attempt to prevail by indicating the monster was buried in a sulfur pit and Ygor was riddled with bullets. The villagers insist on destroying the Frankenstein castle, but when they arrive with explosives, they discover Ygor, alive, on the roof. He attempts to thwart them by throwing rocks down at the villagers but to little avail. As the castle explodes around him, Ygor flees, and the wreckage reveals the monster, preserved in the sulfur. Ygor revives him enough to rescue him from the explosions. As they flee, a thunderstorm erupts, and lightning hits the monster, causing him to gain strength.

Although he was not referred to in previous films, Ygor speaks of a second son of Frankenstein, Ludwig, who lives in Visaria and is achieving success in discovering treatments for mental illness. He and his assistants Dr. Kettering and Dr. Bohmer have been experimenting successfully with removing a damaged brain from a person, altering it with surgery, and reinserting it into the patient. Ygor travels with the monster to Visaria and finds Ludwig Frankenstein, but the doctor is resistant to revisit his father's past. The monster kills Dr. Kettering, and Ludwig plans to destroy the monster. He then sees the image of his father, who advises him to perform the brain-altering operation on the monster. He plans to replace the monster's brain with Kettering's and make the creature one of scientific erudition.

Darling's script shows its research during several scenes in this portion of the movie. Realizing that the monster's response to children had an enor-

Lon Chaney Jr. and Lionel Atwill.

mous impact in previous films, that idea is revisited here. Some bullies are picking on a little girl and kick a ball she's playing with up onto an area that is unreachable. The monster approaches her, and she is more fascinated than frightened. "Are you a giant?" she asks. She also asks if he can get her ball. He gently takes the child into his arms and proceeds to climb steps toward where the ball is. Villagers run to her rescue but are knocked away. Once again, the monster means no harm to the child, but the frightened villagers respond in protective fear. The monster comes down the steps and hands the child to her terrified father.

The monster is then accosted by the villagers and bound to a chair in a courtroom. Ludwig Frankenstein is called due to his working with insane minds, not because they believe him to have any connection. The monster recognizes him. Frankenstein denies any knowledge of the monster. The angry monster escapes his bonds.

Ygor blackmails Frankenstein by threatening to tell his daughter, Elsa, about his family's nefarious past, as he has kept this information from her. However, after doing some snooping in her father's library, she finds her grandfather's notes detailing the creation of the monster. As she is perusing these notes, a shadow appears on the wall, and she sees the monster and Ygor looking in the window. She screams and flees from the room. Director Kenton films this scene very effectively, bathing Elsa in darkness as she quietly sneaks into the library and using lightning and shadows, as well as a cut to the image of the creature and Ygor, to add horror to the sequence. The effective scream of Elsa (actress Evelyn Ankers was known for her scream) adds greater accent to this scene.

Plot elements are nicely tied together via the characters, with police inspector Erik being romantically connected to Elsa. When he hunts for the monster, he questions Frankenstein and searches his home. Although Erik does find the secret room where they stay, both Ygor and the monster fled beforehand. Ygor, meanwhile, tries to manipulate Frankenstein's planned experiment. The doctor's intention to use an intelligent scientific brain in the creature is an attempt to right the wrong of his father's original experiment. Ygor, however, wants to leave his broken, tattered body and have his own brain in the undying monster. He tells Frankenstein's assistant, Bohmer, that he should not be a subordinate, having been the original Frankenstein's teacher and mentor. Ygor gets Bohmer to place Ygor's brain in the monster.

Darling's script adds an element that more deeply explores the monster's connection to a child. It goes to the home of the little girl with the ball and abducts her. Arriving at the castle, it is determined that the monster wants to have the child's brain. The child tells him she doesn't want to lose her brain, so the monster reluctantly places the child in the arms of Elsa, who takes her away. The monster having an opinion on the matter at all is quite a fascinating development that adds another layer to the character.

The script also cleverly presents the conflict regarding Frankenstein being duped into putting Ygor's brain into the monster. The villagers are ready to storm the castle, believing Frankenstein is harboring the monster who has kidnapped the little girl. Inspector Erik convinces the crowd to let him investigate. The doctor takes Erik to the monster, the operation having been completed. He believes Kettering's scientific mind has been transplanted into the monster. The doctor is aghast at hearing Ygor's voice. Ygor triumphantly proclaims he will now live forever. But he quickly loses his eyesight. Frankenstein explains that the blood type not matching would result in a limited use of the brain, thus Ygor's being blind. Ygor weeps that having immortality is useless without his sight and shoves Boehmer into one of the laboratory's electrical devices, electrocuting him. This causes the castle to catch fire, so Elsa and Erik escape as Ygor and the mortally wounded doctor perish.

A script that was filled with good ideas that paid homage to past films and a director who was skillful enough to be inspired by the earlier movies make *The Ghost of Frankenstein* come off as a tight, exciting horror melodrama. Running under 70 minutes, *The Ghost of Frankenstein* is also the shortest film of the Frankenstein series.

Chaney's approach to the monster was to make him more withdrawn as well as more focused. The monster responds well to the child but then is shown as having an ulterior motive regarding the little girl's brain. Chaney also adds the mannerism of the monster holding his arms outstretched as he walks, a gesture that has since become common when one mimics the monster's walk. Because there were children on the set, including the little girl, actor Chaney was concerned that they might be frightened of him, so he would buy them ice cream cones during breaks in filming. Janet Ann Gallow, who played the little girl, recalled in an interview with Dominic Florentino years later,

> I was never frightened with Lon, we got along great. He played with me a lot. Also, he would take me around and show me to everybody. After the film, he and his wife decided they would have me come over to the house. He asked if I could come over to see him and my mom said ok. I went and got pony rides at this other lady's house, and played with these miniature copper things that were all over the coffee table. They would make me fancy drinks with all kinds of different colors. There would be reds and blues. They were soft drinks, like strawberry and grape and pineapple. They were great.[1]

Evelyn Ankers, despite not getting along with Chaney, registers well as Elsa. Ankers was interviewed on the set by Ernest Bell for the April 1942 issue of *Hollywood* magazine. The focus landed on her talent for screaming. She stated,

> I'm proud of my scream. I developed it when I made six mystery pictures in England, and was always being terrified. I hope no one gets the bright idea of calling me the "Boo Girl." That would label me for life—and I hope I eventually get to do something in the movies besides scream.[2]

Bela Lugosi's second turn as Ygor further convinces the viewer that it is his finest horror film character despite being known as the quintessential

Dracula. His performance in *The Ghost of Frankenstein* adds even more of a horrific, sinister element to the narrative than the monster himself. When the monster is overtaken by Ygor's brain, Chaney's incorporating Lugosi's facial mannerisms is one of the performance highlights of the movie. Sir Cedric Hardwicke and Ralph Bellamy, as Frankenstein and Erik, respectively, add their solid talent to the proceedings and are further bolstered by Lionel Atwill as the jealous Bohmer.

Because of its short running time, *The Ghost of Frankenstein* was issued as part of a double feature, sometimes with a comedy as an antidote. In one instance, it was effectively paired with Laurel and Hardy's feature *A-Haunting We Will Go* when that film was released by 20th Century Fox a few months later. Interestingly enough, Scott Darling would soon be hired by Fox to write the screenplay for several Laurel and Hardy features. *The Ghost of Frankenstein* was also paired with the Warner Brothers comedy *Larceny, Inc.* with Edward G. Robinson. This pairing averaged nearly $5,000 at the box office during a nine-day run in Milwaukee, for example, with 35-cent ticket admission prices. When paired with the latest Charlie Chan feature, *Castle in the Desert*, this double feature broke all double-bill house records at a theater in Pittsburgh. In Canada, the film played in conjunction with a beauty contest and did tremendous business. Perhaps the most intriguing show was at a Boston theater, where *The Ghost of Frankenstein* was the sole screen attraction, along with a live act featuring Jimmy Durante. This grossed nearly $25,000.

Promotional ideas for *The Ghost of Frankenstein* were often quite inspired.

As part of his campaign in selling *The Ghost of Frankenstein*, a Pennsylvania theater owner constructed a six-foot set piece made out of a three-sheet poster, mounted it on beaver board, and displayed it two weeks in advance. He put a coffin in his lobby with signs all over it stating, "Don't be afraid to go see *The Ghost of Frankenstein*, for here lies his body, as dead as a doornail." He also had a boy leading a donkey around town with a sign on its back that stated, "I'm the only one in town that's afraid to see *The Ghost of Frankenstein* and I'm a jackass!"

Bosley Crowther of the *New York Times* continued to be dismissive of the entire horror genre. In his April 4, 1942, review, he stated,

> Don't look now, gentle reader, but Frankenstein's monster is loose again. Out of that deadly bed of sulphur into which he was last seen to plunge, Universal has hauled the foul creature and set him to roving once more on the scabrous

Trade ad for *The Ghost of Frankenstein.*

screen of the Rialto in a film called "The Ghost of Frankenstein." Gorgons, hydras and chimeras dire! Aren't there enough monsters loose in this world without that horrendous ruffian mauling and crushing actors? For that, as a matter of fact, is about all he does in this film, except to submit to an operation whereby the sinister Dr. Lionel Atwill removes the brain from Bela Lugosi and pops it into him. To be sure, the replenished monster is being consumed by fire when we see him last, but the thought that he may yet return for further adventures with his body and Lugosi's sconce fills us with mortal terror. That is the most fearful prospect which the picture manages to convey.[3]

However, *The Motion Picture Herald* was decidedly more appreciative:

> The current installment in the continued adventures of Frankenstein main-
> tains a standard of performance, effectiveness, and quality exceeding the aver-
> age for horror films by a considerable margin. Cedric Harwicke gives his usual
> polished performance while Lon Chaney as the monster achieves an equiva-
> lent distinction in point of terrifying uncouthness. Among the best of its kind.[4]

Finally, a theater owner reported in the *Motion Picture Herald*, "These
Frankensteins are all good for my box office. Chaney does a grand job as
the monster."[5]

Because of its low budget and the popularity of the characters and the
cast, *The Ghost of Frankenstein* was another big moneymaker for Universale Studios. Along with the massive popularity Abbott and Costello continued to enjoy at the studio, maintaining their status as top box office stars,
1942 was becoming a very profitable year for Universal. Because of this
success, the monster series continued. And Lon Chaney Jr. was cast to take
a turn as the mummy in *The Mummy's Tomb*, which began filming in June
1942. But first, Universal revisited its *Invisible Man* series.

INVISIBLE AGENT

(1942)

Director: Edwin L. Marin.
Screenplay: Curt Siodmak.
Producer: Frank Lloyd. *Cinematography:* Lester White. *Editing:* Edward Curtiss.
    Art Direction: Jack Otterson. *Music:* Hans J. Salter.
Cast: Ilona Massey (Maria), Jon Hall (Frank Raymond), Peter Lorre (Baron
    Ikito), Cedric Hardwicke (Conrad Stauffer), J. Edward Bromberg
    (Karl Heiser), Albert Basserman (Arnold Schmidt), John Litel (John
    Gardiner), Holmes Herbert (Sir Alfred), Keye Luke (surgeon), Lee
    Tung Foo (General Chin Lee), Walter Tetley (newsboy), Phil Van
    Zandt (SS man), Duke York, Lane Chandler, Donald Curtis (German
    sentries), Wolfgang Zilzer (Van Porten), Henry Zynda (Colonel
    Kelenzki), Sven Hugo Borg (German captain), Paul Bryar (German
    soldier), Mabel Colcord (Gretl), Eddie Dunn (prison guard), Henry
    Guttman, William Pagan (state troopers), Bobbie Hale, Wallace Scott
    (English Tommies), Milburn Stone (German sergeant), John Merton
    (German soldier).
Released: August 7, 1942.
Running Time: 81 minutes.
Availability: DVD (Universal Home Video).

By the time *Invisible Agent* was released, America was involved in World
War II. Wartime propaganda thus became part of the Invisible Man saga.
This time, the grandson of Jack Griffin from the original *The Invisible
Man* becomes involved in the war effort by using his family formula to
become invisible and effectively spy on the enemy. The film is longer than
the most recent horror productions had been and had a larger budget

due to the special effects necessary. But its wartime sentiment assisted in its popularity with moviegoers, and it was yet another moneymaker for Universal's horror unit.

The story opens with the grandson of the original Invisible Man having changed his last name from Griffin to Raymond and running a print shop in Manhattan. Frank Raymond is confronted by four men at his shop, and they indicate they know his true identity and try forcing him to reveal his grandfather's formula for invisibility. They want to use it for the war in Europe. The men, who are armed, reveal themselves to be a lieutenant general for the SS, his henchmen, and a Japanese operative. They are willing to pay for the formula, but Raymond naturally refuses. They threaten to cut off his hand in a large printing press, so he agrees but then manages to escape with the formula.

Soon after this incident, Pearl Harbor is bombed, and Raymond takes his formula to the U.S. government. He agrees to allow use of the formula but only if he himself is the one who becomes invisible and completes the mission. The army would prefer trained professionals, but Raymond insists he do it, as he has a better idea of what the serum can do to a person psychologically.

With the assistance of German espionage agent Maria Sorenson, Raymond attempts to obtain a list of German and American spies stationed in the United States. It happens to be in the hands of Conrad Stauffer, the man who attempted to secure the formula at Raymond's print shop. They do secure the list, and then both Stauffer and his Japanese comrade Ikito

Peter Lorre, Cedric Hardwicke, and J. Edward Bromberg.

separately seek out the "invisible agent." Meanwhile, Raymond goes into a German prison to acquire information about a German attack on New York City. He helps Karl Heiser escape execution in exchange for this information, but they are trapped by Ikito. Raymond and Maria escape, and a conflict between Stauffer and Ikito result in both of them dead. Raymond and Maria then steal one of the German bombers that was set to attack New York and use it to destroy other German planes as they fly to England. They parachute to safety after English aircraft shoot down their plane, believing it to be the enemy. An injured Raymond is hospitalized but recovers.

One of the less interesting films in the monster movie subgenre, *Invisible Agent* is really an action movie with comical touches rather than a horror film. Curt Siodmak's screenplay was inspired by his own experience in Nazi Germany, and his reaction was to present the Nazis as buffoons. Jon Hall, a strong, handsome presence in nearly 50 movies, never liked acting or committed himself to it, but he was quite effective in this rather challenging role, having to be represented only by his voice. His performance is decidedly less effective than predecessors Claude Rains and Vincent Price.

Cedric Hardwicke is effectively sinister as Stauffer, while Peter Lorre's performance as Ikito is essentially a villainous version of his heroic Japanese detective Mr. Moto, which he played in several Fox features during the late 1930s. Lorre was, at this time, using his German accent to play wartime villains in such movies as *All through the Night* and *Background to Danger*. Bolstering every movie in which he appears, Lorre resonated in a very small role in *Casablanca* right around the same time. His work on *Invisible Agent* almost ran too long for him to accept the *Casablanca* role of Ugarte, but fortunately filming wrapped in time. *Casablanca* turned out to be one of the actor's most noted roles. *Invisible Agent* has been generally forgotten.

Ilona Massey is effectively attractive as the female lead, exhibiting romantic interest in scenes that waver from serious to comic. Edwin L. Marin was a curious choice to direct *Invisible Agent*, being best known during this period for helming the *Maisie* series with Ann Sothern at MGM. The special effects by John P. Fulton, who had done the effects for Universal's previous *Invisible Man* films, were good enough to net an Oscar nomination (they lost to *Reap the Wild Wind*).

Despite a budget of over $300,000, due to the intricacies of the special effects, *Invisible Agent* grossed over $1 million at the box office. A sequel, with Jon Hall, was planned and eventually produced. Along with moviegoers, critics were generally pleased with this movie as well, understanding the movie's niche market. The critic for *Film Daily* wrote,

All in all this is the ordinary peace time meller translated into wartime pattern. It should do okay with the adventure fans. The Nazis are made to look pretty stupid and beset with official rivalry, while the Japs appear like slipper villains of the old serial days. Attraction is functional, i.e. made for a specific stratum of fans and in the light has enough on the ball to entertain them.[1]

Photoplay was decidedly more enthusiastic when their critic wrote,

Universal has had lots of fun with its series of invisible men pictures (sometimes more than the audiences have), but now it produces one that everyone—actors, customers, and producers alike—will enjoy.[2]

The only interest in *Invisible Agent* as late as the twenty-first century would be how the film combines action mystery with wartime propaganda. All the studios began making propaganda films of different sorts around this time, and it's interesting to see how Universal took an established franchise and translated it into what is basically an entirely new and different genre. It's not an especially good film, but it's fun to watch and examine within this historical context. The comically silly Nazi stereotypes, the sacrifice and ultimate triumph of the central character, and the overall message of victory all combine to offer something of a cultural artifact that works effectively in its context.

Just as the previous mummy movie, *The Mummy's Hand*, was shot around the same time as *The Invisible Woman*, resulting in limiting the former film's budget, another mummy film was being produced at about the same time as *Invisible Agent*. And once again, the budget for this effects-driven feature was such that it was limited for the mummy movie. *The Mummy's Tomb* has a brief one-hour running time and a much lower budget.

15

THE MUMMY'S TOMB
(1942)

Director: Harold Young.
Screenplay: Griffin Jay, Henry Sucher, from a story by Neil P. Varnick.
Cinematography: George Robinson. *Editing:* Milton Carruth. *Art Direction:* Jack
    Otterson.
Cast: Lon Chaney Jr. (Kharis), Dick Foran (Stephen Banning), John Hubbard
    (John Banning), Elyse Knox (Isobel Evans), George Zucco (Andoheb),
    Wallace Ford (Babe Hanson), Turhan Bey (Mehemet), Virginia Brissac
    (Ella), Cliff Clark (sheriff), Mary Gordon (Jane Banning), Paul Burns
    (Jim), Frank Reicher (Professor Norman), Emmett Vogan (coroner),
    Harry Cording (Vic), Mira McKinney (Vic's wife), Fern Emmett (Laura),
    Vinto Hayworth (Frank), William Ruhl (Nick), Glenn Strange (farmer),
    Charles Trowbridge (Petrie), Janet Shaw, Dick Hogan (boy and girl in
    car), Otto Hoffman (cemetery caretaker), Tom Tyler, Peggy Moran,
    Cecil Kellaway (seen in archive footage).
Released: October 23, 1942.
Running Time: 61 minutes.
Availability: DVD (Universal Home Video).

Lon Chaney Jr. had defined the Wolf Man and offered a different perspective to the Frankenstein monster, so Universal next cast him as the
Mummy. With Boris Karloff busy with other projects (including a good run
on Broadway in *Arsenic and Old Lace*, playing a role written specifically for
him), Chaney became the leading horror movie actor at the studio. Along
with the monster movies, Chaney would be cast in films of other genres
(including westerns and gangster melodramas). A busy actor, Chaney was

accepting of any role and could always do well. But he did not enjoy playing the Mummy. The makeup took a lot of patience, and there was little he could project as an actor. Nevertheless, this is the first of three times he would play the role.

The Mummy's Tomb picks up the story 30 years after the conclusion of the previous film *The Mummy's Hand*. Dick Foran is back as Steve Banning, and the opening scene shows him telling his family (son John, his girlfriend Isobel, and her mother) his exploits years earlier on an expedition in Egypt. As he tells the story, a good portion of the previous film is shown as a flashback, with their confronting Andoheb and Kharis, the mummy. Roughly 10 minutes of footage from *The Mummy's Hand* is shown to bring viewers up to date with the events that are about to take place.

Once this is established, we are shown in new footage that Andoheb, who had controlled the Mummy in the previous film, was not killed but only injured. Now very old and near death, he reveals to his follower, Mehemet, that Kharis is also alive. He places the power of the Mummy in Mehemet's hands, who swears to destroy the living members of the previous expedition and all of their descendants. After Andoheb dies, Mehemet and Kharis journey to the United States.

Mehemet gets a job at a local cemetery, brings Kharis to life with the tana leaves, and instructs him to kill those who stole Princess Ananka from her tomb in the previous movie. Banning is the first victim. He next kills Banning's sister. The police (and several reporters) try to find clues as to the motivation for these murders, but it is Banning's old partner Babe Hanson (Jenson in the previous film but once again played by Wallace Ford) who shows up and indicates it is the work of a mummy. Babe Hanson is unable to convince anyone of the Mummy's existence and is himself killed soon afterward due to Mehemet overhearing him telling his story to reporters in a restaurant.

The way *The Mummy's Tomb* presents the threat of Kharis is much more focused than the exploits of other monsters who kill more randomly. Kharis targets specific victims, under orders, and ignores any other people in his path. People report seeing eerie shadows cascading about them and report it to police (who balk at "seeing shadows" being any kind of threat), but the victims are identified as Banning, his sister, and his son.

The Mummy's Tomb contains what may be the first instance of a couple in a car making out who hear and see something eerie and comment on it. They are not injured, but the Mummy does cross near where they are, resulting in this unsettled reaction. This scene has since become something of a cliché in horror movies, but it appears to be making its first appearance

Lon Chaney Jr. and Elyse Knox.

here. The couple are among those who report to the police. Playing down that they were actually making out, they claim they were "listening to Jan Garber on the car radio." The mention of Garber is a rather poor choice. *The Mummy's Tomb* is set 30 years after the previous *The Mummy's Hand*. Since *The Mummy's Hand* was made in 1940, this would ostensibly mean that *The Mummy's Tomb* would be 1970. Young people in 1970 would not likely be listening to Jan Garber on the radio. In fact, Jan Garber was already passé when this film was made in 1942 (he was popular on the radio in the 1920s and 1930s but not as much after 1940).

Of course, setting a film 30 years after the previous was simply an effort to separate the exploits of one from another and to allow Banning to have an adult son to avenge his murder. It is not specifically identified that the year is 1970. That is what we conclude by Banning indicating his expedition was 30 years earlier. No attempt is made to explain why Andoheb waited 30 years to seek revenge, even considering the fact that he needed a follower to travel to America and carry out his plans. The idea that 30 years have passed as an underlying plot point would have worked much better had the dialogue not insisted on specifying the era by including Garber's name.

John Banning, who has been trying to help investigate the murders, gets his draft orders to report in a matter of days, so he plans to marry his girl, Isobel. Mehemet has inexplicably fallen in love with Isobel and orders Kharis to bring her to him. The townspeople gather at the Banning home and are told about the Mummy and his motivation. One of them is the cemetery caretaker who hired Mehemet. He tells everyone about his new hire's Egyptian background.

Armed with torches, the townspeople head to where Mehemet has Isobel bound. He tells her it is her destiny to become his bride after immortalizing her with the fluid of tana leaves. The townspeople descend on his quarters, so Kharis leaves with Isobel. Mehemet is shot and killed, and the townspeople set out to find Kharis and Isobel, who are headed back toward the Banning estate. The Mummy is held back with a torch so Isobel can escape with John Banning. Kharis pursues them, but the townspeople throw torches at the building, and Kharis burns down with it.

Having Mehemet fall hopelessly in love with Eloise is another convenient plot point similar to Andohep's sudden infatuation with Marta (Peggy Moran) in *The Mummy's Hand*. However, it somehow works better here. Mehemet is a young, exotically handsome man who is both quirky and evil. The idea of his having a sudden infatuation with a pretty lady who is connected to his immediate task is a bit more understandable than Andohep's attraction to Marta, especially when the earlier film was attempting to parallel the ancient relationship of the Princess Ananka and Kharis. Here it is shown as just another portion of Mehemet's wickedness.

A disregard for human life is evident as the townspeople throw torches at the Banning mansion to kill Kharis, who lurks within, despite the fact that the Mummy is still carrying Isobel and John Banning is inside attempting to rescue her. Their escape down a trellis allows for the Mummy's demise.

At a quick 60 minutes, *The Mummy's Tomb* is superficially entertaining despite its lapses in narrative logic. Of course, expecting logic in a movie about a living mummy has some absurdity, but setting the movie 30 years later and specifically identifying things contemporary to 1942, when the film was made, does skew things beyond the usual acceptance of illogical happenings, even for a horror movie. Because of its short running time, *The Mummy's Tomb* usually went out to distributors as a double feature with Universal's *Night Monster* starring Bela Lugosi. The double feature was successful, both films profiting. One notable bit of trivia regarding *Night Monster* is that it was shot in only two weeks in July and was ready for release in October. This impressed Alfred Hitchcock, who attended a screening of this double feature with an interest in casting actress Janet Shaw (from *Night Monster*) in his film *Shadow of a Doubt*. He reportedly enjoyed both films.

The reviews generally accepted *The Mummy's Tomb* for what it was. *The Motion Picture Herald* stated,

> Universal, with this latest spine-chilling melodrama, insures its reputation of leadership in the horror-drama field. The picture manages to somehow maintain a measure of plausibility and the audience should find it "right in the groove."[1]

Film Daily considered the film "a feast for shocker fans" that kept audiences "on the edges of their seats" and that the movie "packs wealth of screams and chills for lovers of horror entertainment."[2]

Universal was now ready to make a sequel to *The Wolf Man* and decided to bolster possible box office success by including the Frankenstein monster. Lon Chaney was glad to get away from the uncomfortable mummy makeup and return to the monster he defined. But the studio also wanted him to play the Frankenstein monster, as he had taken over the role from Karloff in *The Ghost of Frankenstein*. Chaney agreed to the challenge, but it was ultimately decided that the makeup involved for the separate characters would not only make it a difficult shoot but also increase the film's budget.

Bela Lugosi had originally been asked to play the monster in *Frankenstein* (1931) after his success in Dracula but was reticent about portraying a character with no dialogue. Lugosi agreed to play the monster in the proposed sequel *Frankenstein Meets the Wolf Man* with the understanding that the character would have the opportunity to speak. Lugosi was pleased with having dialogue and intrigued with playing the monster being blind, as he had been blinded in the previous *The Ghost of Frankenstein*.

Curt Siodmak put together a screenplay, a cast of available Universal players was assembled, and a sequel to *The Wolf Man*, pitting two noted Universal monsters against each other, was ready for production. Shooting on *Frankenstein Meets the Wolf Man* began on October 12, 1942.

16

FRANKENSTEIN MEETS THE WOLF MAN
(1943)

Director: Roy William Neill.
Screenplay: Curt Siodmak.
Producer: George Waggner. *Cinematography:* George Robinson. *Editing:*
    Edward Curtiss. *Art Direction:* John B. Goodman. *Music:* Hans J. Salter.
Cast: Lon Chaney Jr. (Larry Talbot, the Wolf Man), Bela Lugosi
    (Frankenstein's monster), Ilona Massey (Baroness Elsa Frankenstein),
    Patric Knowles (Dr. Mannering), Lionel Atwill (mayor), Maria
    Ouspenskaya (Maleva), Dennis Hoey (Inspector Owen), Don Barclay
    (Franzec), Rex Evans (Vazec), Dwight Frye (Rudi), Harry Stubbs
    (Guno), Jeff Corey (crypt keeper), Cyril Delevanti, Tom Stevenson
    (grave robbers), Beatrice Roberts (Varja), Martha Vickers (Margareta),
    Lance Fuller (villager), Charles Irwin (constable), Adia Kuzentzoff
    (festival singer), Doris Lloyd (nurse), Spec O'Donnell (man in tavern),
    David Clyde (police sergeant), George Calliga, George Ford, Cosmo
    Sardo (townsmen).
Released: March 5, 1943.
Running Time: 74 minutes.
Availability: DVD (Universal Home Video).

The pairing of the Frankenstein monster and the Wolf Man seems like a clever marketing ploy concocted by eager studio publicity people, but the idea started as a joke. Screenwriter Curt Siodmak told Patrick McGilligan,

> I was sitting at the Universal commissary during the war with a friend of mine who was drafted and wanted to sell his automobile. You couldn't get an automobile in those days since those companies only turned out war material.

I wanted to buy that car but I didn't have the money. George Waggner was sitting with us, and I made a joke about *Frankenstein Wolfs the Meat Man*, I mean *Frankenstein Meets the Wolf Man*. He didn't laugh. He came to my office a couple days later and asked, "Did you buy the automobile?" I said, "For that I need another job!" He said, "You have a job, *Frankenstein Meets the Wolf Man*. You have two hours to accept." That taught me to never joke with a producer.[1]

Frankenstein Meets the Wolf Man opens with two grave robbers going into the Talbot crypt with the intention of stealing from Lawrence Talbot, who was said to have been buried with money on his person. They chose a night during which there is a full moon, so while they are stealing from the body, Talbot turns into the Wolf Man and attacks one of the grave robbers while the other escapes.

There are a few important points regarding this opening. First, the Wolf Man poem is recited once again but with a significant change:

> Even a man who is pure in heart,
> And says his prayers by night,
> May become of wolf when the wolf bane blooms
> And the moon is full and bright

In the original version of the poem, the final line is "And the autumn moon is bright." It is with this film where it is first established that a full moon is what causes Talbot's transformation into a werewolf. The narrative continuity from the previous movie is also addressed. It is explained that John Talbot, Larry's father, shot him accidentally and died of grief soon afterward, which explains what happened to the character Claude Rains played in *The Wolf Man*. But what is not explained is why Talbot does not stay dead. When a werewolf is killed in the manner that Larry was in the previous movie, he is supposed to stay dead. This would become a problem in subsequent Wolf Man appearances as well.

The next day, an injured Talbot is found by police and taken to the hospital, where he undergoes an operation conducted by Dr. Mannering. He attempts to explain his transformation, but the medical staff—and the police—dismiss his ravings as affectations of the mind. They also believe that is the reason he claims his name is Larry Talbot, as they are informed Talbot has been dead for years. That night, there is another full moon. Talbot becomes a werewolf and kills a police constable. For this transformation scene, it is the first time we see Talbot actually change into a werewolf. In *The Wolf Man*, we see him remove his sock and reveal hair growing, but the camera does not stay on him as he transforms. Here, it focuses on his face as he gradually transforms into a beast.

Mannering and police inspector Owen travel to Llanwelly, Talbot's home city, to investigate his background. Meanwhile, Talbot escapes the hospital in an effort to find Maleva, the Gypsy woman who understands his plight. Curt Siodmak told McGilligan,

> You need a gimmick for the story. So the gimmick was that the Wolf Man meets the Monster and they both want to find Dr. Frankenstein because Victor Frankenstein knows the meaning of life and death. The Wolf Man wants to die and the monster wants to live forever.

Talbot finds Maleva, who states that she knows someone who can help him, referring to Frankenstein. They travel to Vasaria, where his castle is. Once they arrive, they are told both Victor and Ludwig Frankenstein are dead and their castle has been burned down.

As they continue their journey, there is a full moon, and Talbot transforms into a werewolf. After killing a woman, he falls into the frozen catacombs of the Frankenstein castle's remains. He awakens there and discovers the frozen remains of the Frankenstein monster. The monster is unable to tell where Frankenstein's papers are, but he is surprisingly willing to help search for them. Talbot decides to seek out Dr. Elsa Frankenstein, the daughter of Ludwig, in hopes of finding the answers to end his suffering.

It is a good 30 minutes into the film before the monster is discovered. Most of the film deals with Talbot's anguish and the Gypsy woman's volunteering to care for him before the eventual discovery of the monster. Chaney plays his role very well, always teetering between frustrated anguish and desperate determination. Maria Ouspenskaya approaches Maleva somewhat differently than in *The Wolf Man*. Here, she is more emotional, whereas in the previous film she was more stoic. But she is every bit as effective and plays off of Chaney nicely. The first half of the film is compelling and goes by quickly.

Talbot locates Elsa Frankenstein and is tracked down by Dr. Mannering. They are all at a festival discussing possibilities when the Frankenstein monster shows up and creates a disruption. Talbot stops him, and they flee to the castle, where Elsa locates the Frankenstein notes. They discover that there is a way to drain all life from both Talbot and the monster, and they intend to do so.

Originally, the part of the Frankenstein monster was going to feature dialogue. Lugosi accepted the role with this intention. There was a scene, alleg-

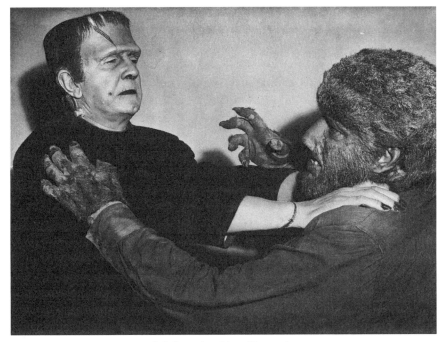

Bela Lugosi and Lon Chaney Jr.

edly filmed, where the monster states his intentions of securing enough energy to rule the world. Siodmak's shooting script featured the monster saying,

> Die? Never! Dr. Frankenstein created this body to be immortal. His son gave me a new brain. A clever brain. I will rule the world!

The studio felt this sounded too much like Adolf Hitler, so the scene was excised, and all scenes featuring the monster talking were removed. Lugosi was so angered by this decision that it was years before he agreed to work at Universal. Photos exist of the scene where the monster speaks, but the footage is said to be lost. At one point, when Talbot finds a photo of Elsa Frankenstein, you can see the monster standing behind him with his mouth moving, but the dialogue was wiped from the sound track.

The fight between Frankenstein's monster and the Wolf Man ensues when Dr. Mannering's interest in seeing the monster at full strength intrigues him too much, and he reverses his decision. Realizing that this decision causes Mannering to fill the monsters with more energy instead of draining them. Elsa tries to stop him. However, a full moon rises, and Talbot transforms into a werewolf. Both Elsa and Mannering are batted aside, and the two monsters battle. Elsa and Mannering leave the castle as the townspeople gather and blow up the town's dam, causing the castle to be destroyed by the cascading waters that drown both monsters.

Frankenstein Meets the Wolf Man is a good, compact horror film, and the combining of two noted Universal monster characters works well. Lugosi's approach to the monster offers more blatant gestures than his predecessors, and one wonders how it might have perhaps been more layered with the intended dialogue. The director, Roy William Neill, had been helming the studio's Sherlock Holmes films and had an idea of how to pace a mystery with dark imagery. Neill's shot composition is quite remarkable, with some good overhead angles and expansively framed sequences that surround the actors with a lot of negative space. His choices are consistently impressive.

Curt Siodmak was, by now, an old hand at creating screenplays for the studio's horror genre, so he decided to have a bit of fun with the process. Siodmak recalled,

> I always put a funny scene in my scripts because I know that the director didn't really study my script before shooting. There was a scene in *Franken-stein Meets the Wolf Man* where the Wolf Man says, "I change into a wolf at night," and the monster says, "Are you kidding?" When they broke the screenplay down on the shooting schedule they finally read it and threw that scene out.

Makeup man Jack Pierce already established the characters of the Wolf Man and Frankenstein's monster, so one of his staff often would do the work. One of these was former silent screen comedian Max Asher, who recalled working with Lon Chaney's father during the silent era:

> Back then Universal used to charge tourists 25 cents to come in and watch a picture being filmed. Mr. Chaney was the only actor who would visit with the tourists during breaks and sign autographs. They loved him.[2]

According to an article in *Photoplay*, there was danger on the set, and it could have had very serious results:

> On a tour of Universale Studios, we happened to witness Lon Chaney Jr. af-fectionately rubbing the head of a weather beaten horse. Lon explained that this horse deserved praise because it remained still in a moment of crisis. He and Ouspenskaya were riding in a heavy iron cart through a wooded path on the set of *Frankenstein Meets the Wolf Man* when suddenly the cart over-turned, pinning them both underneath. Had the horse bolted, the accident would have had unthinkable consequences. Instead he stood still amidst the

confusion until Lon and Maria could be extracted. It occurred to us on our way home that despite Lon's Wolf Man makeup, we'd remember only the kindness and gratitude of this player of monsters.[3]

Frankenstein Meets the Wolf Man was another big box office hit for Universal, and it showed them that combining their monster characters could be a good idea for future projects. *Variety* stated,

> In order to put the Wolf Man and the Monster through further film adventures, scripter Curt Siodmak has to resurrect the former from a tomb, and the Frankenstein creation from the ruins of the castle where he was purportedly killed. But he delivers a good job of fantastic writing to weave the necessary thriller ingredients into the piece, and finally brings the two legendary characters together for a battle climax. Eerie atmosphere generates right at the start, when Lon Chaney, previously killed off with the werewolf stain on him, is disinterred and returns to life. After one transformation, he winds up in a hospital to gain the sympathetic attention of medico Patric Knowles, then seeks out gypsy Maria Ouspenskaya for relief, and she takes him to the continent and the village where Frankenstein held forth. This allows Chaney to discover and revive the monster, role handled by Bela Lugosi, and from there on it's a creepy affair in grand style.[4]

The film was also well received by moviegoers and benefited from strong advertising.

Wartime shortages slashed the budgets of many Hollywood movies, but the monster series were already low-budget B productions, so there was no real change with them. However, *Frankenstein Meets the Wolf Man* is nicely mounted, well directed, tightly written, and very well acted despite any budgetary limitations.

Lon Chaney Jr. was Universal's main horror master now that Lugosi angrily refused to work at the studio and Boris Karloff had been active on projects elsewhere. He had defined the Wolf Man and redefined the Frankenstein monster. He had offered his own approach to the Mummy. So now he was asked to play a variation on the Dracula role. His next film would be *Son of Dracula*.

SON OF DRACULA

(1943)

Director: Robert Siodmak.
Screenplay: Eric Taylor, based on a story by Curt Siodmak.
Producer: Ford Beebe. *Cinematography:* George Robinson. *Editing:* Saul
    Goodkind. *Art Direction:* John B. Goodman, Martin Obzina. *Music:*
    Hans J. Salter.
Cast: Lon Chaney Jr. (Count Dracula), Robert Paige (Frank Stanley), Louise
    Allbritton (Katherine Caldwell), Evelyn Ankers (Claire Caldwell),
    Frank Craven (Dr. Brewster), J. Edward Bromberg (Professor
    Lazlo), Samuel S. Hinds (Judge Simmons), Adeline De Walt Reynolds
    (Madame Zimba), Pat Moriarty (Sheriff Dawes), Etta McDaniel (Sarah),
    George Irving (Colonel Caldwell), Charles Bates (Tommy), Joan Blair
    (Mrs. Land), Jack Rockwell (Deputy Jack), Walter Sande (Deputy Mac),
    Sam McDaniel (Andy), Ben Erway (Charlie), Robert Dudley (Jonathan
    Kirby), Jess Lee Brooks (Stephen), Cyril Delevanti (Dr. Peters),
    Robert Dudley (deputy), Charles R. Moore (Matthew), Emmett Smith
    (servant), George Meeker (party guest).
Released: November 5, 1943.
Running Time: 80 minutes.
Availability: DVD (Universal Home Video).

Lon Chaney Jr. had defined the Wolf Man, brought his own perspective
to the Frankenstein monster and the Mummy, and was now cast in the
role of Count Dracula. Perhaps the strongest and most layered actor of his
horror movie contemporaries, Chaney was being used extensively by Universal not only in their monster movies but also in other films. At around
the same time as *Son of Dracula*, Chaney was about to star in a series of

Inner Sanctum mysteries for the studio, alternating between playing the hero and the villain.

Count Alucard ("Dracula" spelled backward) comes to the United States from Hungary at the invitation of Katherine Caldwell, one of two daughters of Colonel Caldwell, a wealthy plantation owner. Katherine has a fascination for the occult, which does not interest her sister Claire or her boyfriend Frank Stanley. A reception is held in anticipation of the count's arrival, but he shows up in the form of a bat, transforms into a man, and kills the colonel. The others believe the elderly and ailing colonel has died of a heart attack, although Frank remarks, "he looks as though he'd been frightened to death." Count Alucard shows up and is told the family is not receiving due to the colonel's death. He sternly insists on being announced.

Louise Allbritton and Lon Chaney Jr.

Chaney's approach to the Dracula character has immediate differences from the way Bela Lugosi had established it a dozen years earlier. He is a larger and more powerful-looking man, and he is more stern and intimidating than seductive. His mysteriousness is not romantic or attractive. He arouses a great deal of suspicion from Claire and Doctor Brewster, a family friend, who recognizes that "Alucard" is "Dracula" spelled backward. The two have a conversation to indicate Katherine has been seeing Alucard. Brewster suggests putting Katherine in an asylum "to protect her from herself." Claire is unhappy with this idea.

The relationship between Alucard and Katherine is presented as her sneaking around to see him and their eventually eloping. There is no real development of this relationship within the narrative. Katherine, who is said to have met Alucard in Budapest, appears to be quite taken with him in the same seduced manner that women succumbed to Dracula in previous movies. Frank shows up shortly after Katherine and Alucard have been married and confronts the count. Alucard takes Frank by the throat and pushes him away effortlessly. Frank takes out a gun and shoots the count, but the bullets go through him and kill Katherine.

Chaney's very different approach to the Dracula character is further exhibited in these scenes. Where Lugosi retained his emotions to the point where sudden outbursts were jarring, Chaney is more emotionally open, and his outbursts are less effective. His grabbing Frank by the throat and effortlessly tossing him away shows a brute strength that is a new element to the Dracula character.

Frank runs to Dr. Brewster and cries that he shot Alucard but ended up killing Katherine. Brewster goes to their residence and finds Katherine alive, not realizing she is now a vampire, along with Alucard, and simply concludes Frank is overcome with emotion due to losing Katherine to the count. Alucard and Katherine state that they plan to conduct scientific research that will "take up all of our daylight hours" and that they will have "no time for social life at night." They insist that they are not to be disturbed. However, Frank goes to the police to confess to murdering Katherine. Brewster asserts to the police that he saw Katherine alive, but the sheriff insists on investigating. Since it is during the day, he finds Katherine's body and has it sent to the morgue.

The narrative structure that directly connects to the Brewster character is the most satisfying portion of the story. What he witnesses, from the very beginning, effectively pieces together his conclusions that vampirism is a possibility. He is perhaps the central character in the narrative, anchoring the proceedings more so than Dracula.

Brewster invites a Professor Lazlo from Hungary to help him investigate the connection of "Alucard" being "Dracula" spelled backward. Since he saw Katherine alive and she is later revealed as dead, he suspects actual vampirism. The doctor's suspicion is backed up when an injured boy is brought to him. There are bite marks on the boy's neck. When the count appears to confront Brewster and Lazlo, he is driven away with a cross.

In the original *Dracula*, Bela Lugosi played the character as calm and secure. When he is shown a cross, he very suddenly bats it away and lets out a hiss to indicate that the animal within was suddenly unleashed. Chaney plays it differently. When his Dracula is shown a cross, he backs away in terror and disappears in a cloud of smoke.

Katherine appears to Frank in his jail cell as a vampire and claims she still loves him. She reveals that Alucard is Dracula and that she married him to become immortal. She now wants to make Frank immortal in the same way. Frank escapes prison, finds Alucard's coffin, and burns it. Without a way to escape the daylight, Dracula is destroyed. He then does the same thing to Katherine's coffin, realizing he must destroy the one he loves, as she is now a vampire.

One final discussion regarding Chaney's version of the Dracula character is his reaction to Frank's burning of the coffin. Catching him in the act, Dracula frantically shakes Frank and yells for him to "put it out." He is again frightened, unglued, without the secure control the character had as played by Lugosi. Chaney's Dracula is not detached or aloof. It is relatable and compromising.

Chaney, being an excellent actor, is not as effective in this particular role, and it is understandable he never revisited it. However, the supporting cast is very good. Frank Craven as Dr. Brewster does nicely as a curious and ultimately informed central presence. Louise Allbritton is very striking and effective as Katherine. And Robert Paige turns in what may be the finest performance of his career as the jealous and ultimately distraught Frank.

Robert Siodmak's direction provides an effectively eerie atmosphere, but he does not pace the film well. The final third of the story moves much more slowly than the brisk two-thirds that precede it and tends to drag until the climax. However, the death of Dracula is much more gory than previous films, as he is shown melting in the presence of the deadly daylight.

Hans Salter's dramatic score effectively enhances the action, and the special effects by John P. Fulton were quite impressive. For example, this is the first time we actually see, on camera, Dracula transforming to and from a bat. Fulton also shows the count forming and disappearing in a cloud of mist, which is unique to this movie among all the other Universal monster films.

Still, overall, *Son of Dracula* remains one of the weaker Universal monster movies. Curiously, even the title is misleading. Nowhere is Alucard referred to as the son. There is some discussion between Brewster and Lazlo that he may be a descendant, but there is really very little explanation of the character and almost no development of the relationship between the count and Katherine. Since the reliable Curt Siodmak only provided the story and Eric Taylor wrote the screenplay, perhaps the loose holes in the development of the narrative and of the characters falls on him.

Critics were divided in their reaction to *Son of Dracula*. A. H. Weiler of the *New York Times* was underwhelmed:

> Universal, unhorrified by its own horrors and wise to a good box-office thing, again has revived its deathless Dracula series. *Son of Dracula*, like its predecessors, is often as unintentionally funny as it is chilling. Despite all the accepted props, from the lonely Southern plantation set in a miasmic bog to the squeaking bats and creaking coffins, this thriller is a pretty pallid offering.[1]

The critic for the *Motion Picture Herald* was more satisfied with this production, indicating, "For chills, thrills and spine-tingling sensations, this picture hits the mark."[2] The review also praises the actors. The review in the *Film Daily* agreed, stating,

> All the ingredients on which horror gourmets sharpen their cinematic appetite are contained in *Son of Dracula*. Eeriness, mystery and suspense abound in this chiller. . . . The acting in general befits a tale of this sort. While Paige, Chaney, Miss Allbriton, and Evelyn Ankers discharge their duties well, it is Frank Craven and J. Edward Bromberg who contribute the best acting in the film.[3]

Moviegoers had the last word. *Son of Dracula* was a hit at the box office. One exhibitor stated in the *Motion Picture Herald*'s section "What the Picture Did for Me," "Leave it to Universal to make a good horror picture. This is top notch from every angle."

The studio next went into production on another Invisible Man feature. Meanwhile, Lon Chaney Jr., who had shot this film in January and February 1943, was put to work on another Mummy movie. It was a character he did not enjoy playing but still performed much more effectively than he had Count Dracula.

THE INVISIBLE MAN'S REVENGE

(1944)

Director: Ford Beebe.
Screenplay: Bertram Milhauser.
Producer: Ford Beebe. *Cinematography:* Milton Krasner. *Editing:* Saul
   Goodkind. *Art Direction:* John B. Goodman, Harold MacArthur. *Music:*
   Hans J. Salter.
Cast: Jon Hall (Robert Griffin), John Carradine (Peter Drury), Leon Errol
   (Herbert Niggins), Alan Curtis (Mark Foster), Evelyn Ankers (Julie
   Herrick), Gale Sondergaard (Irene), Lester Matthews (Sir Jasper),
   Halliwell Hobbes (Cleghorn), Leyland Hodgson (Sir Fredrick), Doris
   Lloyd (Maud), Ian Wolfe (Feeney), Billy Bevan (sergeant), Jimmy
   Aubrey (Wedderburn), Mildred Dunnock (Norma), Janna DeLoos
   (Nellie), Lillian Bronson (Norma), Skelton Knaggs (Alf), Olaf Hutten
   (Gray), Beatrice Roberts (nurse), Guy Kingsford (Bill), Arthur Gould-
   Porter (Tom Meadows), Tom Dillon (Ned), Ted Billings, Russell
   Cluster, Cap Somers, Dan White (men in pub).
Released: June 9, 1944.
Running Time: 74 minutes.
Availability: DVD (Universal Home Video).

The Invisible Man's Revenge is the last and the weakest of the Invisible
Man films. Jon Hall returns, having also been in the previous *The Invisible
Agent*, and the cast includes John Carradine, who would soon figure promi-
nently as the studio's next Dracula, as well as the welcome appearance of
Evelyn Ankers and Gale Sondergaard. And to lighten the proceedings, the
formidable skills of Leon Errol are also included. But that isn't enough to

make *The Invisible Man's Revenge* any more than a pedestrian outing in Universal's monster cycle.

Despite the return of actor Jon Hall and his character having the last name of Griffin, *The Invisible Man's Revenge* does not connect him to the previous Griffins who created, understood, and operated with the formula for invisibility. In this film, he plays a crazed man who escapes from a mental institution, seeking revenge on the Herricks, a wealthy family that left him in the jungles to die when they were on a safari together five years earlier. He demands they share the diamonds they acquired on the safari.

Griffin still has a written agreement, and with that leverage, he not only wants his fair share from the Herricks but also wants to marry their pretty daughter Julie. They pretend to comply and offer him a drink, by which he is drugged and then thrown off the estate. But first, they take away the written agreement and destroy it. He is found by a passing Cockney, Herbert Higgins, who hears his story and agrees to help him settle a score. An attempt to blackmail the Herricks fails when the chief constable deems Griffin's claims to be without merit. He is told to leave the area.

Griffin intends to go to London, but as he travels on foot to reach some type of affordable transportation, he is caught in the rain and seeks refuge at the home of Dr. Peter Drury. Drury is experimenting with the formula for invisibility, and when he hears Griffin's story about being a fugitive, he asks to experiment on him. Desperate, Griffin agrees, and he uses his invisibility to his advantage. He gets his revenge on the Herricks by forcing Mr. Herrick to write a confession to assign his property and then returns to visibility by knocking out Dr. Drury and giving himself a blood transfusion of Drury's blood. This kills the doctor, so Griffin burns down Drury's home to avoid being charged with murder.

Under a new identity, Griffin pays off Herbert Higgins to kill Drury's dog. The dog escaped the fire and has targeted Griffin as having killed his master. Griffin then tries to reap the rewards of the Herricks' estate, which he now owns, but his invisibility returns. He knocks out Julie's fiancé, Mark Foster, and gives himself another transfusion with Mark's blood. The chief constable arrives at the house, being told of Griffin's return, and stops Griffin from completing the transfusion. Griffin is attacked and killed by Drury's dog, which Higgins never killed. It is determined that Griffin meant no real harm; he just went insane while locked up in an asylum.

While the 1933 film *The Invisible Man* is a genuinely strong horror melodrama, none of its sequels were particularly impressive. *The Invisible Man Returns* was average; *The Invisible Woman* was, at least, amusing with its

John Carradine and Jon Hall.

addition of a comical element; and *Invisible Agent* at least benefited from the presence of Peter Lorre in the cast.

The setup for *The Invisible Man's Revenge* works as a standard B drama but doesn't appear to lead up toward what could be considered a horror movie. But then, this series often flirted with mystery and comedy and did less within the horror genre despite its origin being the 1933 classic. Hall plays an unpredictable psychopath with a basic level of competence, but one imagines what a stronger actor like Lon Chaney Jr. might have done with the role.

The Invisible Man's Revenge is a very trite use of the formula and doesn't work as horror, as suspense, as melodrama, or for the comedy provided by Leon Errol as Higgins. Errol might be the best thing in this movie, filmed when he was quite popular in several different series, including the Joe Palooka movies at Monogram, the Mexican Spitfire series at RKO, and his own starring series of short comedies, also at RKO. Perhaps the highlight of this lackluster effort is a comic dart game in which the invisible Griffin helps Higgins win a pub bet.

Shooting concluded in just over a month, with the special effects once again raising the budget beyond the usual B movie. But despite its budget of over $300,000 and its not being a very good movie, *The Invisible Man's Revenge* still managed to gross over $750,000 at the box office.

Along with the previously mentioned Errol, John Carradine is impressive as Dr. Drury. He was already an established character actor who achieved recognition and respect for his work in films like *The Last Gangster* (1937) and *The Grapes of Wrath* (1940). He had essayed small roles in earlier Universal monster movies, including *The Bride of Frankenstein* and, ironically, *The Invisible Man*. The rest of the formidable cast is wasted, given little to do.

Producer/director Ford Beebe had an interesting background for helming a Universal horror movie. He was best known for helming westerns and serials, most notably the *Flash Gordon* and *Buck Rogers* cliffhangers featuring Buster Crabbe and the *Junior G-Men* serial featuring the Dead End Kids. These were also done for Universal. Beebe also wrote several screenplays and had an impressive and accomplished career that dated back to silent movies. But he offers nothing to this unremarkable effort.

While audiences enjoyed *The Invisible Man's Revenge*, it didn't impress the critics. Bosley Crowther often had a snobbishly dismissive reaction to popular movies without pretension but was pretty accurate in his *New York Times* review on June 10, 1944:

> A mild exercise in trick photography is Universal's *The Invisible Man's Revenge*. And, as one might vaguely suspect, it is best when the principal character is present on the screen but can't be seen. Then there is comical oddity in the fanciful maneuvers of Jon Hall as a man rendered into a vacuum by the abracadabra of Dr. John Carradine. It is fun when this unseen hunk of thin air carries darts hurled by Leon Errol straight to the bulls-eye of a target or makes comments which startle the guests. But when Mr. Hall in person or with a towel wrapped around his unseen head gets serious with folks who stole his gold mine, it is just plain old-fashioned ham. Unfortunately, trick photography is not sufficient to maintain a whole film, and this one reveals quite plainly that you don't see much when you see an "Invisible Man."

The Universal monster movies continued to be popular and made good money at the box office, especially since they could be made very cheaply. But since the special effects increased the budget on the Invisible Man series, it was determined that no more would be made despite the financial success of this film.

THE MUMMY'S GHOST

(1944)

Director: Reginald Le Borg.
Screenplay: Griffin Jay, Henry Sucher, Brenda Weisberg, from a story by Jay and Sucher.
Producer: Ben Pivar. *Cinematography:* William Sickner. *Editing:* Saul Goodkind. *Art Direction:* John B. Goodman, Abraham Grossman. *Music:* Frank Skinner.
Cast: Lon Chaney Jr. (Kharis), John Carradine (Yousef Bey), Robert Lowery (Tom Hervey), Ramsay Ames (Amina Mansouri), Barton MacLaine (Inspector Walgreen), George Zucco (Andoheb), Frank Reicher (Professor Norman), Harry Shannon (Sheriff Elwood), Emmett Vogan (coroner), Lester Sharpe (Dr. Ayad), Claire Whitney (Mrs. Norma), Oscar O'Shea (watchman), Mira McKinney (Mrs. Evans), Dorothy Vaughn (Mrs. Blake), Eddy Waller (Ben Evans), Steve Barclay, Martha Vickers, Carl Vernell (students), Jack Rockwell, Jack Smith (deputies), Fay Holderness (policewoman), Oliver Cross, William Desmond (museum tourists), Kid Chissell, Caroline Cooke, Bess Flowers, Michael Jeffers, Jack Perrin (townspeople).
Released: July 7, 1944.
Running Time: 61 minutes.
Availability: DVD (Universal Home Video).

The third sequel to *The Mummy* and second featuring Lon Chaney Jr. as Kharis benefits from a better script and a stronger cast than the previous *The Mummy's Tomb*. Unlike its immediate predecessor, *The Mummy's Ghost* does not rely on lengthy flashback sequences to connect its narrative to the previous film. *The Mummy's Ghost* is perhaps the best of the sequels to the original 1932 classic.

The film opens in Egypt, where Andoheb tells Yousef Bey that Kharis is alive and must be retrieved along with the body of Ananka and returned to their resting place. Andoheb informs Yousef Bey that he is to brew the fluid from nine tana leaves at each full moon. This will attract Kharis. Yousef Bey sets off for America.

Meanwhile, in a Massachusetts college, a Professor Norman is lecturing about the expedition that discovered and brought home Ananka's remains and how Kharis killed everyone connected with that expedition. When a student inquires with some skepticism, the Professor insists he examined Kharis. Tom Hervey is one of the students in this class. His girlfriend Amina is of Egyptian descent and acts mysteriously anytime the story of Kharis is discussed. She claims an odd feeling comes over her whenever Kharis is mentioned.

The moon is full when Professor Norman conducts a study of Egyptian hieroglyphics on a case of tana leaves, following their instructions to brew nine of the leaves. This attracts Kharis, who enters the professor's home and murders him. On his way, he passes Amina's home, and she goes into a trance and follows him. She faints, and when she is revived, she has no recollection of the night's events. This arouses the suspicion of the police who are investigating Professor Norman's murder.

The original script began with the professor's lecture, but director Reginald Le Borg suggested the prologue featuring Andoheb and Yousef Bey would offer greater clarity to the backstory. The resulting lecture scene verifies the narrative connection to the previous films in the series.

Le Borg had been directing Chaney in his Inner Sanctum mysteries, such as *Calling Dr. Death* and *Weird Woman*, and had connected well with the actor. As a result, he listened to Chaney's complaints regarding his misgivings about playing Kharis. Not only did he have to endure the hours of makeup, but his ability to emote as an actor was camouflaged. Le Borg used more close-ups, and the intimacy of the camera gave Chaney the opportunity to convey some emotion. In some ways, this gave more substance to the character, but the clarity of the Mummy's eyes in close-up, rather than the deadened blackness used in earlier films, can be disconcerting.

Le Borg's choice to shoot the professor's murder by cross-cutting between Kharis approaching the camera in close-up and the professor backing away from the camera in a similarly tight shot made the scene that much stronger. Not only do we get a closer and clearer look at Kharis, we also see the real fear in the professor's eyes. The scene is more stirring and frightening as a result.

The narrative is rather formulaic, relying on that which had been established in previous films. But the connection of Amina to Ananka is explored very gradually and is presented as tangential to the main story until the movie reaches its conclusion.

Once Yousef Bey arrives in Massachusetts, he summons Kharis with the tana leaves. Kharis is distracted by a barking dog and commits another murder along the way, this time a farmer. This second murder causes the sheriff to develop a search party for the Mummy. Yousef Bey enters a museum as part of a tour group and hides until closing. Once it is closed, he allows Kharis in, and they find the remains of Ananka. Her remains disintegrate as Kharis approaches, so it is determined she has reincarnated into another form. An enraged Kharis destroys the museum. When the night watchman comes out to investigate the disruption, he is murdered.

The gradual connection of Amina and Ananka is again presented when, as Kharis approaches Ananka's remains, Le Borg cuts to a quick shot of Amina jumping up in bed and then returns to the proceedings in the museum. It is a good, effective brief cutaway.

While investigating the watchman's murder, Inspector Walgreen and Dr. Ayad of the museum are unable to explain how Ananka's remains could have disappeared without the wrappings being cut. The hieroglyphics are translated, and the concept of Ananka having been reincarnated is discussed. With the help of Dr. Ayad's understanding of Egyptian culture, Inspector Walgreen decides to attempt attracting Kharis with the tana leaves in order to either capture or destroy him.

Unlike previous Mummy films, the characters in *The Mummy's Ghost* are well aware of Kharis's existence, and when these random murders occur, they make that conclusion rather comfortably. Even when the student earlier in the movie offers some skepticism to Professor Norman's lecture, his logic is dismissed out of hand. It is established that the Mummy is at large once again and murders are being committed. Amina's connection cannot yet be determined.

Although Amina has been told to remain in town during the investigation, Tom insists she elope with him to New York. They plan to do so the next morning. Meanwhile, Yousef Bey conducts a séance, asking the spirits to guide him to Ananka's incarnate. He sends Kharis to find her. But Kharis is distracted by the tana leaves being burned by Inspector Walgreen and Dr. Ayad. On his way, he passes Amina's house, causing her to go into a trance and follow him. When Kharis sees Amina, he recognizes her as Ananka's incarnate and carries her away.

From this point, *The Mummy's Ghost* starts to resemble the other Mummy films. Tom and several townspeople seek out to find Amina, who has been presented by Kharis to Yousef Bey. Recognizing a birthmark on her arm, Yousef Bey tells Amina as she awakens that she is the carrier of Ananka's soul. A voice-over informs us that the gods are convincing Yousef Bey to give Amina the tana leaves and keep her immortal so she can go through life with him. As he is about to do so, Kharis stops him and throws

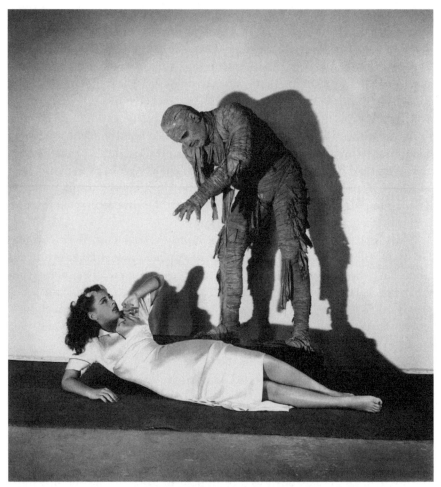

Lon Chaney Jr. stands over Ramsay Ames.

him out a window. Tom arrives in time to witness Yousef Bey falling to his death. Tom struggles unsuccessfully with the Mummy, who escapes with Amina. The townspeople pursue them as we see Amina slowly age into the 3,000-year-old Ananka. As she and Kharis are chased deep into the swamps, Tom sees that Amina's beauty is gone and she is now the very old Ananka. Kharis and Ananka sink into the swamp's waters and drown.

At this point, the connection to the 1932 classic *The Mummy* was very basic. It is *The Mummy's Hand* that established the narrative from which all subsequent sequels relate. There are some continuity problems here as there are with most of the Mummy series. First, Andoheb died of old age in the previous film before instructing his follower to travel to America with Kharis and secure the remains of Ananka. Andoheb is back again to give the same instructions to another follower, but this time he doesn't die. Actor George Zucco was hired each time to play the role of Andoheb.

The aging of Amina into the character of Ananka is handled nicely, beginning on her capture and continuing until she and Kharis drown. First, we see white highlights in her hair, then her hair is completely white. Her hands and feet are shown to have aged as the Mummy carries her deeper into the swamps. The last shot of her face as she and Kharis sink into the water is striking and effective.

The Mummy films are not examples of good cinema as the 1932 original had been, but as B movies they remain disarming and enjoyable viewing. *The Mummy's Ghost* is perhaps the best of the sequels with better direction and a stronger cast. The narrative follows the same formula, but that is really what moviegoers wanted. The June 26, 1944, *Motion Picture Herald* noticed that Lon Chaney offered more to the title character, stating in their review. "Chaney's performance in this film advances his claim to a large following." *The Mummy's Ghost* was a success at the box office.

However, according to the July 8, 1944, issue of *Harrison Reports*, not all audiences were pleased:

> At the Rialto theater in New York, a house noted for its avid mystery and horror fans, the audience greeted the actions of the characters with derisive laughter. And one cannot blame them, for the proceedings become ludicrous to the extreme as the players strain to inject creepiness and all the other well known nonsense identified with pictures of this type.[1]

For their next monster movie, Universal extended beyond combining two monster characters in the same film, as they had with *Frankenstein Meets the Wolf Man*, and decided to include the Frankenstein monster, the Wolf Man, Dracula, and the Mummy together into one story. While this concept became fairly common in the twenty-first century with the Avengers movies, Universal's decision to do this with its monster franchises was a unique and innovative idea.

Along with securing the talents of Lon Chaney as the Wolf Man, Boris Karloff agreed to appear. Bela Lugosi was then sought for the Dracula part, and although he was still angry over his dialogue being cut from *Frankenstein Meets the Wolf Man*, he agreed to reprise his most famous role. Preproduction began on the ensemble monster movie that was tentatively titled *The Devil's Brood*.

20

HOUSE OF FRANKENSTEIN

(1944)

Director: Erle C. Kenton.
Screenplay: Edward T. Lowe, story by Curt Siodmak.
Producer: Paul Malvern. *Cinematography:* George Robinson. *Editing:* Phillip
   Cahn. *Art Direction:* John B. Goodman, Martin Obzina.
Cast: Boris Karloff (Dr. Nieman), Lon Chaney Jr. (Larry Talbot), J. Carroll
   Naish (Daniel), Glenn Strange (the monster), Elena Verdugo (Ilonka),
   John Carradine (Dracula), Anne Gwynne (Rita Hussman), Peter Coe
   (Carl Hussman), Lionel Atwill (Arnz), George Zucco (Lampini), Sig
   Ruman (Hussman), Phil Van Zandt (Muller), William Edmunds (Fejos),
   Charles Miller (Toberman), Phil Van Zandt (Muller), Julius Tannen
   (Hertz), Hans Herbert (Meier), Dick Dickinson (Bjorn), George Lynn
   (Inspector Gerlach), Michael Mark (Strauss), Olaf Hytten (Hoffman),
   Frank Reicher (Frederick Ullman), Brandon Hurst (Dr. Geissler), Joe
   Kirk (Schwartz), Belle Mitchell (Urla), Charles Wagenheim (jailer),
   Edmund Cobb (coachman), Gino Corrado (audience member), Anne
   Sterling (Gypsy).
Released: December 1, 1944.
Running Time: 71 minutes.
Availability: DVD (Universal Home Video).

The success of pitting the Frankenstein monster against the Wolf Man in
Frankenstein Meets the Wolf Man resulted in this ensemble, which includes
not only the two of them but also Dracula. Boris Karloff, the original Frankenstein monster, is back but not in the monster role as intended. Karloff
felt he was too old to play the monster as well as the character deserved, so
he took the role of mad scientist Dr. Nieman. The monster role was given

to a tall, imposing western stuntman named Glenn Strange, whom Karloff patiently coached throughout the production.

Veteran character actor J. Carroll Naish plays the role of Nieman's murderous hunchback partner Daniel. Naish had just been nominated for an Oscar for Best Supporting Actor the previous year for his performance in *Sahara* (he lost to Charles Coburn for *The More the Merrier*). Lon Chaney Jr. commands his classic role as the Wolf Man, and while Bela Lugosi was originally considered to play Count Dracula, he was still performing in a play when shooting began and was not available to take the role. The part went to John Carradine, Universal having been pleased with his work in other movies for the studio. Carradine was a very busy actor, appearing in 11 different films for six different studios in 1944 alone. Plans to include the Mummy in this story was deemed to be too much, so that part was cut out before production began.

House of Frankenstein turns out to be half of an excellent horror movie, while the other half is only fair. The film opens with Nieman and Daniel in prison, Nieman having forcefully obtained a block of chalk by reaching through the bars and clutching a guard's throat. He uses it to outline his plans to emulate Dr. Frankenstein, to whom he refers as "a genius in whose footsteps I shall follow when I get out of here." Daniel watches from an adjacent cell; a worshipful pupil who cannot comprehend the scientific intricacies of Nieman's plans but looks on them with wonder and fascination. Nieman offers drawings, diagrams, and other study guides as he explains his ideas to bring the dead back to life as Dr. Frankenstein had. He indicates to Daniel that while he never met Dr. Frankenstein, "my brother who assisted him learned his secrets, and before he died, he passed them on to me." Daniel hopes that Nieman's experiments can rid him of his hunched back and "make me like other men." Nieman promises, "If I had Frankenstein's records to guide me, I could give you a perfect body."

The characters of Nieman and Daniel are immediately understood on being introduced. Nieman is the sort of controlled madman who is driven to experience the power of controlling life and death. Daniel is his worshipful servant who agrees to kill for him for the promise of deliverance from his handicap.

A raging storm is too much for the dungeonlike structure in which Nieman and Daniel are imprisoned, and it collapses, allowing them to escape. They hitch a ride on a horse-drawn wagon advertising a traveling house of horrors. They kill Lampini, its owner, allowing Nieman to take his name and take over his exhibit, which includes a coffin containing the skeletal remains of Count Dracula. While Daniel is concerned that police will be looking for them when they do not find their bodies in the destroyed dungeon, Nieman believes they should hide in plain sight. Before his journey to obtain Dr. Frankenstein's records, Nieman first intends to seek vengeance on Bürgermeister Hussman, the man who'd caused his imprisonment.

Nieman and Daniel roll into the town where Hussman resides and set up their shop of horrors. This allows for an initial encounter with Hussman, who, with his granddaughter, her fiancé, and his friend the police inspector, attend the house of horrors. Since it has been 15 years, Hussman does not recognize Nieman as the man he once sent to prison. He does see a familiarity, something he indicates while scoffing at the fakery of the horrors on display, including Dracula's skeletal remains.

Nieman revives Count Dracula by removing the stake from the skeleton and instructs him to kill Hussman, promising his services if he does so, stating,

> If you move I'll send your soul back to the limbo of eternal waiting. But do as I say and I will serve you. I will protect the earth on which you lie so that before sunrise your coffin will always be ready for you.

Dracula responds by saying, "For that I will do whatever you wish." This sets up the dynamic between Dracula and Nieman.

The aristocratic count approaches the Hussman party and offers them a ride in his horse-drawn carriage, which they accept. Dracula introduces himself as Baron Latos and exhibits an irresistible charisma that attracts the Hussman party. Dracula seduces Rita, Hussman's granddaughter, and kills Hussman just as he realizes that Lampini is indeed Nieman, whom he had sent to prison 15 years earlier. When Dracula attempts to flee with Rita, her fiancé and the inspector and his men chase him. Nieman and Daniel want to evade police and leave town, so they take this opportunity to destroy Dracula by tossing his coffin out of their moving carriage. Dracula's own carriage crashes, and he does not reach his coffin before the sunlight destroys him.

This portion of the film takes up roughly the first half hour of the feature, and other than a connecting thread with the Nieman character, it doesn't blend cohesively with the second half. It appears to be a featurette unto itself, introducing Dracula, presenting his exploits, and concluding his story. Even the other characters in this segment (Hussman, his granddaughter, her fiancé, and the inspector) are only within its confines, never again referred to after this portion of the movie concludes.

From that point, *House of Frankenstein* becomes a direct sequel to *Frankenstein Meets the Wolf Man* as Nieman and Daniel come on the ruins

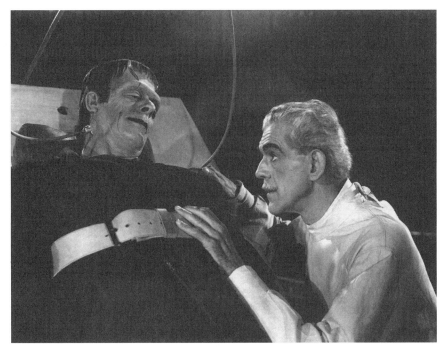

Glenn Strange and Boris Karloff.

where the monster and the werewolf had been killed in the previous film. They revive the Wolf Man, Larry Talbot, who shows them where to find Dr. Frankenstein's records and helps them bring the monster to Nieman's laboratory with the promise that Nieman will also rid Talbot of his curse.

What sets *House of Frankenstein* apart from the other films is its melo-dramatic subplot featuring Ilonka, a Gypsy girl whom Daniel rescues from an abusive man he sees whipping her. Daniel falls in love with her, and while she is grateful to him and fond of him, she is repulsed by his hunch-backed appearance. He understands her revulsion and believes that when Nieman's experiments make him "like other men," she will accept him ro-mantically—and beyond merely stating, "You've been kind to me, and I like you." Nieman continues to lead Daniel on, stating, "To please your little gypsy girl, Daniel, I'll make you an Adonis." The conflict has her attracted to Larry Talbot, inspiring jealousy in the murderous Daniel, who realizes he can do nothing, as Talbot is an essential part of Nieman's experiments.

This dynamic forces tenderness in the murderous Daniel that adds greater depth to the character. There is a tragic layer beneath the mur-derous servitude he extends to Nieman. Ilonka's beauty and innocence succeed in bringing the troubled Talbot out of his shell. Both men are impatient, Daniel wanting to be like other men and Talbot wanting to be freed from the curse of the werewolf. The Ilonka character is also not a one-dimensional point of conflict. She rejects Daniel's unfortunate handicap but continues to accept Talbot even after she realizes he is a werewolf.

Daniel is the most complex character. We see the most change in him throughout the film, as in the beginning he blindly follows Nieman but soon shows us that he is capable of love with Ilonka. Finally, we see him turn on Nieman.

The Nieman character has his own complexities. He is focused, driven, intelligent, but mad. He says what is necessary to inspire loyalty but discards people once they have given him the service he desires. Count Dracula is destroyed after he kills Hussman. Daniel is no longer promised to be "like other men" once his services have been sufficient. Nieman is on a selfish quest for power and control.

Boris Karloff being cast as the mad scientist Nieman instead of the monster turned out to be an excellent idea. Karloff's being a classically trained actor whose ability to convey the right amount of madness in voice and expression is really effective in bringing Nieman to life. Even when he is in a position to convey normalcy, his madness is always evident immediately beneath the surface. Karloff brilliantly exhibits a consistent evil tension.

This was Glenn Strange's first appearance as the monster, and, arguably, he does nearly as good of a job as Karloff had and much better than either Chaney or Lugosi. Boris Karloff was very helpful to Strange, carefully coaching his movements and gladly answering any questions the actor had. Strange was a veteran of western films, but this was his first horror movie, and the fact that he was playing an iconic monster made it essential that he do the best possible job. Karloff helped make that happen. Strange's approach to the character is exactly like Karloff's had been, showing the monster as a lumbering, clumsy presence who is capable of utilizing enormous strength. Naturally athletic, Strange did his own stunt work.

House of Frankenstein has a great ending, likely inspired by the drowning climax of *The Mummy's Ghost*. The film's conclusion has Ilonka putting Talbot out of his misery by shooting him with a silver bullet but not until after he attacks her on turning into a werewolf. She crawls over and dies in his arms. A tearful Daniel carries her body to the laboratory, stating that she was "the only thing I ever loved." He starts to strangle Nieman, but the Frankenstein monster breaks away from his restraints, lifts Daniel high over his head, and throws him out the window as he falls to his death. The monster then cradles Nieman, and they try to escape villagers with fiery torches, but they walk into quicksand and sink as the film concludes.

House of Frankenstein was the first ensemble monster movie. While the footage in which the mad scientist, the hunchback, the monster, and the werewolf all appear is some of the best Universal's horror unit had to offer, the film is hampered by its being so remote and separate from the footage featuring Dracula.

John Carradine does an exceptional job in the role that had been defined by Bela Lugosi. Carradine plays Dracula in a much more refined and sophisticated manner. None of Lugosi's affected speech or florid gestures is part of his definition of the role. And while it is different, it is also effective. With very little makeup, Carradine displays wickedness, anger, and terror using his expressive eyes.

Lon Chaney Jr. had long made the Wolf Man character his own, and this might be his finest portrayal of the role. Unlike the consistent characters of Dracula or the monster, Chaney's Wolf Man is portrayed as both the werewolf he becomes and the shattered man he truly is. Larry Talbot is another very complex character in the narrative, wanting to lead a normal life but suffering from the terrors that the full moon brings to him. He even confesses to Ilonka that when he transforms, he not only kills but also genuinely wants to kill.

Lon Chaney Jr. and Elena Verdugo.

In the book *Confessions of a Scream Queen*, Elena Verdugo, who played Ilonka, told author Matt Beckoff,

> Lon Chaney broke the ice. Not so much with the others. They were not interested in talking to an eighteen-year-old girl. Lon was just darling. We would go out to his wagon off the set. He would have a beer and I would have a coke. There he was in his makeup and I was in my outfit. He was a doll.[1]

Ms. Verdugo also recalled the arduous process of filming Talbot's transition from man to werewolf:

> It took a lot of time, several hours. It was done in stages. His hands were always in gloves and the feet were covered wearing boots, all of which had fur.

Ms. Verdugo got the role of Ilonka shortly after losing out on a role in the film *The Story of Dr. Wassell*. Verdugo would always be thankful that she lost the role in that film, allowing her to play in *House of Frankenstein*, which became an enduring classic with so many admirers.

House of Frankenstein was Boris Karloff's final appearance in the Universal monster movie cycle, which itself was beginning to wind down. After having saved the studio from bankruptcy in the 1930s, the series was now at the point of choosing marketing strategies over creative ones by putting several "name" monsters together even if it meant a lack of continuity with the film's narrative structure. Apparently at this point, the studio believed that the attraction of several monsters in one movie was a necessary marketing ploy to attract moviegoers.

Still, the intent is to make a good movie. Erle C. Kenton was a studio director who never established a truly individual style. He helmed some good movies in all genres, including *The Ghost of Frankenstein* (1942), so he knew how to effectively frame the action for this type of film. When Daniel approaches Lampini to kill him, Kenton shoots it as a close-up with actor J. Carroll Naish coming toward the camera until his image fills it to where it's a black screen. Kenton shoots the quicksand finale in close-up, revealing that it is indeed Boris Karloff, not his stuntman Cary Lofton, actually sinking.

By now, critics were beyond taking these films too seriously, but they remained fond of the productions, which, they believed, were now relegated to B status. *Independent Exhibitor's Bulletin* stated,

> *House of Frankenstein*, Universal's horror classic starring all its Titans of Terror, has broken all existing records at the Rialto Theater on Broadway in NY.

This again proves that Universal knows when and how to make this type of box office bonanza. We really believe that *House of Frankenstein* is headed for an all time record for horror pictures.[2]

The critic for the *Motion Picture Herald* wrote,

In this excellent horror film, each member of the cast portrays his part effectively. Skilled makeup, clever photography, lighting effects, and musical background all add to the weird and striking effect.[3]

House of Frankenstein was a success at the box office, and this was enough to warrant yet another ensemble horror feature the following year, with director Kenton and actors Chaney, Carradine, and Glenn Strange all returning. But *House of Dracula* would be the final movie in the Dracula–Frankenstein–Wolf Man series. Production was to begin in September 1945, and as a cost-cutting measure, director Kenton was instructed to utilize footage from earlier films.

However, while *House of Dracula* was in preproduction, Lon Chaney Jr. had one more turn as the Mummy in *The Mummy's Curse*. It would be the final film in the Mummy series. After years of box office success, the age of the actors, the expiration of contracts, and other factors combined to cause the inevitable conclusion of the Universale Studios monster series.

㉑

THE MUMMY'S CURSE

(1944)

Director: Leslie Goodwins.
Screenplay: Bernard Schubert, from a story by Dwight Babcock and Leon
   Abrams, with Oliver Drake and Ted Richmond.
Producer: Ben Pivar. *Cinematography:* Virgil Miller. *Editing:* Fred Feishans Jr. *Art
   Direction:* John B. Goodman, Martin Obzina.
Cast: Lon Chaney Jr. (Kharis), Peter Coe (Dr. Zandaab), Virginia Christine
   (Princess Ananka), Kay Harding (Betty), Dennis Moore (Dr. Halsey),
   Martin Kosleck (Ragheb), Kurt Katch (Cajun Joe), Addison Richards
   (Mr. Walsh), Holmes Herbert (Dr. Cooper), Charles Stevens
   (Achilles), William Farnum (sacristan), Napoleon Simpson (Goobie),
   Herbert Heywood (Foreman Hill), Ann Codee (Tante Berthe), Tony
   Santoro (Ulysses), Eddie Abdo (Pierre).
Released: December 22, 1944.
Running Time: 60 minutes.
Availability: DVD (Universal Home Video).

The Mummy's Curse ends the Mummy series after five films, and, like the
other four sequels to the 1932 classic, this one attempts to be a compact,
entertaining B movie with no pretensions beyond this status.

This one has an engineering company planning to drain the swamp in
Louisiana Cajun country, but the workers are fearful because of the legend that surrounds the swamp. This is where Kharis and Ananka drowned
20 years earlier.

There are some problems right away with the establishing scene. While
The Mummy's Curse is careful to take up where *The Mummy's Ghost* left

off, suddenly we are in Louisiana, whereas the swamp in the previous movie was set in Massachusetts. Also, a couple of films earlier, *The Mummy's Tomb* was set 30 years after the events of its immediate predecessor *The Mummy's Hand*, making it 1970. Then *The Mummy's Ghost* was set around that same time. But *The Mummy's Curse* is 20 years later. So it is around 1990. Nothing about the manner of dress, for example, makes any attempt to bring the setting outside of 1944, when it was filmed and released.

It also relies on flashbacks of earlier movies to connect the narratives, something each Mummy sequel does except for *The Mummy's Ghost*. In the flashbacks, featuring footage taken from *The Mummy* and *The Mummy's Hand*, we see both Boris Karloff and Tom Tyler as Kharis.

A couple of museum representatives, Dr. Zandaab and Dr. Halsey, arrive at the swamp with an interest in getting some of the mummy remains that are said to be buried within the area where the engineering company is digging. As they arrive, a man is murdered on the construction site. It is determined by the workers that this is the work of Kharis.

That night, it is revealed that Zandaab is actually a high priest who is concealing his identity. He connects with one of his followers, Ragheb. They go to a monastery where Ragheb is hiding the unearthed Kharis. They are confronted by the monastery's sacristan, who is killed by Kharis, who has risen due to Zandaab's brewing of the tana leaves.

In one of the most striking scenes in the film, we see Ananka emerge from the dirt of the swamp's remains at the work site, slowly emerging from the earth and wandering in a trancelike state. She washes away the dirt by which she is covered by submerging herself in a pond and emerges as a beautiful woman. She wanders the woods saying, "Kharis," when she is found by Cajun Joe, who takes her to the pub owned by Tante Berthe. Kharis finds her there and kills Tante. Ananka runs away while Kharis pursues her.

The pacing of this film is very taut, with Kharis approaching in the slow, methodical manner of the other films. Director Leslie Goodwins shows Kharis carefully opening a door to enter the room where he finds Ananka and Tante. He approaches the shocked Ananka slowly and kills the screaming Tante because she leaps up and gets in his way.

Ananka faints in the woods near the side of the road, and as Kharis approaches, Dr. Halsey and Betty Walsh, daughter of construction foreman Pat Walsh, find her and bring her home to care for her. They believe she has amnesia but are impressed with her thorough knowledge and understanding of ancient Egypt. She occasionally lapses into a trance and calls for Kharis, but when shaken, she remembers nothing about it.

Lon Chaney Jr. and Kurt Katch.

Goodwins's directorial career was mostly comedy, having helmed everything from Ben Turpin silents to sound shorts with Edgar Kennedy and Leon Errol. He has some fun with visual humor as he shows Kharis approach Betty just as she and Halsey have loaded the dazed Ananka into their car. The Mummy reaches for her, but she doesn't see him. He approaches the vehicle, but it drives off. These situations are staged the way one would present a comic scene featuring a monster and the amusing close calls of the lead comedian.

Kharis tracks Ananka to the Halsey camp, and she feels the vibes and flees to the tent of Dr. Cooper. She tells him, "It's as though I were two different people. Sometimes it seems as if I belong to a different world. I find myself in strange surroundings with strange people. I cannot ever seem to find rest! And now Kharis!" The Mummy enters and kills Cooper, and Ananka again flees.

The script is slowly allowing Ananka to try to understand why her mind thinks something but cannot specifically reason why she has such thoughts or feelings. In a brief 60-minute running time, the actress has little opportunity to add much depth to this character other than what we know from the backstory and previous films.

Ananka goes to Betty Walsh's tent, where Kharis finds her and takes her away, ignoring Betty and not killing her like the others. The reasoning behind this would seem that while the others got in the way of the Mummy, Betty backs away in terror. Betty asks Ragheb to help her find Dr. Halsey so they can go after the Mummy, but Ragheb takes her to the monastery. Halsey and Goobie, one of the workers, find Betty's tent destroyed, and an errant bandage causes them to conclude Kharis has her. Halsey follows the Mummy's tracks while Goobie runs to get Mr. Walsh.

The character of Goobie is played by black actor Napoleon Simpson, who usually only did bit roles in films. While he does present some level of stereotyping, he does not so much present himself as a comic character who reacts in fear to every situation. When he hears a suspicious noise, he goes to help and bravely crawls into the remains of Betty's destroyed tent to investigate. When he gets Mr. Walsh and others to help find the Mummy, he joins them, entering the monastery armed like the rest. He is part of the group, not a comical outsider. It is an interesting presentation of an African American character during a time when stereotypical characters abounded in B movies. Goobie does not wallow so specifically within those limitations.

Kharis brings Ananka to the monastery, where Zandaab administers the tana leaves so that she and the Mummy can be together for eternity. Ragheb makes advances toward Betty and is caught by Zandaab, who admonishes his disciple for betraying his trust. He orders him to kill Kay, but Ragheb kills Zandaab. Halsey arrives and Ragheb tries to kill him, but Kharis comes after Ragheb, who locks himself in a cell. The Mummy continues after him, and it causes the walls to fall on top of them, burying them alive. Walsh, Goobie, and the others arrive and find a mummified Ananka. Realizing her identity, arrangements are made to return her to the museum.

Despite another formulaic script and the setting changes and year being rather dubious, *The Mummy's Hand* was reasonably entertaining and offers some good action during its 60-minute running time. The budget was only $123,000 for a 12-day shooting schedule, with Lon Chaney being paid $8,000 for what amounted to two days of work. And according to Virginia Christine, who played Ananka, he was so drunk during some of the shooting that the director had to replace him with a double for fear that he'd drop the actress.

However, Chaney was still able to be supportive of his fellow actors. William Farnum, who had been a star in silent movies, was relegated to bit parts by this time and has a very small role as the sacristan of the monastery. Despite having little dialogue, Farnum was having trouble mastering his lines, and the director became impatient. Chaney told the director that

Farnum was once a star, a friend and contemporary of his father, and deserved better treatment. Despite Farnum playing only a bit role, Chaney also insisted that Farnum get a chair on the set with his name on it, threatening to walk off the set if that wasn't arranged. It was.

The Mummy's Curse is filled with strong performances, including Chaney, Christie, and such welcome character actors as Addison Richards (late of MGM's Andy Hardy series), Martin Kosleck, Dennis Moore, and Kay Harding. Kurt Katch, whose long career dated back to silent movies in Germany and extended into the early days of television, is a standout as Cajun Joe.

Chaney was continuing to appear in the Inner Sanctum mysteries as his contract with Universal moved toward its expiration. Kharis the Mummy continued the one role Chaney really did not like to play. It was very hot under all of the heavy bandages and makeup, he never had dialogue, and he was rarely able to emote. He was essentially doing stunt work despite receiving actor's pay. The only reason he continued to agree playing the role is because he realized the series had a lot of fans.

The Mummy's Curse had originally been titled *The Mummy Returns*, but that was changed during postproduction. After its 12 days of shooting, the film was ready for release by December and was another hit for Universal. Its short running time made it good for double features, and it was usually paired with *The House of Fear*, one of the same studio's popular Sherlock Holmes films. *Motion Picture Daily* stated,

> The very original story of two mislaid mummies who rise from the swamps of the Louisiana Bayou country to plague the natives with their strange "courtship" provides a good hour or intriguing and terrifying fantasy tailored to please the horror followers. An atmosphere of mystery and suspense, achieved through eerie settings and frequent shots of strange rituals, pervades the entire production. Exhibitors can't go wrong on this one.[1]

However, while the box office remained good, Universal realized its horror series was coming to an end. Neither Bela Lugosi nor Boris Karloff was under contract, and Lon Chaney Jr.'s contract was heading toward expiration. Chaney made it clear he wanted to branch out and do other things once that happened.

Universal then decided to have another ensemble monster movie similar to the popular *House of Frankenstein*. Lon Chaney would be back as the Wolf Man, and John Carradine would return as Count Dracula. The studio wasn't sure if it should call the film *The Wolf Man Meets Dracula* or *Dracula Meets the Wolf Man*. They eventually decided on *House of Dracula*.

22

HOUSE OF DRACULA

(1945)

Director: Erle C. Kenton.
Screenplay: Edward T. Lowe Jr., story by Dwight V. Babcock and George
    Bricker. *Producers:* Joseph Gershenson, Paul Malvern.
Cinematography: George Robinson. *Editing:* Russell Schoengarth. *Art Direction:*
    John B. Goodman, Martin Obzina.
Cast: Lon Chaney Jr. (Lawrence Talbot/the Wolf Man), John Carradine
    (Dracula), Glenn Strange (Frankenstein's monster), Martha O'Driscoll
    (Milizia Morelle), Lionel Atwill (Inspector Holtz), Onslow Stevens
    (Dr. Franz Edelmann), Jane Adams (Nina), Ludwig Stossel (Siegfried),
    Skelton Knaggs (Steinmuhl), Joseph Bernard (Brahms), Gregory Marshall
    (Johannes), Fred Cordova, Harry Lamont (Gendarmes), Jane Nigh, Anne
    Sterling, Robert Robinson, Harry Lamont, Dick Dickinson (villagers).
Released: December 7, 1945.
Running Time: 67 minutes.
Availability: DVD (Universal Home Video).

Another ensemble monster movie that takes up where *House of Frankenstein* left off, *House of Dracula* is, like the Mummy sequels, a bit sloppy in its attempt to connect to its predecessor. While the Frankenstein monster is found in the quicksand that ended him in *House of Frankenstein*, still clutching the skeleton of Dr. Nieman, who perished with him, the appearances of both the Wolf Man and Dracula are sudden, with no acknowledgment of how they resurrected from their respective deaths in the earlier movie.

The film opens with Count Dracula arriving at the castle of Dr. Franz Edelmann, who is at work with his assistants Milizia and Nina, the latter a hunchback. Introducing himself as Baron Latos, the count is seeking a cure for his vampirism. Later that night, Larry Talbot shows up seeking a cure for his lycanthropy. Talbot must wait while Edelmann uses his own blood to transfuse into Dracula, believing that this series of transfusions will cure his vampirism. Meanwhile, Talbot realizes the moon will be full that night, so he asks to be incarcerated by the police. When Edelmann and Milizia arrive at the jail, they witness Talbot turning into the Wolf Man.

John Carradine's approach to the Count Dracula character concentrates more on the nonvampire air of aristocracy that Lugosi also effectively exuded. Carradine does a good job of combining this with the creepiness of a vampire stalker, but his choice to wear a top hat seems a bit disconcerting. That Dracula is introspective enough to want to be cured of his vampirism adds another element to the character. Talbot, of course, has long wanted to rid himself of his lycanthropy, but this appears to be the first time such an opportunity seemed possible. Attempts to find an answer through the Frankenstein papers were futile in past movies. The ability of the others to witness his transformation within the safety of the jail cell allows them to realize he is not a crackpot who imagines such things but rather an actual beast whose transitions must be stopped.

During this portion, the film introduces Steinmuhl, played by the delightfully creepy Skelton Knaggs, whose suspicions center on the curiosity of the townspeople. The inspector shoos them away, wanting to keep the identity of the locked-up Wolf Man a secret so as not to frighten the villagers.

John Carradine and Martha O'Driscoll.

The next morning, once again in human form, Talbot is transferred to the castle. Edelmann believes Talbot's problem is mental and has nothing to do with the moon. However, Talbot must wait while the doctor gathers enough mold from certain spores to create a formula that may relieve pressure on his brain. Talbot does not want to wait and go through the transformation again, so he jumps into the ocean. He survives the jump but is washed away into the basement of the castle. When he is discovered, he has turned into the Wolf Man. He returns to human form after attacking Edelmann. Talbot and Edelmann discover in the bottom of the castle that the walls are filled with the necessary mold spores for a formula that cures the Wolf Man curse. They also find, submerged in quicksand, the Frankenstein monster. The monster is taken back to Edelmann's lab, but it is believed that it's best to not revive him.

The special effects of the Wolf Man's transition are shown in reverse as he gradually changes back to human form before causing any real damage to Edelmann. They discover the monster in quicksand, still clutching the skeleton of Dr. Nieman, who sank with him at the conclusion of *House of Frankenstein*. As with any other scientist, Edelmann is fascinated by the concept of bringing the dead back to life and allows this discovery to distract him from his continued transfusions to help Dracula. However, the discovery of the mold spores progresses the story regarding the Wolf Man's cure. The idea to not revive the Frankenstein monster shows a more pragmatic reaction by Edelmann than scientists in previous monster films.

The count is attracted to Milizia and attempts to overtake her but is warded off by a cross she wears around her neck. Still, she remains in a daze, affected by Dracula's presence. Nina notices Milizia's erratic behavior and that the count has no reflection in the mirror. She informs Edelmann, who plans to destroy Dracula with the next scheduled transfusion. However, Dracula uses his powers to overcome Edelmann and Nina and reverses the transfusion. He then carries Milizia away. Edelmann and Nina come to and, with the help of Talbot, use a cross to overpower Dracula and rescue Milizia. The sun comes up, and Dracula returns to his coffin, pursued by Edelmann, who drags the coffin into the sunlight, opens it, and destroys Dracula.

It is a curious choice to destroy Dracula at this point in the film rather than continuing to cure him. One would think that the count's pursuit of Milizia would end once he was no longer under the spell of his vampirism. The reaction of Nina and then Edelmann at the fact that Count Dracula is acting like Count Dracula seems a bit off pace from the narrative, where the intention was to remove the very thing to which they are now reacting. In any case, Dracula is destroyed.

Of course, the narrative explains this by showing Dracula knocking out Edelmann and Nina and reversing the transfusion so he can remain a vampire and pursue Milizia. It is not explained if the count reacts this way due to realizing that Edelman intends to kill him with this next transfusion or if he simply changed his mind and wanted to remain a vampire. In either case, it is a curious development on the part of the screenwriters.

Now evil, Edelmann revives the Frankenstein monster but soon returns to his normal demeanor. Like Talbot, he is consumed by a separate personality, but it is a vampire and not a Wolf Man. Edelmann operates on Talbot, who is cured of the Wolf Man's curse. Edelmann, however, changes regularly into his evil vampire personality and continues to kill, including Siegfried the gardener. He is chased by villagers back to the castle but returns to his normal state. The police question him and Talbot to find the killer of Siegfried. When they leave, Edelmann confesses to Talbot and asks to be killed before he kills again.

In one of the most stirring scenes in *House of Dracula*, Larry Talbot looks up at a full moon and is relieved to have no transition. He can now live his life as a man, the curse of the werewolf having been removed. It is an excellent culmination for the character, and Chaney plays it beautifully. Conversely, Edelmann's confession to him shows that he now lives much like Talbot once had. Edelmann's vampirism causes him to become evil, to want to kill, but when he returns to his normal state, he is ashamed of what he has done.

When Edelmann again becomes evil, he is found reviving the Frankenstein monster by Nina. She tries to stop him, but he breaks her neck and throws her aside just as Talbot, Milizia, and the police enter. The Frankenstein monster subdues the police, throwing the inspector into a device that electrocutes him. Talbot then shoots Edelmann in order to save the other survivors but also fulfilling the doctor's request to him earlier. The castle catches fire, and the villagers flee as the roof caves in on the Frankenstein monster, who is destroyed.

House of Dracula is much more interesting as the sum of its parts than as a whole. The scene in which Edelmann, in vampire mode, confronts and kills Siegfried is one highlight. Edelmann confronts the man by approaching him in a friendly manner and becoming more and more bizarre as they talk. Siegfried becomes frightened and is ultimately attacked. His brother is Steinmuhl, and Skelton Knaggs responds in his creepiest monotone, stating, "Doctor Edelmann killed my brother" in another one of the film's most noted moments.

It is also interesting that the screenwriters chose to make Nina, the hunchback character, both sympathetic and pretty (played by model and actress Jane "Poni" Adams). Usually, disfigured characters were not attractive. This was originated partially by J. Carroll Naish's hunchback character Daniel in *House of Frankenstein*. The Gypsy girl is attracted to him until he reveals himself enough to show that he has a hump. Although a tragic figure, he is also an evil one who kills on command. Nina is none of those things.

Erle C. Kenton had directed both *Ghost of Frankenstein* and *House of Frankenstein*, so he was familiar with the territory and did okay with a script that was not as tightly written as those by Curt Siodmak, Eric Taylor, or Scott Darling. He bathes each scene in darkness and allows for medium shots to frame the larger portions of action, switching to close-ups when examining characters.

Along with the previously mentioned actors, Onslow Stevens does a good job as Edelmann, and Martha O'Driscoll registers nicely as Milizia. Lionel Atwill was suffering from the cancer that would soon kill him while playing the inspector in *House of Dracula*. He would die a few months after this film's release. Glenn Strange is back as the Frankenstein monster and would later recall he was so cold in the scenes where the monster was buried in quicksand that he eventually couldn't feel his legs. Lon Chaney tried to help by sharing a bottle of whiskey he always seemed to have handy.

This was one of six films Lon Chaney made for Universal in 1945. He also appeared in a drama, in two Inner Sanctum mysteries, and with Abbott and Costello in *Here Come the Coeds* (which also featured Martha O'Driscoll). Chaney liked Abbott and Costello and would work with them again in the future in films and on TV. But after finishing his work on *House of Dracula*, his contract was finished at Universal and was not renewed. Chaney was off-screen in 1946 but would return for a cameo in the Bob Hope comedy *My Favorite Brunette* in 1947, playing a comical variation of his Lenny character from *Of Mice and Men*.

Theaters continued to promote the horror films when they appeared. One theater in Elkhart, Indiana, converted its box office into a miniature house of horrors, increasing ticket sales. An Augusta, Georgia, theater decorated its lobby weeks in advance featuring papier-mâché heads of the Frankenstein monster and the Wolf Man with blinking red and green eyes. Dracula was hanging above them in the center. This display was placed in front of the theater when the film was playing. And the critic for *Film Daily* found the movie's entertainment value, stating,

House of Dracula is a horror picture to end horror pictures. The film brings together all the top characters in Universal's prize horror exhibitors—Dracula, Frankenstein's monster, the chap with the cure of the werewolf, the scientist who tampers with the laws of nature. All the prize stock situations so dear to the creators of shockers have been dumped into the footage to make a Roman holiday for those who have a taste for this sort of entertainment.[1]

With the original horror masters getting older and going or having gone in other directions at different studios, Universal realized it was time to wrap up its lucrative monster series. It would have been good if *House of Dracula*, with its destruction of Dracula, the Frankenstein monster, and the cure of the Wolf Man, had been the series culmination. However, the monster series was such a moneymaker that the studio tried to find some way to keep it going even without the now iconic performers that had defined the genre with its previous films. This attempt resulted in the B-movie variation on the werewolf theme. It was called *She-Wolf of London*.

23

SHE-WOLF OF LONDON

(1946)

Director: Jean Yarbrough.
Screenplay: George Bricker, from a story by Dwight Babcock.
Producer: Ben Pivar. *Cinematography:* Maury Gertsman. *Editing:* Paul Landres.
    Art Direction: Abraham Grossman, Jack Otterson.
Cast: Don Porter (Barry), June Lockhart (Phyllis), Sara Haden (Martha), Jan
    Wiley (Carol), Lloyd Corrigan (Latham), Dennis Hoey (Pierce), Martin
    Kosleck (Dwight Severn), Eily Malyon (Hannah), Frederick Worlock
    (Constable Hobbs), Clara Blandick (Mrs. McBroom), Olay Hytten
    (Alfred), David Thursby (Herbert), Joan Wells (Phyllis as a child).
Released: May 17, 1946.
Running Time: 61 minutes.
Availability: DVD (Universal Home Video).

It is unfortunate that such a weak film as *She-Wolf of London* became the movie that culminated the Universal monster series. *House of Dracula* would have been a rather inauspicious culmination as well, but at least it featured top monsters, actors, and the cure of the Wolf Man. Shot in two weeks, *She-Wolf of London* is nothing more than Universal's attempt to keep its horror cycle going with younger stars. It doesn't work.

The film deals with 20-year-old Phyllis Allenby, an orphaned woman who lives in her parents' mansion with her aunt and cousin and is engaged to the wealthy Barry Lanfield. There is a series of murders taking place in the woods near the mansion, the victims' throats being ripped apart. The head inspector of Scotland Yard believes it is some sort of animal, while his subordinate insists it is a werewolf. Phyllis is unsettled whenever

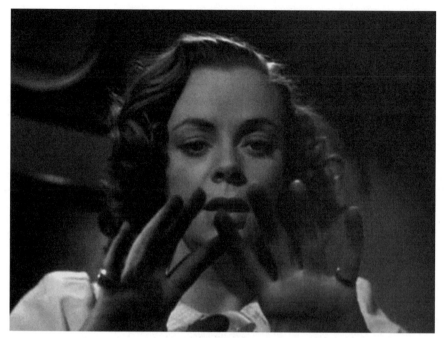

June Lockhart.

any discussion of these events takes place, as she believes she is the one committing these murders. Phyllis's aunt Martha is the only one to whom Phyllis confides, and she tries to convince her niece that a so-called curse of the Allenbys is silly. However, she continually keeps Barry from seeing Phyllis when he calls on her.

After one of the Scotland Yard detectives is killed, Barry insists on seeing Phyllis, and she goes riding with him. She confides in him and states that, as a result, they cannot be married. Barry becomes highly suspicious and does some investigating with the help of Phyllis's cousin Carol, who decides to get the police to assist them. When the aunt discovers this, she drugs Phyllis, and it is revealed that Martha has been committing the murders. Martha wanted to convince Phyllis she was insane and commit her into an asylum. Then Martha planned to continue living in the mansion with her daughter. The servant discovers this information and goes for the police. Martha realizes this and chases her with a knife. Martha falls down the stairs and stabs herself with her own knife.

June Lockhart had just left her longtime studio of MGM when she was cast as Phyllis, along with another MGM actress, Sara Haden who plays Aunt Martha. The cast is rounded out with familiar names like Don Porter,

Martin Kosleck, and Lloyd Corrigan replacing Forrester Harvey (who died a week before production began). June Lockhart recalled in an interview,

> I got the part through Jean Yarbrough, the director. What was nice about that movie was that some of the other people in it, like Dennis Hoey, Lloyd Corrigan, Eily Malyon, Sara Haden and Frederick Worlock, were all pals of my family, so doing the picture was sort of like hanging out with people who were always around the house! They were good actors, of course they were prepared, they were English-trained, and one of the reasons we could shoot *She-Wolf* so quickly was because we knew how to come in and do it in one take. We shot the whole thing in 12 fat days! Jean Yarbrough was a very nice man, I liked him a lot, and he was a good director. But—on *She-Wolf*, the staging was so unimaginative. The shots were full-on, everybody goes in and faces each other in profile and recites the lines.[1]

When the film was released in May 1946, it was paired up with another Universal suspense drama, *The Cat Creeps*. Because of its low budget of less than $135,000, the film turned a reasonable profit. But Universal realized by this time that its horror franchise was just not the same with actors who did not identify with the genre. Martin Kosleck was the closest they came, and this turned out to be his last movie for the studio.

The year 1946 was something of a transition for Universale Studios. The war had ended, and the culture had changed. The horror films were strong during the Depression and continued their strength during the war years, as the monsters represented the evil that American audiences battled, be it tangible or intangible. But after the war, there was a sense of triumph and victory, and moviegoers wanted upbeat stories. This, along with the previously mentioned fact that the actors who had created and defined the monster icons were no longer available, made continuing the series with new variations on Dracula, Frankenstein, the Invisible Man, the Mummy, or the Wolf Man less feasible. They did not completely abandon the idea, but they did shelf it, thinking that this particular time was no longer good for monster movies. Universal had just merged with International Pictures to form Universal-International, and the new president, William Goetz, had other ideas for the company's productions.

Also at this time, the studio was experimenting with their popular Abbott and Costello films. This comedy team's rat-a-tat style of humor fit the war years perfectly, but they had done so many variations on the same themes that the public was growing tired of their antics. Although in 1945 they released the very funny *Here Come the Coeds*, in which Lon Chaney scored as the heavy, and *The Naughty Nineties*, featuring what may be their best version of the classic "Who's on First?" routine, their box office receipts were slipping. In 1946, the duo attempted a couple of films in which the team was split and playing separate roles, including *Little Giant* and *The Time of Their Lives*. Lou Costello came off well as a solo comic but needed to play off of his costars. But Abbott fared even better as a supporting character actor.

In 1948, someone got the bright idea to combine the classic monsters and the comedy team of Abbott and Costello, with the possibility of securing a great box office by having both of Universal's most lucrative franchises occupy one movie. Along with Abbott and Costello, Universal still had access to Glenn Strange as the Frankenstein monster and sought out Bela Lugosi to finally play Count Dracula once again by having the vampire be the monster's keeper and master. They secured the talents of Lon Chaney Jr. as Larry Talbot to warn the boys. Originally set to be called *Abbott and Costello Meet the Monsters*, executives recalled that having a monster's name in the title would likely mean a stronger box office. *Abbott and Costello Meet Frankenstein* became, in its own way, a classic on par with the original *Frankenstein, Dracula,* and *The Wolf Man*.

(24)

ABBOTT AND COSTELLO
MEET FRANKENSTEIN

(1948)

Director: Charles Barton.
Screenplay: Robert Lees, Frederic Rinaldo, John Grant.
Producer: Robert Arthur. *Cinematography:* Charles Van Enger. *Editing:* Frank
    Gross. *Art Direction:* Hilyard Brown, Bernard Herzbrun. *Music:* Frank
    Skinner.
Cast: Bud Abbott (Chick Young), Lou Costello (Wilbur Grey), Lon Chaney
    Jr. (Lawrence Talbot), Bela Lugosi (Count Dracula), Glenn Strange
    (the Frankenstein monster), Lenore Aubert (Dr. Sandra Mornay),
    Jane Randoph (Joan Raymond), Frank Ferguson (McDougal), Charles
    Bradstreet (Dr. Stevens), Howard Negley (insurance man), Harry
    Brown (photographer), Clarence Straight (man in armor), Helen
    Spring (lady at baggage counter), Bobby Barber (waiter), Vincent Price
    (voice of the Invisible Man).
Released: June 15, 1948.
Running Time: 83 minutes.
Availability: DVD (Universal Home Video).

The idea to match Universale Studios' horror franchise with its most popular comedy team came as a whim to producer Robert Arthur, who needed
a good idea for his next Abbott and Costello movie. Once the top box office
stars in America, Bud Abbott and Lou Costello's style became somewhat
less popular after the war, and their recent experiments to change their style
had netted little interest. Bud and Lou were burlesque comics who were
comfortable with their old routines, such as the classic "Who's on First?"
Having to adapt their basic comedy dynamic of the sharp straight man and

the comic patsy into acting roles in situations that relied on character and narrative was a bit of a challenge. But they no longer could simply rely on their old routines. Since the studio remained noted for its horror films, the idea for another Frankenstein movie with the addition of Abbott and Costello seemed like a fun idea. After a couple of unsuccessful drafts, the idea was turned over to screenwriters Robert Lees and Frederic Rinaldo, who had already penned several Abbott and Costello features.

Blending horror and comedy was not at all an innovative idea by 1948. Abbott and Costello themselves had already starred in *Hold That Ghost* (1941), which had been penned by Lees and Rinaldo. Even as far back as the silent era, Harold Lloyd's *Haunted Spooks* (1920) and Buster Keaton's *The Haunted House* (1921) are among the better early examples of this concept. These comedians were enormously creative and didn't simply rely on mechanical gags. *Abbott and Costello Meet Frankenstein* had to also be clever. The idea was that Bud and Lou would be part of the narrative but as a functional team with funny wordplay and slapstick. The monsters would play it straight, as if in a horror movie. The challenge would be to blend these elements cohesively so that horror fans as well as comedy fans were satisfied.

Originally, the title was to be *The Brain of Frankenstein*, and the idea was to promote it as another Universal monster movie, as part of the studio's horror cycle, only with added comedy. The idea to change the title to *Abbott and Costello Meet Frankenstein* was decided during preproduction, with the understanding that the movie was playing more as a comedy with horror elements instead of a horror movie with some added comic relief.

When first given the script, Lou Costello thought it was a terrible idea and told the producers that his youngest child could write a better screenplay. Even though he had already exhibited a real flair for doing scare comedy, he wanted no part of this production. But he was under contract, realized past experiments like splitting up the team had been ineffective, and ultimately agreed to give this one a try. Despite his misgivings, Costello obviously worked hard on the film and did his best with the material.

Universal wanted all of the original horror masters to appear, but Boris Karloff not only refused play the monster but also was somewhat chagrined at its being placed in a comedy. Glenn Strange, who had played the monster twice before and been coached by Karloff, took the role. Lon Chaney Jr. was pleased to appear in the film and revisit his Wolf Man role. Bela Lugosi accepted the chance to once again bring his Dracula role to film. However, both Chaney and Lugosi wanted it understood that neither of them were to burlesque their characters or to make fun of them. They agreed to appear straight in a narrative that had them frightening the comedians.

Abbott and Costello play Chick Young and Wilbur Grey, two baggage clerks. They are assigned to deliver two exhibits to McDougal's House of Horrors, where Mr. McDougal will inspect the packages with his insurance man and accept delivery. The exhibits are said to contain the Frankenstein monster and the remains of Count Dracula. Larry Talbot, living in London, calls the baggage office to warn them, but a full moon causes him to turn into a werewolf before he can fully explain.

The film's opening scenes immediately show us that both horror and comedy elements will be utilized. The comedy in the baggage office has typical slapstick bits, such as Wilbur pulling a suitcase from the bottom of a large stack, causing all of the luggage to topple onto him. It also features the harried McDougal impatiently arguing with Wilbur, allowing for some comic wordplay:

> *Wilbur:* If I am going to deliver these crates at night, you're going to pay overtime, because I am a union man and I only work sixteen hours a day.
>
> *McDougal:* A union man only works eight hours a day!
>
> *Wilbur:* I belong to two unions!

This amusing dialogue exchange does not appear in the script, showing how the comedians would often work out wordplay routines as they filmed.

When Wilbur takes the call from Talbot, the blending of the comedian and the serious character is first presented. Chaney once again plays Talbot as serious, tragic, and, in this scene, very concerned. As he tries to explain the danger of McDougal's crates and their contents and is interrupted by his transformation, Wilbur hears only the growling, snarling Wolf Man. Wilbur amusingly suggests that Talbot keep his dog away from the phone, stating, "It's silly of you to call all the way from London to have your dog talk to me!"

This scene also introduces Sandra, an exotically attractive woman with an accent who appears to be Wilbur's girlfriend. Chick is completely baffled how someone like Wilbur could have such an attractive girlfriend. There is some level of ominous foreshadowing when Sandra shows concern after Wilbur is hit by the luggage and complains that he hurt his head. "Your head?" Sandra asks with concern, and gently starts rubbing it. Chick remains baffled.

The next scene allows the fear element to enter the comedy. Chick and Wilbur arrive at McDougal's House of Horrors ahead of McDougal. They open the first crate and discover it is a coffin bearing Dracula's crest on its cover. Chick leaves to get the other crate, and as he brings it in, Dracula attempts to leave the coffin without being noticed. Wilbur does notice and tries to alert Chick but to no avail. Chick leaves again to greet McDougal's arrival when Dracula reveals himself, hypnotizes Wilbur, and reanimates the Frankenstein monster, who is resting in the other coffin. They hide as the others enter.

At this point, the combination of Universal monsters and Abbott and Costello comedy is fully established. Lugosi plays Dracula with all of the seriousness and commitment as he had in 1931 and likely did onstage originally. Glenn Strange, having dialogue for the first time as the monster, addresses him as master. Frank Skinner's brilliant musical score helps to create the mood. The hypnotized Wilbur is still as the count brings the monster to an area of the House of Horrors that will seclude them from others.

The comedy deals with Wilbur being frightened while Chick dismissively scoffs at the silliness of the entire concept:

> *Chick:* Do you realize people actually pay McDougal to come in here and get scared?
>
> *Wilbur:* I'm cheating him. I'm getting scared for nothing.

As Chick reads from the accompanying card about "Dracula's Legend," Wilbur becomes more and more frightened. They also do a variation on the moving candle bit from *Hold That Ghost* where Dracula opens the casket to peer out and it causes the candle atop the lid to slide. Chick doesn't see it. Wilbur does. And Wilbur tries in vain to convince Chick what he saw.

It is especially funny when McDougal enters with his insurance man and discovers both coffins empty. He believed the coffins should contain the remains of Dracula and the monster, even if only exhibits. Chick insists they were always empty. As they argue, Wilbur, too frightened to speak, is making wild gestures attempting to convey what he saw, mimicking the monster's walk, and Dracula's hypnotizing gestures.

This is followed by a more serious scene in which Count Dracula goes to an island castle and is greeted by Sandra. It is revealed that Sandra has been posing as Wilbur's girlfriend because she finds him to be simple enough for his brain to be a good fit for the monster. She has studied Dr. Frankenstein's notes and gets the idea to replace the monster's defiant abnormal brain with Wilbur's more pliable one. She has an assistant who is described as so engrossed in the scientific work that he does not stop to realize the underlying desires of Sandra, who is acting at Dracula's behest.

Bud Abbott, Lou Costello, Glenn Strange, Lon Chaney Jr., and Bela Lugosi.

By this point, the blending of horror and comedy is complete and can now respond to the continuing narrative. Count Dracula is referred to as Dr. Lejos, and Lugosi again carries himself with an air of aristocracy when removed from the Count Dracula persona, just as he had in the 1931 film. Sandra takes the role not unlike Gloria Holden in *Dracula's Daughter*, although that is not the role she is playing. She is unlike the various Frankenstein offspring who researched his notes in previous films and is presented as closer to the Dracula persona despite not being a vampire. She has the same sort of aloofness.

Wilbur and Chick are actually arrested for the disappearance of the exhibits, and McDougal plans to press charges, but they are bailed out of jail. When they are told they were bailed out by a woman, they believe it to be Sandra but discover it to be Joan. She also pretends to be enamored with Wilbur but is actually working undercover for the insurance company and is trying to find out what happened to the contents of McDougal's exhibits. Chick is completely beside himself that Wilbur has two attractive women interested in him, which is a consistently amusing comic conflict. It allows Abbott and Costello to dig up one of their comedy exchanges:

Wilbur: How about those two girls we had last night? You got the good lookin' one—yours had teeth . . .

Chick: What? Well, yours had teeth too.

Wilbur: Did you see that tooth?

Chick: Well, yes, I did happen to see it . . .

Wilbur: Mine had so much bridge work, every time I kissed her, I had to pay toll.

The dichotomy between the horror and comedy elements is brought together once again when Talbot visits Chick and Wilbur at their apartment, indicating he has taken the room across the hall. When Wilbur describes what he saw, Talbot identifies them as Dracula and the Frankenstein monster. Chick remains skeptical, stating, "Look, bub, I have my own troubles." But Wilbur is sympathetic. When Talbot asks him to lock him in his room, he agrees. Talbot doesn't have time to explain that the moon will be full and his transformation will soon take place.

This sets up a comedy scene between Wilbur and the Wolf Man. After locking Talbot in his room, Wilbur discovers he forgot his suitcase. He goes across the hall and unlocks the door and, on entering, calls out for Talbot, who does not answer. "Now how did he get out of here?" Wilbur wonders. He puts the suitcase down, takes an apple from a fruit basket, and starts to leave. During this time, it is revealed to the audience that the transformation has taken place and Talbot is now the Wolf Man. He stalks behind Wilbur, lunges at him, and keeps missing him. Wilbur goes about his business completely oblivious to the monster's presence. It is an expertly filmed scene that manages to be the ultimate blend of horror and comedy. Wilbur doesn't perform this task quickly. He looks for paper and a pen and leisurely writes a note for Talbot explaining that he returned the suitcase. He ponders before taking the apple, even looking around. But he still manages to keep from seeing the Wolf Man. After he leaves, he stops and asks himself, "I wonder if I counted these?" Director Charles Barton cuts back to the Wolf Man on the other side of the door, sure to pounce if Lou reenters. Fortunately, this bout with his conscience is brief, and Wilbur returns to his room.

Abbott and Costello Meet Frankenstein could easily have been an uneven narrative that fluctuated back and forth from serious horror scenes to amusing comedy sequences. Its choice to establish both genres and then blend them within the same narrative is what makes this film so successful. Somehow, the elements remain true to form and never clash. This scene between Chaney and Costello is one of the best examples during the progression of the narrative.

The culmination occurs when all attend a masquerade ball. Somehow, Wilbur is escorting both Joan and Sandra, while each woman believes the other is Chick's escort (he'd be willing to take either but is frustrated by their complete indifference to him over Wilbur). Wilbur, Chick, and Joan arrive at the castle to pick up Sandra for the masquerade ball. The two women leave to get ready when the phone rings. Wilbur picks it up and hears a voice asking for Dr. Lejos. It is Talbot, who recognizes Wilbur's voice and states, "I believe you're in the house of Dracula right now. If you could find the monster." The scene then cuts to the phone receiver discarded on the ground and Wilbur running for the door. Chick stops him, angry that Talbot keeps filling his head with such nonsense, and suggests they search the castle.

This allows another scene blending horror and comedy. A door leads to a winding staircase into a dank cellar. Wilbur and Chick venture down the stairs when Wilbur pushes against a wall that revolves and places him on its other side. He sits down, not realizing he is on the monster's lap. When he notices, he reacts big and is then confronted by Dracula. He pushes against the wall, which again revolves and places him back with Chick, who once again is skeptical as to Wilbur's frightened description of what he just saw.

There are existing outtakes for the scene where Wilbur is sitting on the monster's lap. During the scene, Wilbur notices a third hand. He pounds on it and wonders why he doesn't feel anything. He then pounds his own hand and hurts himself. As the outtakes reveal, this scene required several takes because Glenn Strange kept laughing. This revealing footage, naturally cut from the released movie, offers the delightful image of the Frankenstein monster laughing at Lou Costello's comedy.

The women and men get ready to leave for the masquerade, and Dracula comes down dressed in regular clothes, introducing himself as Dr. Lejos. His naive helper, Professor Stevens, comes out of the laboratory and questions some of the special equipment that has arrived. Stevens appears to be taken by Joan and is invited to accompany the others to the masquerade. Sandra, however, tries to get out of it by faking a headache. She believes Joan knows too much. While the women were getting ready, Sandra found Joan thumbing through some of Dr. Frankenstein's notes. Lejos takes Sandra aside, away from the others, and bites her neck, putting her under his spell. They arrive at the masquerade together, shortly after the others get there. Lejos is dressed as Dracula. Talbot is at the masquerade ball, too, but not in costume. As Lejos and Sandra meet up with Chick, Wilbur, Joan, and

Stevens, Talbot confronts him as Count Dracula. Lejos chuckles and states, "My costume, you mean." He then asks Joan to dance and moves away with her from the others. Sandra then asks Wilbur to go for a walk in the woods.

During these scenes, Lon Chaney Jr.'s concentration on the seriousness of his role is especially significant. It begins when Chick reveals that his mask for the ball is a wolf. Talbot begs him not to wear it, stating, "When the moon gets full, I turn into a wolf." Wilbur retorts, "You and twenty million other guys." Talbot reacts angrily. At no time does he settle into the lightheartedness of his comic surroundings, and never do Chick or Wilbur comment on the tragic aura he projects. As the elements of the horror and comedy blend cohesively, the actors remain connected to their own genres.

As the narrative journeys to its climax, Sandra and Wilbur are shown sitting together in a secluded area of the woods. She goes to bite him but is interrupted by Chick and Talbot, who are looking for the missing Joan. Wilbur joins their search just as Talbot transforms into the Wolf Man. Wilbur thinks it is Chick under his wolf mask, but when the Wolf Man tries to attack him, he flees. The Wolf Man attacks another guest at the masquerade who turns out to be McDougal. Chick, holding his wolf mask in his hand, is blamed. Wilbur runs over to the scene and confronts Chick about attacking him in the woods. McDougal insists on arresting both, stating, "Don't listen to the little guy, that's his accomplice!" Chick and Wilbur then flee into the woods, where they are confronted by Dracula and an entranced Joan. He puts a spell on both. Chick faints, and Wilbur is taken to the castle. Chick comes to the next morning and finds Talbot, who reveals it is he who attacked McDougal. Talbot offers to turn himself in, but first they must find Lou and Dracula.

The conclusion of *Abbott and Costello Meet Frankenstein* perfectly wraps up the narrative as well the horror and comedy elements. Sandra reveals to a trapped Wilbur their plans to place his brain in the monster. Stevens finds Joan, brings her around, and goes to the castle to confront Lejos, who he now realizes is Dracula. He is knocked out from behind by Sandra. Wilbur is strapped to a table next to the monster, and the experiment is about to take place when they are interrupted by Chick and Talbot. As Talbot goes to unstrap Wilbur, we see his hands are furry. The camera rises up to reveal he has transformed into the Wolf Man. His battle with Dracula causes them to bang into the laboratory equipment, setting off a current to reanimate the monster. The monster breaks from its restraints, picks up Sandra, and throws her through a window.

Lou Costello and Lenore Aubert.

From this point, the film relies on action but continues to offer both the thrill of horror and the merriment of comedy. Chick and Wilbur run though the castle in an attempt to escape, but whatever door they open reveals either the battling Dracula and Wolf Man or the marauding Frankenstein monster. They barricade themselves in a room by pushing a bed in front of the door, but the door opens from the other way. They shut the monster in a closet, but he puts his hand through the door and escapes. The fast movement, the editing, and the musical score all combine to make this an especially funny and exciting ending.

Dracula transforms into a bat and flies out a window, pursued by the Wolf Man, who grabs the bat and falls far down into the rocky waters below. The pursuing Frankenstein monster chases Chick and Wilbur off a pier into a boat. Stevens and Joan pour buckets of gasoline on the pier, set it on fire, and destroy the monster. The last shot shows Chick and Wilbur in a boat, glad that the monsters have been destroyed. Suddenly a voice says, "Oh, I was hoping to get into the action," revealing himself as the Invisible Man. The voice is Vincent Price, who played that character in *The Invisible Man Returns*. Chick and Wilbur jump into the water and swim away as the film ends.

Costello's dislike of the script continued throughout the production, yet he somehow turns in one of his most amusing performances. Abbott did not have the same misgivings but rather supported his partner. He also does an excellent job as the angrily confused buddy who scoffs at the idea of monsters and offers bemused frustration at Wilbur's apparent success as a lady's man. Director Charles Barton connected well with Abbott and Costello, having directed them in the past.

The duo's movie sets were known for a lot of practical jokes, including pies in the face and squirting seltzer bottles. Because of his makeup, Glenn Strange was considered off limits to such tomfoolery, and Bela Lugosi usually avoided the action as well. But since he spent most of the movie out of costume, Lon Chaney delighted in joining the others with off-screen gags and silliness. It kept the spirit of the proceedings high and helped with Costello's dislike of the script. He felt that the entire idea was stupid and that the movie would fail at the box office. In fact, *Abbott and Costello Meet Frankenstein* was an enormous hit and was instrumental in bringing Abbott and Costello back among the very top box office stars, a status they had not enjoyed in recent years.

Bela Lugosi and Glenn Strange, in costume, share a laugh on the set.

The comedy team's children visited them on the set and years later recalled their experiences for Bob Furmanek and Ron Palumbo for their book *Abbott and Costello in Hollywood*. Paddy Costello recalled,

> Glenn Strange was so sweet. "Frankenstein" was always walking around with a smile. I always got a big kick out of that—seeing the monsters between scenes sitting in a chair reading a newspaper or chewing gum, or laughing and smoking like regular people. And then how that reality was suspended so this fantasy could come to life. He was the nicest, sweetest gentleman and very, very friendly.[1]

The reaction to the actors while in costume was intimidating even to other professionals shooting at the studio. Lugosi, Strange, and Chaney were asked not to eat lunch in the cafeteria while working in their makeup. They would have food delivered to the set. This didn't stop them from having some fun with that concept. At one point during a break, actress Lenore Aubert, who played Sandra, put a rope around a fully made-up Glenn Strange's neck and walked him around the studio lot as a tour of the studio was in progress.

Along with Lees and Rinaldo, John Grant contributed to the script as a gag man. Grant had been with Abbott and Costello since their first movies and recalled most of the old burlesque routines they enjoyed doing. On this movie, he contributed to the moving candle bit, which dated back to burlesque, and other such sequences.

One particular gag was written but not performed. When Wilbur is summoned to the cave by Dracula, the idea was for him to resist by trying to run away but getting nowhere. They were going to have a treadmill stationed in the ground out of the frame to create this effect. This gag was cut before production. Robert Lees told Furmanek and Palumbo,

> I was absolutely furious, because I thought that it would have been one of the funniest pieces of business. Costello trying to fight this invisible force. It was like a gag Buster Keaton would have done. Either they felt it was too hard to do or too expensive.[2]

The makeup that had originally been designed by Jack Pierce was the inspiration for the Frankenstein monster and the Wolf Man. Pierce was no longer at Universal, having been replaced by Bud Westmore of the noted Westmore brothers in 1946. Westmore created effective rubber masks for both Glenn Strange and Lon Chaney, reducing their time in the

Lou Costello and Lon Chaney Jr. between scenes.

makeup chair from several hours to just one hour. Their appearance is no less effective here than in any earlier movie.

The use of animation to present the transformation of Count Dracula from bat to man (and vice versa) was nicely done under the supervision of Universal cartoon producer Walter Lantz. Famous for the Woody Woodpecker cartoons produced by the studio, Lantz's presentation of the vampire's transformation is perhaps the most effective one in all of the Universal monster movies featuring Count Dracula as a character.

The music by Frank Skinner used some cues from his work on *Son of Frankenstein* and *The Wolf Man*, but much of the music was especially for this movie. His music enhances every scene, adding horror elements to the comedy so that an underlying eeriness is always evident, even in the lighter scenes where Abbott and Costello are just being funny. It might be the most effectively scored film in his long career.

Filming of *Abbott and Costello Meet Frankenstein* was not without its mishaps. In the scene where the monster throws Sandra through the window, the glass didn't break, causing stuntwoman Helen Thurston to fly back at the actor, knocking him down and fracturing his ankle. The next day, Lon Chaney volunteered to get behind the Frankenstein monster makeup and do the scene, having played the monster before. This time, the breakaway glass broke, but shards of it got in Miss Thurston's eyes, and she had to be rushed to the hospital.

There are also some continuity issues. Lees and Rinaldo were comedy writers and Barton was a comedy director, so it is impressive that their work on the horror elements of this story are done so well. However, there is a shot where Dracula's reflection is clearly evident in a mirror, and there is no discussion over the fact that in his last movie appearance (*House of Dracula*) Talbot had been cured of his curse. But this film, despite being more a comedy than a horror movie, is significant to the genre for having Lugosi repeat his role as the count and for being the only time Glenn Strange's version of the monster has dialogue (he says "Master" and "Yes master" at different times in the film). It is also important as being the final Universal monster movie of this era to feature Dracula, the Wolf Man, or the Frankenstein monster.

Costello attended the premiere with his family, still being dismissive of the content and believing the film would be a misfire. At the end of the film, Lou's own mother ran up and hugged producer Robert Arthur, stating, "That is the hardest I laughed in years." According to Arthur, "Lou got furious. He had just taken a position early on, and he wasn't going back on it." According to Chris Costello in an interview with Ethan Alter,

> Dad hated it! He thought that Universal no longer had any faith in Abbott and Costello and therefore just wanted to bring in all these monsters. He was not very partial to that film, but I think if he could come back and see new generations of fans locking onto Abbott and Costello because of the film, he would just glow.[3]

The budget for *Abbott and Costello Meet Frankenstein* was just under $760,000, which is fairly high for an Abbott and Costello movie but low overall. It went more than $30,000 over budget and ran seven days past its proposed 32-day shooting schedule. But its worldwide gross in 1948 was over $3 million, making it the third-largest box office hit that year.

The reviews for the movie were strong in nearly all of the trades and newspapers, except, once again, stodgy old Bosley Crowther in the *New York Times* on July 29, 1948, who stated,

> Most of the comic invention in *Abbott and Costello Meet Frankenstein* is embraced in the idea and the title. The notion of having these two clowns run afoul of the famous screen monster is a good laugh in itself. But take this gentle warning: get the most out of that one laugh while you can, because the

picture, at Loew's Criterion, does not contain many more. That is to say, the situations which the wags at Universal have contrived for their two untiring comedians in this assembly-line comedy are the obvious complications that would occur in a house of horrors. Costello, the roly-poly and completely susceptible one, shudders and shakes in standard terror to behold the assembly of ghouls—which includes not only the monster but Count Dracula and the Wolf Man. Abbott, prevented from seeing the creatures until near the end, scoffs and snorts at his partner from behaving so curiously. After a thorough exhaustion of this play on frustration and fright, the story is brought to a climax with the intended transference of a brain. Whose brain is tagged for what monster we leave you to surmise.

This caused the reviewer for the June 28, 1948, *Hollywood Reporter* to state,

> New York critics bore us stiff sometimes. One of those sometimes is when they get around to reviewing Abbott and Costello. The chief critical complaint is that if you've seen one of those flickers, you've seen them all. Well, if you've read one review on an Abbott and Costello comedy, you've read them all.

Most reviewers agreed with the June 25, 1948, *Variety*, which stated,

> The comedy team battles it out with the studio's roster of bogeymen in a rambunctious fracas that is funny and, at the same time, spine-tingling.

While looking at the success of this movie, Universal realized that subsequent monster movies would not be the direction to go, as the monster actors were not under contract to the studio and were getting too old to continue playing these challenging roles in an active series. In addition, new studio head William Goetz decided the newly defined Universal-International would be for more prestigious pictures. He claimed he did not care for horror movies or for Abbott and Costello.

Abbott and Costello, however, were still under contract, and their status at being the third-highest box office stars in the nation on the strength of *Abbott and Costello Meet Frankenstein* meant that their film careers remained secure. The following year, Universal was able to secure the services of Boris Karloff to make a movie with the comedy team. The success of *Abbott and Costello Meet Frankenstein* changed the actor's mind. However, Karloff was not cast as an iconic monster. He is cast as a hypnotic swami in the comedy/mystery *Abbott and Costello Meet the Killer Boris Karloff*, managing to secure his name in the title as well. That movie was also a hit, so the studio decided to have the comedy team deal with another one of their horror franchises. So, in 1951, *Abbott and Costello Meet the Invisible Man* was released.

ABBOTT AND COSTELLO MEET
THE INVISIBLE MAN

(1951)

Director: Charles Lamont.
Screenplay: John Grant, Robert Lees, Frederic I. Rinaldo, from a story by
 Hugh Wedlock and Howard Snyder.
Producer: Howard Christie. *Cinematography:* George Robinson. *Editing:* Virgil
 Vogel. *Art Direction:* Bernard Herzbrun, Richard Riedel.
Cast: Bud Abbott (Bud Alexander), Lou Costello (Lou Francis), Nancy Guild
 (Helen Gray), Arthur Franz (Tommy Nelson), Adele Jergens (Boots
 Marsden), Sheldon Leonard (Morgan), William Frawley (Roberts),
 Gavin Muir (Dr. Gray), Paul Maxey (psychiatrist), Herb Vigran
 (Stillwell), John Day (Rocky Hanlon), Jack Perry (Rocky's handler),
 Frank Dae (Colonel Duffie), Ed Gargan (Milt), Harold Goodwin
 (bartender), George J. Lewis (Torpedo Al), Carl Sklover (Lou's
 handler), Frankie Van (referee), Billy Wayne (Rooney), Walter Appler
 (Professor Dugan), Sam Balter (radio announcer), Bobby Barber
 (Sneaky), Milt Bronson (ring announcer), Steve Carruthers, Russ
 Conway, Sayer Dearing, George Ford, Billy Snyder (reporters).
Released: March 7, 1951.
Running Time: 82 minutes.
Availability: DVD (Universal Home Video).

The original script for *Abbott and Costello Meet the Invisible Man* was
originally penned years earlier as a proposed new sequel to the actual Invisible Man series. It was shelved but resurrected as an idea for Abbott and
Costello after the success of *Abbott and Costello Meet Frankenstein*. The
existing screenplay was used only as an idea, and a new script was written
by the duo's usual writers: John Grant, Fredric Rinaldo, and Robert Lees.

Because the actual films in the Invisible Man series had only a tangential connection at best, with little of the continuity found in the Frankenstein or even the Mummy series, using the concept of invisibility as a plot point in an Abbott and Costello feature works well. There is reference to John Griffin, the creator of the concept, and he is even referred to with a photo of Claude Rains, the actor who played the role in the 1933 film. Otherwise, *Abbott and Costello Meet the Invisible Man* is another attempted combination of the horror/suspense genre and the duo's comedy.

Since making *Abbott and Costello Meet Frankenstein*, Bud and Lou appeared in *Mexican Hayride, Africa Screams, Abbott and Costello Meet the Killer Boris Karloff*, and *Abbott and Costello in the Foreign Legion*. Reviewers were becoming less interested in the sameness of the team's work, which was appearing to be less innovative and more forced. The new young team of Dean Martin and Jerry Lewis had started making films at Paramount and became an immediate sensation. Abbott and Costello needed another solid hit that was somewhat different than what they had been doing but still retained the comedy they did best. *Abbott and Costello Meet the Invisible Man* expands their scope in that, once again, the fantasy and suspense elements are taken seriously while the duo handle the comedy.

Abbott and Costello's characters are named for their actual first and middle names. Bud Alexander and Lou Francis are recent detective school graduates. Their first case is to help a former boxer who escaped from jail after being framed for murder. He wants Bud and Lou to bring him to the home of his fiancée, Helen, so he can ask her uncle, Dr. Gray, to inject him with a serum that will make him invisible. This, he believes, will allow him to spy on those who framed him and ultimately clear his name. Dr. Gray doesn't want to inject Tommy, recalling that John Griffin, the man who first developed the serum, went insane. The police arrive, and Tommy injects himself with the serum. Lou is present when Tommy starts to become invisible, but the police—and Bud—don't believe him. He is taken to the police psychiatrist for evaluation

Unlike *Abbott and Costello Meet Frankenstein*, the Invisible Man character does get involved with the comedy to an extent. When Bud starts to berate Lou for letting Tommy escape, the invisible fugitive kicks Bud. But the first big comic highlight takes place in the psychiatrist's office. First, there is the usual comic banter:

Psychiatrist: How often do you see things?

Lou: Whenever I have my eyes open.

Psychiatrist: Do you ever hear strange voices?

Lou: Every time I dial the wrong number.

Eventually, Lou gets hold of the psychiatrist's watch and ends up hypnotizing him—and anyone who comes into the room—into a deep sleep.

Bud and Lou eventually agree to help Tommy find the actual killer of his manager and clear his name. At first, Bud is presented as unscrupulous enough to phone the cops in an attempt to capture Tommy but is eventually convinced to help him. From this point, the film plays like a typical suspense mystery, using the same type of narrative and conflicts as the other Invisible Man sequels but with comic touches by Abbott and Costello. The film has elements of a boxing drama as well as a suspense mystery and comes off as more serious than other Abbott and Costello movies that expand to include other genres.

It is explained that Tommy's manager was killed because of his and Tommy's refusal to purposely lose (or throw) a fight against rival Rocky Hanlon. The manager was beaten to death, and Tommy was framed for his murder. Now the invisible Tommy is at the gym gathering information by listening

Abbott and Costello meet the Invisible Man (Arthur Franz).

to conversations unnoticed, while Lou poses as a fighter. Lou pretends to punch the bag while the invisible Tommy punches it. When Rocky Hanlon confronts Lou, the invisible Tommy knocks him out, and Lou is given credit. A fight between Rocky and Lou is arranged, so gangster Morgan attempts to fix the fight, just as he had attempted with Tommy. He sends his girl, Boots Marsden, to seduce Lou into throwing the fight. Lou plays along.

There are two particular highlights worth noting, one involving Bud and the other involving Lou. First, Bud and Lou are out with the invisible Tommy. Tommy keeps drinking and becomes increasingly more intoxicated. In order to cover up the Invisible Man's audible voice, Bud must act like he is drunk, and it is his voice saying these things. While not a particularly funny scene and not very long, it is quite well acted and shows the scope of Abbott's acting ability.

The other highlight is more comical when a fight is arranged between Rocky and Lou. Tommy stands beside Lou and hits Rocky, calling out the punches so Lou can mimic the moves. Tommy will say "right cross" or "uppercut," and Lou will respond with those punches, but it is actually Tommy who is hitting Rocky. It is both funny and exciting, playing off of the comedy of the narrative as well as the dramatic element. At one point, Lou throws a wild punch and accidentally knocks out Tommy. Then both he and Rocky trip over Tommy's invisible body lying on the canvas.

When Lou wins the fight, Morgan orders Bud's murder. Tommy protects him and is stabbed when his image becomes visible in a rush of steam from a burst pipe. He starts to bleed profusely, and a transfusion becomes necessary. Lou gives Tommy the transfusion, but some of Tommy's blood backs up into Lou, and he starts to become invisible. The movie ends on an effects-driven visual gag, with Lou becoming visible again, only to find that his legs are now on backward.

Abbott and Costello Meet the Invisible Man seems to connect better to the Invisible Man series than it does to the Abbott and Costello comedies. Like the previous Invisible Man sequels, the narrative features a man wanting to become invisible to clear his name, his personality becoming affected along the way. This is because the original story by Hugh Wedlock and Howard Snyder had initially been written as an Invisible Man film. The comedy of Abbott and Costello appears to have been added to the idea rather than redefining it. *Abbott and Costello Meet the Invisible Man* is really a serious story with comic touches rather than a comedy with an underlying serious narrative. It is one of the most unusual Abbott and Costello movies but is a fairly typical Invisible Man movie.

There are a lot of amusing moments in *Abbott and Costello Meet the Invisible Man* provided by William Frawley as a harried police detective trying to capture Tommy. Frawley had appeared with Abbott and Costello in their first movie, *One Night in the Tropics* (1940). Only months after the release of *Abbott and Costello Meet the Invisible Man*, Frawley began his iconic role as Fred Mertz on the *I Love Lucy* series.

Sheldon Leonard, who plays Morgan, was a quintessential tough-guy actor who appeared in comedies such as this as well as dramas like *Come Fill the Cup* (1950) with James Cagney. He is probably best remembered as Nick the bartender in Frank Capra's holiday classic *It's a Wonderful Life* (1946). He later became a top-level TV producer, responsible for such programs as *The Andy Griffith Show* and *The Dick Van Dyke Show*, and made strides in interracial relationships on TV with his series *I Spy* featuring Robert Culp and Bill Cosby as costars.

Arthur Franz as Tommy does an effective job in the challenging role of the invisible prizefighter. He alludes to the shaky sanity of past invisible men, with dialogue such as "Invisibility gives me a feeling of power—for good or for evil." Nancy Guild is an attractive presence as his girl, while Adele Jergens is at her wily best as Morgan's moll. Paul Maxey is very funny as the befuddled psychiatrist.

Universal executives were pleased that director Charles Lamont finished shooting on *Abbott and Costello Meet the Invisible Man* four days ahead of schedule and $70,000 under budget—this despite the necessity for expensive special effects provided by David Horsley, who had also worked on several of the earlier Invisible Man films. Fred Rinaldo and Robert Lees wrote the screenplay for the comedy sequel *The Invisible Woman*, so they were familiar with the studio's concept of invisibility as well as with Abbott and Costello. Everything ran smoothly during production, and the comedy duo had no problem expanding the parameters of their roles by venturing outside of their comedy and responding to the dramatic element of the screenplay.

Abbott and Costello Meet the Invisible Man was well received by both critics and moviegoers and enjoyed as something different. The critic for *Motion Picture Daily* stated,

A rainy Monday night at the Ritz Theater in Los Angeles promptly forgot about the unusual California weather outdoors when this brightly-conceived and alertly-executed Abbott and Costello comedy followed a sternly-militaristic March of Time subject upon the screen. Laughter that got rolling within the first minute of *Abbott and Costello Meet the Invisible Man* rippled steadily along the first hour and then broke into crashing waves when Costello entered a boxing ring to meet the title challenger, with the Invisible Man alongside to deliver the knockout punch. Foyer comment in the theater tended to suggest that this may be their best all-around comedy in years.[1]

At a budget of $625,000, *Abbott and Costello Meet the Invisible Man* grossed over $1.5 million, so, while not the enormous profit *Abbott and Costello Meet Frankenstein* had been, it was still a solid moneymaker that pleased studio executives. Abbott and Costello would now spend time doing TV work as well as movies, not revisiting a classic monster series until 1955 with *Abbott and Costello Meet the Mummy* (although they would "meet" Dr. Jekyll and Mr. Hyde the year before).

While Abbott and Costello continued making comedies, the monster series seemed to have effectively ended. While there were no further plans to bring back any of the iconic creatures from earlier movies, there were some new pop culture developments that caused studio executives to take notice.

Right around this time, the early 1950s, a science fiction craze started to enter American culture and would continue to pick up momentum as the decade progressed. Usually, science fiction movies dealt with visitors from outer space, but in other instances the narratives featured mutants that developed elsewhere. Such was the concept when, three years later, Universal decided to both jump on the sci-fi bandwagon and investigate the popular 3-D novelty by creating one more monster before dispensing with the genre entirely.

The Creature from the Black Lagoon created yet another monster. Combining the popular science fiction genre with Universal's experience making horror movies, the creature has lived on as an iconic figure alongside Dracula, Frankenstein, the Mummy, the Invisible Man, and the Wolf Man. And its success spawned a couple of sequels that fit neatly into the continued popularity of the science fiction genre and also maintained its status as a horror movie.

26

CREATURE FROM THE BLACK LAGOON
(1954)

> *Director:* Jack Arnold.
> *Screenplay:* Arthur A. Ross, Harry J. Essex, based on a story by Maurice Zimm.
> *Producer:* William Alland. *Cinematography:* James C. Havens, William Snyder.
> *Editing:* Ted Kent. *Art Direction:* Hilyard Brown, Bernard Herzbrun.
> *Cast:* Richard Carlson (David Reed), Julie Adams (Kay Lawrence), Richard
> Denning (Mark Williams), Antonio Moreno (Carl Maia), Nestor Paiva
> (Lucas), Whit Bissell (Edwin Thompson), Ricou Browning (the Gill
> Man in water), Ben Chapman (the Gill Man on land), Ben Gozier
> (Zee), Henry Escalante (Chico), Rodd Redwing (Louis), Sydney Mason
> (Dr. Matos), Perry Lopez (Tomas).
> *Released:* March 5, 1954.
> *Running Time:* 79 minutes.
> *Availability:* DVD (Universal Home Video).

Universal-International decided to connect with the current science fiction craze and also the popularity of 3-D movies. While the 3-D gimmick's popularity had died down by the time the movie was released (resulting in some theaters simply running a straight 2-D print), the science fiction genre was enjoying its greatest era.

While much of science fiction dealt with visitors from outer space, Universal realized its background was in monster movies. So its science fiction film would likely feature a monster. The result was the title character who, although coming along decades after the studio's other iconic monsters had been established, became every bit as popular and with the same lasting significance.

Trade ad for *Creature from the Black Lagoon*.

The film opens with a geologist, Carl Maia, on an Amazonian expedition discovering a fossilized hand with webbed fingers that he believes proves an evolutionary connection between sea animals, land animals, and, ultimately, humans. He contacts a former student at a California aquarium who secures funding for a return expedition to, it is hoped, find the rest of the skeleton that goes with the fossilized hand discovered. The members of the expedition include the original geologist, Maia; his student David Reed; Reed's boss, Mark Williams; Reed's girlfriend and colleague, Kay; and a fellow scientist, Edwin Thompson.

Prior to the expedition sailing off on a craft run by a man named Lucas and his crew, we are shown Maia's expedition team, stationed in the Amazon, being attacked and killed by the Creature. When the others arrive at the camp and find the dead bodies, Lucas suggests it was done by a wild animal, perhaps a jaguar. During this discovery, the Creature's hand emerges from the waters and reaches toward Kay, who walks away before contact is made, oblivious to its presence.

The Creature at this point is an ominous presence that we know little about. The mystery of the character is coupled with our knowledge of the violence it is capable of inflicting. Naturally, the director shows it reaching for the woman, who has no idea she came close to being captured.

The crew searches on land in the vicinity of where the fossil had been found but to no avail. Mark and David then dive into the water to search, but Lucas warns them not to enter what he calls "the black lagoon." Mark and David, in full scuba gear, search the ocean floor for revealing fossils. They return with what little they've discovered, not realizing the Creature has been watching them. Kay then goes for a swim, also oblivious to the fact that the Creature is swimming nearby and watching her.

Julie Adams is an attractive presence, and this is used as a ploy to attract the Creature in the film's narrative. There is a great underwater shot of Kay swimming and the Gill Man swimming on his back beneath her, unnoticed as he gazes longingly at her figure. This is a long, drawn out scene that is suspenseful and unsettling. We don't know if the Creature will suddenly strike or if he will be content with stalking Kay while remaining in the shadows of the lagoon. Some of the footage here might have influenced what Steven Spielberg later did in *Jaws*.

The Creature gets caught in the boat's net but escapes as they try to pull up whatever it is. They find a broken claw and realize the existence of a creature, but they do not know the details. The creature is eventually caught and locked in a cage aboard the expedition crew's boat. It escapes and attacks Dr. Edwin. The remaining crew decide to leave, but the Creature has used logs to block their exit from the lagoon. David and Mark go after the Creature. It kills Mark and then captures Kay, bringing her to a cavern. The other crew pursue them, and she is rescued. The Creature is shot several times, reenters the lagoon, and sinks into the murky waters.

A new and interesting monster movie for the modern sci-fi era, *The Creature from the Black Lagoon* was solid sci-fi entertainment and was generally appreciated by most critics. *Variety* stated,

> This 3-D hackle-raiser reverts to the prehistoric. After the discovery of a web-fingered skeleton hand in the Amazon region, a scientific expedition heads into the steaming tropics to hunt more fossils. In the back-washes of the Amazon they come across a still living Gill Man, half-fish, half-human. The 3-D lensing adds to the eerie effects of the underwater footage, as well as to the monster's several appearances on land. The below-water scraps between skin divers and the prehistoric thing are thrilling and will pop goose pimples on the susceptible fan, as will the close-up scenes of the scaly, gilled creature. Jack Arnold's direction does a first rate job of developing chills and suspense, and James C. Havens rates a good credit for his direction of the underwater sequences. Richard Carlson and Julie Adams co-star in the William Alland production and carry off the thriller very well.[1]

Also,

> *Creature From the Black Lagoon* is a good piece of science-fiction of the beauty and the beast school, the beast in this case being a monstrous combination of man and fish. It makes for solid horror-thrill entertainment. Screenplay by Harry Essex and Arthur Ross, from a story by Maurice Zimm, is soundly developed, leading to an exciting climax.
>
> Lovely Julie Adams reveals a gorgeous pair of gams in a swimming sequence and turns in her customary fine performance. Richard Carlson, who seems to appear in most of the good science-fiction pictures, is convincing as the male lead, and Richard Denning is strong as the commercial-minded head of the expedition. Nestor Paiva contributes an excellent stint as the skipper of the river boat, and Antonio Moreno and Whit Bissell handle their roles capably. The production was shot in black-and-white 3-D, the process adding some small value to the underwater shots which don't make up for the eyestrain. William E. Snyder's photography is good. Underwater sequences were ably directed by James C. Havens.[2]

Regarding the movie's backstory, Tom Weaver recalled in his book *Monsters, Mutants, and Heavenly Creatures* that producer William Alland attended a 1941 dinner party during the filming of *Citizen Kane* (in which

Alland has a role as a reporter). At the dinner, cinematographer Gabriel Figueroa of Mexico told Allard a myth about a race of half-fish, half-human creatures in the Amazon. Alland recalled Figueroa's story ten years later and, partly inspired by Beauty and the Beast, wrote the basis for a story called *The Sea Monster*. Maurice Zimm expanded Alland's notes into a treatment that was then made into a screenplay, *The Black Lagoon*, by Harry Essex and Arthur Ross. Jack Arnold was hired to direct the film in 3-D due to the success of *House of Wax*. Arnold had previously scored with the sci-fi hit *It Came from Outer Space*.

The designer of the approved Gill Man was Millicent Patrick, a former Disney illustrator. Patrick was a very attractive woman, so the studio sent her out on a publicity tour to help promote the film, billing her "The Beauty Who Created the Beast." According to the website Tor.com,

Westmore had sent memos to the Universal front office taking exception to the studio's intention to bill her as "The Beauty Who Created the Beast," by claiming that the Creature was entirely the product of his own efforts. In February, while the tour was in full swing, Westmore went to great lengths to secure clippings of her numerous newspaper interviews, some citing her as the Creature's sole creator, without mention of Westmore or of the other members of the make-up department staff. Westmore made it clear in his complaints to Universal executives that he had no intentions of engaging Ms. Patrick's services as a sketch artist again. In correspondence between executives Clark Ramsey and Charles Simonelli dated the first of March 1954, Ramsey noted that Westmore was behaving childishly over the matter, and that Patrick had done everything possible to credit Westmore during her interviews. He further expressed regret at Westmore's intention to penalize her. True to his threat, however, Westmore stopped using her after she completed drawings for Douglas Sirk's Captain Lightfoot, released by the studio the following year.[3]

The Creature was played by two different people: Ben Chapman played the Gill Man on land, while Ricou Browning played him during the underwater scenes. Chapman recalled for The Astounding B-Movie Archive,

I do feel that I brought life to the Creature. Jack Arnold was known as a very tough director. Good, but tough. I said to him, "Just tell me how you want me to portray him." He said, "I don't want him to be like a cartoon. I don't want him going clump, clump, clump, like some kind of cartoon monster. Don't walk. Don't pick up your feet. I want you to glide." They put ten pounds of lead under each foot, stuck to the soles. When I went to walk, ten pounds would remind me, "Don't pick up your feet."[4]

Ricou Browning is perhaps the better known Gill Man actor, having done all of the underwater scenes. He also appeared in all three of the Creature movies, while three different actors played the Creature on land. Browning also outlived all of the actors who played the Creature on land and continued to appear at conventions and autograph shows. When he would be presented with a photo from one of the Creature movies featuring one of the other actors as the Gill Man, he still would agree to sign it.

The original script had planned to have the Creature die from his wounds on camera, not just slink back into the lagoon after being riddled with bullets. But the producer realized the movie would likely be a hit and would warrant a sequel. As a result, it is very ambiguous as to the Creature's ultimate fate. Thus, a sequel was planned even before this movie was released. *Creature from the Black Lagoon* grossed over a million dollars, making a reasonable enough profit for the proposed sequel to be a good investment.

The Creature from the Black Lagoon was not the first appearance of the Gill Man. In one of the promotions for the movie, it was decided that the Creature would appear on TV's *Colgate Comedy Hour* with hosts Bud Abbott and Lou Costello. Because Abbott and Costello had become noted for meeting up with monsters in their most recent movies, the idea was that featuring the Creature with them in a TV skit would be a good way to promote Universal's new monster. The skit features Bud and Lou ending up in the Universal prop department, where all the monster props are kept. The prop manager (played by Bud's nephew Norman Abbott, an actor and prolific film and TV director) shows the duo the various props and then indicates that their latest monster is the Creature. The comedy team goes through their usual routine with Lou noticing monsters that are hidden once Bud tries to look. Glenn Strange was on hand to once again play the Frankenstein monster in the sketch. And Ben Chapman played the Creature.

While technically *The Creature from the Black Lagoon* is a science fiction movie, not a horror film, it does feature an iconic monster. Approaching the films of this series in the postwar 1950s, we see how Universal-International responded to its past legacy of monster movies and adapted that perspective for another type of monster in another setting and a different era. With the classic era of vintage monster movies having ended years earlier, the idea that a new monster from a different era could comfortably fit in with the same iconic status as Frankenstein, the Wolf Man, Dracula, the Invisible Man, and the Mummy is quite impressive. While neither of its sequels would be as good as this first movie, the Gill Man would live on over time and generations just as strongly as the other monsters.

27

REVENGE OF THE CREATURE

(1955)

Director: Jack Arnold.
Screenplay: Martin Berkeley, from a story by William Alland.
Producer: William Alland. Cinematography: Charles S. Welbourne. Editing: Paul
    Weatherwax. Art Direction: Alexander Golitzen, Alfred Sweeney.
Cast: John Agar (Professor Clete Ferguson), Lori Nelson (Helen Dobson),
    John Bromfield (Joe Hayes), Nestor Paiva (Lucas), Grandon Rhodes
    (Jackson Foster), Dave Willock (Lou Gibson), Robert Williams
    (George Johnson), Charles Cane (police captain), Ricou Browning
    (the Gill Man in water), Tom Hennesy (the Gill Man on land), Clint
    Eastwood (Jennings), Brett Halsey (Pete), Don Harvey (Mac), Robert
    Hoy (Charlie), Robert Nelson (Dr. McCuller), Bob Wehling (Joe), Jack
    Gargan (Skipper), Ned LeFevere (newscaster), Sydney Mason (police
    announcer), Charles Victor, Charles Gibb (cops), Jere Beery Sr.
    (photographer), Loretta Agar (bit role).
Released: May 13, 1955.
Running Time: 82 minutes.
Availability: DVD (Warner Home Video).

Universal was now Universal-International, which was interested in producing more prestigious pictures but also found itself temporarily in the
monster business again. *The Creature from the Black Lagoon* was a big hit,
but a sequel was ordered even before the first production was completed.
Revenge of the Creature was also shot in 3-D, but by 1955, the 3-D craze
was pretty much over. In fact, *Revenge of the Creature* was the only 3-D
feature released that year. The 3-D idea would be revived a few years later

and would be technologically revamped in the twenty-first century, but *Revenge of the Creature* was the last 3-D film to be released during the gimmick's so-called golden era. It was also the only 3-D sequel to a film that had also been shot in 3-D. A flat, 2-D film was also released. According to the book *The Creature Chronicles* by Tom Weaver, David Schecter, and Steve Kronenberg, *Revenge of the Creature* was not originally shown in theaters in the format for 3-D where red-and-blue glasses were used to see the images. Its 3-D process was created by the polarized light method and viewed through glasses with gray polarizing filters.

Nestor Paiva returns from the previous *Creature from the Black Lagoon*, assuming his role from the previous movie, as does Ricou Browning, who plays the Creature in the underwater scenes (Tom Hennesy plays him on land). All the others are new characters.

Revenge of the Creature opens with an expedition searching for the Creature, who has been spotted and thus causes everyone to realize the bullets from the previous movie did not kill him. The Gill Man is captured and brought to a Florida ocean research center headed by Professor Clete Ferguson. He and his colleague, ichthyology student Helen Dobson, study the Creature, who becomes taken by Helen. The Creature escapes, killing his keeper, and returns to the ocean. It remains enamored with Helen, returning to land to kidnap her and return to the water. She is rescued when Dr. Ferguson goes to the ocean with police and the Creature is again riddled with bullets.

The film was originally going to feature the first Creature attack almost immediately, but it was decided in postproduction that an introductory scene was necessary. According to Tom Weaver, this scene was shot and directed by Joseph Pevney, as Jack Arnold was on another project and unavailable.

Despite a few entertaining action sequences, the appealing presence of Lori Nelson, and the reliable acting of John Agar, *Revenge of the Creature* is a rather weak sequel to the original. The narrative doesn't build a great deal of suspense, so it is only the stalking of the Creature and the use of music that sustains it. There are some tangential scenes to lighten up the proceedings, including an amusing cameo by a young Clint Eastwood, but overall the film does not generate a great deal of sustained interest and really pales when compared to the vintage horror films Universal had released two decades earlier.

The Creature does not appear to be as dangerous as the other monsters. We learn nothing new about the Creature despite his being captured for study and remaining chained for a great portion of the film. He also appears

The Creature on a rampage.

to be somewhat less resilient than he had been in *Creature from the Black Lagoon*. The Gill Man seems easier to catch, and when it stalks the Professor and Helen swimming, quietly watching them underwater, the focus is on how enamored he is by Helen, with no discernible interest in killing the professor. The motivation is not offered as to why the Gill Man would have human desires for a human female, but the conflict is pretty basic otherwise.

There are a number of exciting sequences, such as the Creature's attempt to grab Helen during the underwater research and his eventually capturing her. During the scenes where the escaped Gill Man is rampaging through the beachfront area and people are running away, there is some excitement when a fleeing child falls in front of the Creature and is quickly rescued by her mother in the nick of time. The climax where Helen is captured and eventually rescued is good visceral entertainment, and the underwater cinematography is once again amazing. *Revenge of the Creature* was shot on location in Florida and repeats a lot of what was successful in the previous film. But, as Tom Weaver points out, the film is, overall, a rather pallid reworking of the King Kong story, where a beast escapes, rampages, captures the girl with whom he is enamored, and is ultimately killed.

The reviews for *Revenge of the Creature* were not too impressed, the *New York Times* stating,

That man is here again, Universal's "gill-man," who made such an unmemo-rable debut last year in *Creature From the Black Lagoon*. In *Revenge of the Creature*, he again is hauled from the Amazon, then deposited in the famous Marineland, Fla., aquarium. Escaping he terrorizes the coast citizens and, of course, a pretty girl, this time Lori Nelson. For this waterlogged exercise is the umpteenth version of Beauty and the Beast. Indeed, the poor, camouflaged actor of the title role still sports a rubberized facsimile of an earlier Jean Cocteau headgear. Close scrutiny will disclose two mild assets—some sharp nocturnal photography toward the end, as a posse destroys the visitor, and a low-keyed unpretentiousness in the earlier scenes at the Marine Studio. What is probably the most unusual aquarium in the world makes a nice, picturesque background indeed. Mr. Agar, a scientist, and Miss Nelson, an ichthyology student (from Texas, yet!), and Mr. Bromfield, as their sidekick, all stumble around foolishly in trying to subdue the tank's rebel. But they and their prey, and eventual nemesis, are the least interesting swimmers, as glimpsed through those beguiling subterranean portholes for tourists. As for the rest—away we go, as before. Two incidents in this dead-serious escapade are hilarious. Yesterday's audience was convulsed when Gill, let's call him, spying on Miss Nelson's preparations to retire, gives a tremendous adenoidal gulp. Even fun-nier is his roaring invasion of a hot jam session, scattering "cats" all over the place. In his own place, the bottom of the Amazon, Gill is strictly okay.[1]

However, Murray Horowitz for *Motion Picture Daily* thought the film succeeded within its own parameters, stating,

A 3-D entry is offered in this Universal release, concerning the horrors of a pre-historic half-man, half-fish, that runs (and swims) amok in civilized Florida. It is the only 3-D entry of any studio this year and smart showmen may capitalize on its uniqueness to revive interest in the medium. Whether the public will be receptive to 3-D again remains to be seen. While the picture does contain a number of weaknesses, there appears to be sufficient suspense and horror ingredients to register in most situations, especially if its exhibition is geared to a proper exploitation campaign. Shock elements on the screen appeal to many patrons and the Creature, gills and all, is shocking indeed.[2]

The 3-D gimmick had been quite successful from 1952's *Bwana Devil* and for the next couple of years. *House of Wax* with Vincent Price, *Money from Home* with Dean Martin and Jerry Lewis, and even a couple of Three Stooges shorts (*Spooks* and *Pardon My Backfire*) used the 3-D concept.

The fact that the classic era of 3-D movies concludes with *Revenge of the Creature* gives it at least some marginal historical significance.

Any bad reviews that *Revenge of the Creature* endured did not hamper its box office success. Despite its shortcomings and the 3-D gimmick having run its course by 1955, *Revenge of the Creature* was a box office hit, grossing over a million dollars. In fact, this film is the highest grossing of all the Creature movies.

One amusing footnote to *Revenge of the Creature* is its being the only Creature movie to be parodied on the TV show *Mystery Science Theater 3000*, on which a host and several puppets watch a movie and make amusing, derisive comments. For example, when *Revenge of the Creature* was presented on the program and Clint Eastwood's cameo appears, the commentary states, "This guy's bad, this is his first and last movie!"

28

**ABBOTT AND COSTELLO
MEET THE MUMMY**

(1955)

Director: Charles Lamont.
Screenplay: John Grant, based on a story by Lee Loeb.
Producer: Howard Christie. *Cinematography:* George Robinson. *Editing:* Russell
  Schoengarth. *Art Direction:* Alexander Golitzen, Bill Newberry.
Cast: Bud Abbott (Peter), Lou Costello (Freddie), Eddie Parker (Klaris the
  mummy), Marie Windsor (Madame Rontru), Michael Ansara (Charlie),
  Richard Deacon (Semu), Kurt Katch (Zoomer), Richard Karlan
  (Hetsut), Mel Welles (Iben) George Khoury (Habid), Peggy King
  (singer), Carole Costello (flower girl), Michael Vallon (Azzui), Veola
  Vonn (French girl), Robin Morse, Jan Arvan, Hank Mann, Jean Hartelle
  (waiters), Paul Bradley, Ralph Brooks, Jack Chefe, Franklyn Farnum,
  Hans Moebus (café patrons), Kem Dibbs, Kenneth Alton, Michael
  Cowell (police), Duke, Fred, and Harry Johnson (jugglers), Mazzone-
  Abbott Dancers, Chandra Kaly and Dancers (themselves).
Released: June 25, 1955.
Running Time: 79 minutes.
Availability: DVD (Universal Home Video).

Bud Abbott and Lou Costello had settled into a formula after the success
of *Abbott and Costello Meet Frankenstein*, with several films that had them
"meet" everyone from Dr. Jekyll and Mr. Hyde to the Keystone Cops. Per-
taining to this book, we have discussed the two films where Bud and Lou
met monsters whose films are discussed within the text. This is the last of
those films, as well as the final movie the duo made for Universal, after 15
years with the studio.

Abbott and Costello are two American photographers in Egypt who need money to get back to their country. They overhear Dr. Zoomer planning to ship Klaris, an Egyptian mummy, to America and want to get a job accompanying it. This will allow them to get back to America and also get paid. The mummy is wearing a valuable medallion that reveals where the treasure of Princess Ara is located. Madame Rontru wants to steal the treasure, while disciples of Klaris, led by Semu, want to defend it.

Unlike *Abbott and Costello Meet Frankenstein*, there is no real horror element as the narrative conflict is established. And unlike *Abbott and Costello Meet the Invisible Man*, the suspense elements do not flirt with film noir. *Abbott and Costello Meet the Mummy* is a far more typical comedy for the duo. There is an underlying story that is punctuated by humor and gags. Bud and Lou will lapse into their typical wordplay at any point:

Bud: How stupid can you get?

Lou: How stupid do you want me to be?

Abbott and Costello go to the doctor's house, but two of the disciples of Klaris kill the doctor and steal the mummy. They bring it to their leader, Semu, but discover it is without the medallion. Costello photographs the dead doctor but with Abbott in the picture. The photo is printed in the newspaper, and Abbott is wanted by police for the doctor's murder.

Several comic elements are at work here. First, Costello has a chance to do his scare reactions as he walks into a closet and finds the doctor's corpse. When he goes to get Bud, the body has been removed. Lou then goes into an office and sees the doctor slumped over his desk. The film borrows from a highlight scene in Abbott and Costello's 1942 comedy *Who Done It* where Lou is confused by the audio from several audio cues in a radio station. In this scene, a recorded message from a tape plays alongside the doctor's body, making Costello believe the dead doctor is speaking to him.

Once the comedians are back in the population, Bud's picture in the paper with the doctor's corpse forces them to disguise themselves and evade the police and various other forces out to get them. This is done with a lot of maneuvering and close calls that are nicely blocked and a throwback to a similar scene in *Abbott and Costello in the Foreign Legion* where the boys are evading evil.

The duo go back to the doctor's place to clear Bud's name, but Madame Rontru is there with her henchmen searching for the medallion. The duo escape with the medallion. They try to sell it but are told it is cursed. Madame Rontru offers $100, but Abbott shrewdly asks for $5,000. Rontru

Abbott and Costello meet the Mummy (Eddie Parker).

agrees to that amount and asks them to meet her at a café. Bud then starts to map out how they can get home by writing down plans and saying aloud to himself, "Let's see. I'll go first class, you go third class. I'll need a new suit of clothes, you can get your shoes shined." Each scene is punctuated with this kind of typical Abbott and Costello comedy.

When at the café to meet Rontru, a waiter informs the boys that the medallion is cursed "death to whoever holds it." This results in a funny routine where the duo, dining on hamburgers, keep passing the medallion to each other. Abbott sneaks it into Costello's pocket. Then Lou puts it in Bud's hamburger. Bud points out a pretty girl to Lou and switches the plates while he is distracted. Lou does the same to Bud but only taps the plates on the table without switching. Bud responds by switching them again and does a double take when discovering he has the medallion. This rather timeworn gag is given an extra energy due to Abbott and Costello's brilliant execution. But it concludes with Costello actually swallowing the medallion and Rontru, on arriving, insisting he be X-rayed so they can read the hieroglyphics that reveal the treasure's location.

Semu disguises himself as a guide and leads them all to a tomb where he plans to cut Lou open to get the medallion. Klaris is brought back to life, one of Rontru's men disguises himself as a mummy, and Abbott also disguises himself as a mummy, each with a different motivation. Lou, in fear, coughs up the medallion, but when all three mummies end up in the same place, dynamite intended to mine for the treasure explodes, killing Klaris and revealing the treasure. The movie concludes with the temple turned into a nightclub with the boys as proprietors.

Abbott and Costello Meet the Mummy is filled with a lot of hectic silliness that is both diverting and engaging. The duo have ample opportunity to perform several typical, fun routines. At one point, when digging for treasure, Costello holds out a shovel and a pick and asks Bud to take his pick. Bud takes the shovel, indicating that the shovel is his pick. "How can a shovel be a pick?" Costello demands with humorous frustration. There is also a running gag where anytime Lou plays a snake charmer's pungi (the musical instrument), a snake comes slithering out of the nearest basket. This leads up to a funny closing gag where a woman emerges from a basket for Bud but Lou conjures up an actual snake.

There are a few curious things about *Abbott and Costello Meet the Mummy*. First, Abbott and Costello are billed in the credits as Pete Patterson and Freddie Franklin, but throughout the film they refer to each other as their actual names. Costello even hollers, "Hey Abbott," which is how he opened the duo's popular radio show for years but never used it in films. Also, the Mummy is referred to as Klaris rather than Kharis. There is no explanation why.

Bud and Lou enjoyed the work of a strong supporting cast, including veteran actors Marie Windsor as Rontru and Michael Ansara as her henchman. The Mummy was played by stuntman Eddie Parker, who had doubled for Lon Chaney in the earlier movies. Newcomer Richard Deacon, who would soon become a household name for his work on TV's *Leave It to Beaver* and *The Dick Van Dyke Show* as well as film appearances ranging from Alfred Hitchcock to Jerry Lewis, appears as Semu. He replaced veteran actor H. B. Warner, who left the production due to illness. Lou Costello's oldest daughter, Carole, has a cute cameo as a flower girl.

During this period in his career, Lou Costello expected new actors assigned to his movies to sign a loyalty oath supporting Joseph McCarthy's anticommunist witch hunts. Richard Deacon told Bob Furmanek and Ron Palumbo in their book *Abbott and Costello in Hollywood* that he was approached by Lou's assistant Bobby Barber to sign the oath:

> From my standpoint, I knew that Lou was thinking of America, which is fine. But I happen to think that McCarthy was the most evil thing that ever happened. So I refused. (Barber) said, "If this gets back to Bud and Lou, you'll never work on this lot again." I said, "Be my guest. If that's what I have to do to stay in the business, then I don't want any part of it." But it was never mentioned to me by Bud or Lou, and, of course, I worked at Universal again and again.[1]

Lou's youngest daughter, Chris Costello, stated in an interview with Ethan Alter,

> Had Dad really investigated a little bit further and really knew what was going on with the McCarthy era, I know he would never have supported it, but he got so caught up in this idea of communists infiltrating Hollywood. He was so patriotic and so much for his country that I think he just kind of went a little bit overboard on it. Lucille Ball told me that when she was questioned by the House Un-American Activities Committee, "Everyone in Hollywood, the ones that I thought were my friends, turned their backs on me. Not one person came to my door except your father. I opened up the door and he looked at me and said, 'What can I do?' I just broke out crying." So he supported people, especially the people that he knew.[2]

Abbott and Costello Meet the Mummy wrapped up filming the day before Thanksgiving in 1954 because Bud and Lou were scheduled to appear in the first float of the annual Macy's Thanksgiving Day Parade. Director Charles Lamont, directing his ninth Abbott and Costello movie, brought the film under budget by one day and $12,000. The studio had, by this time, considered Abbott and Costello movies to be B films rather than top-level comedies despite the fact that the duo had once helped earn millions for the studio when they were among the nation's top box office stars. Their films were still popular and turned a profit, but Universal spent less than $20,000 on advertising for *Abbott and Costello Meet the Mummy*.

Abbott and Costello's contract was up when they finished filming this movie, and they believed the studio still supported them since a street on the back lot had been dedicated to them only a year earlier. However, when they tried to negotiate for more money, the studio dropped their contract. Abbott and Costello made one more film together, *Dance with Me Henry* (1956) for United Artists, then split up as a team the following year. Lou Costello made one solo film, *The 30 Foot Bride of Candy Rock* (1959), but died before it was released.

Universal-International continued to be more interested in prestigious pictures and less interested in its series films. But the science fiction trend remained popular in the mid-1950s, so they continued to release profitable films in his genre, including what would be the last of the Creature series.

29

THE CREATURE WALKS AMONG US

(1956)

Director: John Sherwood.
Screenplay: Arthur A. Ross, from his story.
Producer: William Alland. *Cinematography:* Maury Gertsman. *Editing:* Edward
  Curtiss. *Art Direction:* Alexander Golitzen, Robert E. Smith.
Cast: Jeff Morrow (Dr. Barton), Rex Reason (Dr. Morgan), Leigh Snowden
  (Marcia Barton), Gregg Palmer (Jed Grant), Maurice Manson (Dr. Borg),
  James Rawley (Dr. Johnson), David McMahon (Captain Stanley), Paul
  Fierro (Morteno), Lillian Molieri (Mrs. Morteno), Larry Hudson (state
  trooper), Frank Chase (steward), George Sowards (ranch hand), Ricou
  Browning (the Gill Man in water), Don Megowan (the Gill Man on land).
Released: April 26, 1956.
Running Time: 78 minutes.
Availability: DVD (Universal Home Entertainment).

As we went past the mid-1950s, Universal-International prepared to conclude whatever series were still in production, along with ceasing production on their Abbott and Costello films. The studio's popular Francis the
Talking Mule movies lost its leading man when Donald O'Connor left in
1955 (amusingly citing to the press that it was because the mule received
more fan mail). They tried to continue with Mickey Rooney in the lead,
but *Francis in the Haunted House* was not a success, so this August 1956
release ended the series. The same year O'Connor left the Francis movies,
the popular Ma and Pa Kettle films lost Percy Kilbride, who had played Pa
for the entire series, sputtering to a close with 1957's *The Kettles on Old
McDonald's Farm* and Parker Fennelly replacing Kilbride as Pa. Despite

Poster for *The Creature Walks among Us*.

the theater trade magazine *Independent Film Exhibitor Bulletin* stating in its September 5, 1955, issue that the Creature series would run "as long as the Frankenstein group," *The Creature Walks among Us* was to be the final movie featuring the Gill Man.

This does not mean the studio totally eschewed science fiction. It continued until the end of the decade with such one-shot efforts as *The Deadly Mantis, The Incredible Shrinking Man, The Monolith Monsters, The Mole People,* and *The Leech Woman,* which concluded the studio's sci-fi output in 1960. Of course, science fiction is a genre unto itself, with the Creature series the only monster hybrid that would fit comfortably in this study. Thus, as far as the monster movies of Universale Studios are concerned, *The Creature Walks among Us* is the final entry.

The Creature Walks among Us is directed by John Sherwood. Jack Arnold, the director of the last two Creature films, had gone on to other projects but recommended that Sherwood be his assistant director. The movie was filmed from late August into mid-September 1955. *The Creature Walks among Us* is the only Creature movie to not be filmed in 3-D.

Picking up from where *Revenge of the Creature* left off, *The Creature Walks among Us* has the Gill Man having escaped into the Florida waters and being pursued by a group of scientists on a boat. The leading scientist is Dr. Barton, who is not the intrigued researcher the others are but rather an angry, unstable individual whose character is not too far from the crazed scientists of the studio's earlier horror movies. He even evokes Dr. Frankenstein by stating at one point, "We can create an entirely new form of life."

His colleague is Dr. Morgan, who wavers between agreeing with Barton's madness regarding control of the Creature and a more grounded approach to their project. There is an element of jealous tension when his wife, Marcia, becomes attracted to their flirtatious guide Jed Grant, and Barton's paranoia increases.

Mental instability becomes something of a theme here as Marcia swims too deeply while exploring the ocean depths with Jed and Dr. Morgan and is overcome by what is described as "the raptures of the deep." Her mind snaps to the point where she starts to remove her scuba equipment while underwater and has to be rescued and returned to the ship. She is okay once brought aboard.

Along with taking an odd approach to its human characters, *The Creature Walks among Us* also presents its monster in an unusual manner. Having been burned during its capture, doctors notice while bandaging the Gill Man that he is breathing oxygen successfully and his gills are evolving into lungs. They attempt to continue the transition by mainstreaming him into a more human lifestyle, including getting him clothes. The movie responds to this rather remarkable development with the confused Gill Man attempting to escape into the ocean, not realizing his lungs will no longer allow him to breathe underwater. Shots of the Gill Man actually drowning are among the most harrowing underwater images in this film.

The Creature Walks among Us isn't so much about the Creature as it is about the people, with the Creature serving as a catalyst for their actions. The horror in this film seems to stem more from the love triangle involving Marcia, Jed, and Dr. Barton, the last of whom murders the guide in a jealous rage. He tries to blame the Creature, who responds with a rampage of his own, killing Barton. He returns to the sea, but unlike the previous two films where his return could signify that he remains alive, he now has lungs rather than gills, so it is assumed he drowns at the end.

While certainly the most offbeat of the Creature movies, *The Creature Walks among Us* has its own merit. Because he had been an assistant director, Sherwood does nicely with second-unit footage in establishing shots, offering vast long shots of the ship coasting on the water with Henry Mancini's pleasant music backing up the image. This more tranquil shot dovetails into similar underwater footage as Mancini's relaxed score enhances the camera following Jed, Marcia, and Dr. Barton as they swim underwater. The Creature's first appearance disrupts this rhythm, and Mancini's score emphasizes this first appearance with a loud crescendo that adds the initial shock element for the audience.

Sherwood continues this method in a later scene where the research team goes out on a smaller boat and is confronted by the Creature. The director allows for the boat to glide slowly along in a long shot, then switches to a medium shot of the characters within the craft. Sherwood then abruptly edits to a close-up of the Creature rising out of the water and slapping away the boat's motor, with Mancini's music again reaching a crescendo to enhance the action. Then it's back to a medium shot of the full boat, as the Creature rises again, pushing the boat up from the bottom and causing two of the men to fly into the air and land in the ocean. It is during this confrontation that the Creature is burned: he lifts an open gas container over his head to throw at the others and causes the gasoline to pour over his body. He is easily enflamed and jumps into the water.

The action sequences in *The Creature Walks among Us* are perhaps better than the previous films. But the characters are not. There is no hero. All of the doctors have the same Dr. Frankenstein feelings of creating a series of mutants over which they assume control. The woman is more sexually attracted to Jed than to her husband, who becomes an unsettling figure as the story goes on. During the scenes between these characters, Mancini's score and Sherwood's shot composition resemble film noir more so than science fiction or horror. While the isolated scenes are nicely presented, they don't blend successfully with the sci-fi or horror elements of the production.

Some of the more interesting scenes are the attempts to assimilate the Creature into a more mainstream lifestyle where he could somehow live among humans. Putting him in a cage with electronically charged bars, the Creature spends most of his time looking longingly at the waters, exhibiting a sort of pathos that adds further depth to the character. It can be argued that transforming the Creature from a majestic monster who lives in the water into a hulking brute who lumbers about on land destroys the essence of the character. But it plays as an extension rather than a redefinition.

There is a scene where the Creature destroys an attacking mountain lion that killed some sheep in an adjacent cage. While the film presents this as the Creature having enough of a heart to protect the weaker animal, the scientists who arrive after the lion has been killed believe the Creature was either exhibiting a random killing instinct or defending his own life. This culminates when Barton kills Jed and throws him into the Creature's cage. The Creature has enough cognitive ability to realize he is, in fact, being framed. The shot of him violently lifting Barton over his head and throwing him to his death is another one of the film's more shocking sequences. While Ricou Browning returns to his role as the underwater Gill Man, actor Don Megowan played the role on land. Stuntman Al Wyatt doubles in some scenes. It is he who is playing the Creature during much of the boat attack, including when the Gill Man is set on fire.

Director Sherwood chooses to conclude the film dramatically, showing the Creature walking toward the waters but fading the film out before we see him enter. This is perhaps his attempt to allow for some ambiguity in the event that another sequel might be forthcoming. Since there was not, we can assume the Creature did drown at the conclusion of this movie.

The acting here is handled by some capable performers with solid resumes in B movies and television. Jeff Morrow as Barton, even in his more relaxed scenes, presents a manner of unstable tension that permeates his character. Gregg Palmer slinks about in typically smarmy manner. Leigh Snowden balances between a sci-fi heroine and a film noir femme fatale. Rex Reason has perhaps the most challenging role as Morgan. He is outside of the love triangle, but his attraction to Marcia is palpable. He is supportive of Barton's research but unsettled by his behavior. Morgan is the closest thing to a hero that this film has—he has the best intentions out of everyone, and his attraction to Marcia contrasts nicely with the semiabusive relationship she has with Barton.

While *The Creature Walks among Us* tries to explore too many genres that don't meld sufficiently, the sum of its parts offers a lot of interesting elements. John Sherwood's vision and his approach to each scene offered real potential, making it sad that he had the opportunity to direct only two other films in his lifetime (the Rory Calhoun western *Raw Edge* and the sci-fi thriller *The Monolith Monsters*). Sherwood continued to work as an assistant director until his death in 1959.

The Creature Walks among Us effectively concludes the various monster series from Universale Studios. In the studio's history, despite many top-level films, it is these movies for which it remains best known. The idea of filming horror stories from the likes of Bram Stoker, Mary Shelley, and H. G. Wells resulted in a series of films incorporating several iconic characters that have been essentially defined by the actors who played them at this studio.

Although the films would no longer be produced, the existing movies that had already been filmed would enjoy continued fame due to magazines, television, home movies, and other such merchandising. That is the continuing legacy of the monster movies of Universale Studios.

EPILOGUE:
THE CONTINUED LEGACY OF
THE UNIVERSAL MONSTER MOVIES

In 1957, a year after Universal ended its monster series, the studio leased 550 of its pre-1948 films to Screen Gems, the television subsidiary of Columbia Pictures. Screen Gems grouped these films according to genre and proceeded to distribute them to various TV outlets. One of these groups was the Shock Theater package, which contained 52 features. They were not all monster movies. Along with such films as *Frankenstein*, *Dracula*, *The Mummy*, *The Invisible Man*, and *The Wolf Man*, the package also included mystery and suspense films, such as the Inner Sanctum series with Lon Chaney Jr., as well as nonmonster horror movies, such as *The Invisible Ray* with Bela Lugosi and Boris Karloff. The Shock Theater package became available to TV stations in October 1957.

These films were often shown on weekend nights, usually late, and with local talent playing hosts. The hosting became quite creative. Hosts such as John Zacherle (known on TV first as Roland, then as Zacherly), first in Philadelphia, then in New York; Maila Nurmi (Vampira) in Los Angeles; Jack DuBlon (Dr. Cadaverino in Milwaukee); and Terry Bennett (Marvin in Chicago) would dress in costume and elaborate makeup to introduce the films. Their hosting would sometimes include skits during the commercial breaks, which allowed a 90-minute or two-hour format to effectively fill time for features that ran anywhere from 100 minutes down to only 55 minutes. These shows were extremely popular, boosting the local market ratings by as much as an astonishing 1,000 percent in some markets.

In 1958, another collection of 20 films, called the Son of Shock package, was released to TV markets, expanding the cinematic base of the late-night shows to include some Columbia releases, such as *Before I Hang* with Boris

Karloff. Monster movies left off the first package, such as *House of Frankenstein* and *Ghost of Frankenstein*, were included this time.

Also in 1958, horror movie aficionado Forrest J. Ackerman started the magazine *Famous Monsters of Filmland*. Ackerman and James Warren planned to release just one issue of the magazine in February 1958 to commemorate the popularity of the old horror movies on TV in the 1950s. However, the enormous popularity of this first issue inspired Ackerman and Warren to continue publishing the magazine. The magazine's demographic was mostly teenagers (and some preteens), featuring well-written and thoughtful articles, rare photos, and clever graphics. Ackerman extended beyond the popular TV broadcasts and educated his readers about silent horror films, promoting the work of Lon Chaney Sr. The magazine was extremely popular throughout the 1960s, but by the 1970s it was often reprinting articles from past issues.

Forrest Ackerman became something of a cult hero among horror movie fans. He acquired a magnificent collection of horror and sci-fi memorabilia that he put on display in a museum known as the Ackermansion and, later, the Son of Ackermansion when Ackerman moved into an 18-room home where the materials were housed.

Famous Monsters of Filmland ceased publication in 1983 after 191 issues but was resurrected 10 years later by Ray Ferry, who acquired the rights to use the name and hired Ackerman as editor in chief. Ackerman eventually sued Ferry for breach of contract, causing Ferry to file for bankruptcy after Ackerman won the suit. The magazine was taken over by Phillip Kim in 2008. Forrest Ackerman died in December of that year at the age of 92.

One of the popular merchandising deals regarding the Universal monsters was when Aurora Plastics Corporation acquired a license from Universal Studios to offer models of their iconic monster characters. These plastic models were assembled by potent model glue and could be painted with special tempera paints. The giant Frankenstein monster was the first model to be released in 1961, standing a full 19 inches high when assembled. Others included Dracula, the Mummy, and the Wolf Man. These were the most lucrative figures among all the company's models.

Before the days of video, there were home movie distributors that offered condensed versions of their feature films, showing highlights, an isolated scene, or an abridged version of the entire movie. This originally started in the 1940s when Universal leased the 1945 Abbott and Costello feature *Here Come the Coeds* to the home movie company Castle Films. Castle had originally released news footage for historical purposes in 16mm and 8mm for people with home movie equipment but by the end of the

1940s had expanded to entertainment films as well, including Hollywood highlights and cartoons. Castle took a scene from *Here Come the Coeds* where Costello is trying to eat oyster stew despite an aggressive oyster in his bowl and coupled it with a scene where he has to wrestle Lon Chaney Jr. for charity and called the 10-minute reel *Oysters and Muscles*. They also took a comic basketball sequence from the same movie and titled it *Fun on the Run*. This resulted in a lawsuit against the studio by Abbott and Costello for money they felt was due them from the sales of these movies.

Castle began releasing abridgements of their sci-fi films with *It Came from Outer Space* in 1957, followed by *Creature from the Black Lagoon.* These 10-minute movies would feature highlights from the feature and were available in 16mm sound versions as well as 8mm silent (with subtitles) for the many home movie enthusiasts who had this more affordable equipment. In 1960, an abridgement of *Abbott and Costello Meet Frankenstein* was released, and it became one of the company's biggest sellers. *Bride of Frankenstein* came out later that year, and others followed. There were also short 50-foot abridgements, showing a mere five minutes of silent 8mm highlights, for children's toy projectors. Seeing brief, silent highlights from the monster movies seems pretty useless to people of the modern era of home video and live streaming.

In 1974, Mel Brooks directed *Young Frankenstein*, and although it was not a Universal movie (it was released by 20th Century Fox), it traded on the Universal monster series for its parody. Mel Brooks told the *Los Angeles Times* on October 1, 2010,

> I was in the middle of shooting the last few weeks of Blazing Saddles somewhere in the Antelope Valley, and Gene Wilder and I were having a cup of coffee and he said, I have this idea that there could be another Frankenstein. I said not another—we've had the son of, the cousin of, the brother-in-law, we don't need another Frankenstein. His idea was very simple: What if the grandson of Dr. Frankenstein wanted nothing to do with the family whatsoever. He was ashamed of those wackos. I said, "That's funny."

Brooks further stated in a 2016 interview with *Creative Screenwriting*,

> Little by little, every night, Gene and I met at his bungalow at the Bel Air Hotel. We ordered a pot of Earl Grey tea coupled with a container of cream and a small kettle of brown sugar cubes. To go with it we had a pack of British digestive biscuits. And step-by-step, ever so cautiously, we proceeded on a dark narrow twisting path to the eventual screenplay in which good sense and caution are thrown out the window and madness ensues.[1]

Young Frankenstein parodied elements of *Frankenstein*, *Bride of Frankenstein*, *Son of Frankenstein*, and *Ghost of Frankenstein*. Unlike *Abbott and Costello Meet Frankenstein*, which was a comedy that incorporated horror elements with the monsters, *Young Frankenstein* was straight satire. Kenneth Mars played a version of Lionel Atwill's one-armed inspector from *Son of Frankenstein*. Marty Feldman does a wildly funny comic version of Bela Lugosi's Igor character from the same film. And in one of the movie's highlights, Gene Hackman has a cameo as a blind hermit, as he and Peter Boyle, as the monster, do a hilarious send-up of the scene between Boris Karloff and O. P. Heggie in *Bride of Frankenstein*.

By the time *Young Frankenstein* was released, the most prominent leading actors of the Universal monster movies had gone. Bela Lugosi died in 1956, Boris Karloff in 1968, and Lon Chaney Jr. in 1973. During the 1960s, when the films were popular on TV, produced as Aurora models, promoted in monster magazines, and available as home movies, both Karloff and Lugosi would make appearances on TV programs saluting their past work. The two of them appeared together, along with Peter Lorre, in a classic 1962 episode of TV's *Route 66* titled "Lizard's Leg and Owlet's Wing." The actors play themselves, wondering if their old monster characters would be scary to modern audiences.

Lon Chaney Jr. appeared throughout the 1950s and 1960s in many films and TV shows, often westerns, but sometimes in an effort to trade off of his image in horror movies. His last theatrical release was *Dracula vs. Frankenstein* and reunited him with J. Carroll Naish from *House of Frankenstein*. Both he and Naish died two years later.

Boris Karloff worked often in Roger Corman productions, sometimes with a young Jack Nicholson, in movies such as *The Raven* (1963) and *The Terror* (1963). He also did a great deal of TV work, including providing the narration for the 1966 animated version of Dr. Seuss's book *How the Grinch Stole Christmas*. This show is often revived on TV during the Christmas holidays.

Lugosi, Karloff, Chaney, Lorre, Naish, Claude Rains, and so on were versatile actors whose careers extended to several different roles and in many different genres. But each will be remembered for their defining versions of iconic monster characters in American movies. Since the 1980s, the monster movies have been released as single titles and in various box sets and packages on VHS tape, DVD, and Blu-ray. Well into the twenty-first century, the monster movies of Universale Studios continue to win new generations of fans.

NOTES

CHAPTER I

1. Staff Writer, "Is He the Second Chaney?," *Silver Screen*, January 1931.
2. Mordaunt Hall, "Dracula," *New York Times*, February 13, 1931.
3. Staff Writer, "Dracula," *Variety*, February 18, 1931.
4. Mark A. Vieira, *Hollywood Horror: From Gothic to Cosmic* (New York: Harry N. Abrams, 2003), 35.

CHAPTER 2

1. Susan Tyler Hitchcock, *Frankenstein: A Cultural History* (New York: Norton, 2007).
2. Richard Lamparski, *Whatever Became Of? Tenth Series* (New York: Crown, 1988), 103.
3. Gregory William Mank, *Women in Horror Films, 1930s* (Jefferson, NC: McFarland, 1999), 72–73.
4. Mordaunt Hall, "Frankenstein," *New York Times*, December 5, 1931.
5. Kyle Edwards, "Morals, Markets, and 'Horror Pictures': The Rise of Universal Pictures and the Hollywood Production Code," *Film & History* 42, no. 2 (2012).

CHAPTER 3

1. Phillip K. Riley, *Cagliostro: King of the Dead* (Albany, GA: BearManor Media, 2009), 28.
2. Mark A. Vieira, *Hollywood Horror: From Gothic to Cosmic* (New York: Harry N. Abrams, 2003), 55–58.
3. Andre Sennwald, "The Mummy," *New York Times*, January 5, 1933.

CHAPTER 5

1. Variety Staff, "Bride of Frankenstein," *Variety*, May 1, 1935.

CHAPTER 6

1. Bartlomiej Paszylk, *The Pleasure and Pain of Cult Horror Films* (Jefferson, NC: McFarland, 2009).
2. Frank Nugent, "Werewolf of London," *New York Times*, May 10, 1935.
3. Staff Writer, "Werewolf of London," *Silver Screen*, June 1935.
4. Staff Writer, "Child Ban Is Put on 'Werewolf' for K.C.," *Motion Picture Daily*, May 28, 1935.

CHAPTER 7

1. Biography at the Internet Movie Database (www.imdb.com).
2. Vito Russo, *The Celluloid Closet: Homosexuality in the Movies* (New York: HarperCollins, 1981), 48.
3. Frank Nugent, "Dracula's Daughter," *New York Times*, May 18, 1936.
4. James McCarthy, "Dracula's Daughter," *Motion Picture Herald*, May 1936.

CHAPTER 8

1. Gregory William Mank, *Karloff and Lugosi* (Jefferson, NC: McFarland, 2009).
2. Scott Nollen, *Boris Karloff: A Gentleman's Life* (Parkville, MD: Midnight Marquee Press, 2005).
3. Mank, *Karloff and Lugosi*.
4. Variety Staff, "Son of Frankenstein," *Variety*, January 31, 1939.
5. Frank Nugent, "Son of Frankenstein," *New York Times*, January 30, 1939.

CHAPTER 9

1. Frank Nugent, "The Invisible Man Returns," *New York Times*, January 16, 1940.

2. Variety Staff, "The Invisible Man Returns," *Variety*, January 21, 1940.

3. Victoria Price, *Vincent Price: A Daughter's Biography* (New York: St. Martin's Press, 1999).

CHAPTER 10

1. Bosley Crowther, "The Mummy's Hand," *New York Times*, September 20, 1940.

CHAPTER 12

1. Keith Alan Deutsch, "Curt Siodmak: The Black Mask Interview," www.black maskmagazine.com.

2. Patrick McGillian, ed., *Backstory 2: Interviews with Screenwriters of the 1940s and 1950s* (Berkeley: University of California Press, 1991).

3. Gregory William Mank, *Women in Horror Films, 1940s* (Jefferson, NC: McFarland, 1999).

4. Doug McClelland, *The Golden Age of B Movies* (New York: Hippocrene Books, 1978).

5. Ibid.

CHAPTER 13

1. Dominic Florentino, "The Monster and Me," *Monster Kid Magazine* #5.

2. Ernest Bell, "Screaming Success," *Hollywood*, April 1942.

3. Bosley Crowther, "The Ghost of Frankenstein," *New York Times*, April 4, 1942.

4. Staff Writer, "The Ghost of Frankenstein," *Motion Picture Herald*, March 1942.

5. "What the Picture Did for Me," *Motion Picture Herald*, September 1942.

CHAPTER 14

1. Staff Writer, "The Invisible Agent," *Film Daily*, August 7, 1942.

2. Staff Writer, "The Invisible Agent," *Photoplay*, October 1942.

CHAPTER 15

1. Staff Writer, "The Mummy's Tomb," *Motion Picture Herald*, October 24, 1942.
2. Staff Writer, "The Mummy's Tomb," *Film Daily*, October 19, 1942.

CHAPTER 16

1. Patrick McGilligan, ed., *Backstory 2: Interviews with Screenwriters of the 1940s and 1950s* (Berkeley: University of California Press, 1991).
2. Erskine Johnson, "Hollywood Newsreel," *Hollywood*, February 1943.
3. Cal York, "Cal York's Inside Stuff," *Photoplay*, February 1943.
4. Variety Staff, "Frankenstein Meets the Wolf Man," *Variety*, March 11, 1943.

CHAPTER 17

1. A. H. Weiler, "Son of Dracula," *New York Times*, November 6, 1943.
2. Staff Writer, "Son of Dracula," *Motion Picture Herald*, November 13, 1943.
3. Staff Writer, "Son of Dracula," *Film Daily*, November 22, 1943.

CHAPTER 19

1. Staff Writer, "The Mummy's Ghost," *Harrison Reports*, July 8, 1944.

CHAPTER 20

1. Matt Beckoff, *Confessions of a Scream Queen* (Albany, GA: BearManor Media, 2010).
2. "House of Frankenstein," *Independent Exhibitor's Bulletin*, January 15, 1945.
3. "House of Frankenstein," *Motion Picture Herald*, December 23, 1944.

CHAPTER 21

1. Helen McNamara, "The Mummy's Curse," *Motion Picture Daily*, December 22, 1944.

CHAPTER 22

1. Staff Writer, "House of Dracula," *Film Daily*, December 3, 1945.

CHAPTER 23

1. Tom Weaver, "June Lockhart on She-Wolf of London," http://classic-horror
.com/newsreel/interview_june_lockhart_on_she_wolf_of_londonClassic-Horror
.com.

CHAPTER 24

1. Bob Furmanek and Ron Palumbo, *Abbott and Costello in Hollywood* (New York: Perigee Books, 1991).
2. Furmanek and Palumbo, *Abbott and Costello*.
3. Ethan Alter, "Memories of Abbott and Costello: Chris Costello Talks 'Who's on First,' Frankenstein, and Growing Up in Old Hollywood," http://ethanalter
.tumblr.com.

CHAPTER 25

1. William Weaver, "Abbott and Costello Meet the Invisible Man," *Motion Picture Daily*, March 7, 1951.

CHAPTER 26

1. Variety Staff, "Creature from the Black Lagoon," *Variety*, March 11, 1954.
2. Staff Writer, "Creature from the Black Lagoon," *Hollywood Reporter*, February 9, 1954.
3. Vincent Di Fate, "The Fantastic Mystery of Milicent Patrick," www.tor.com/
2011/10/27/the-fantastic-mystery-of-milicent-patrick.
4. Marty Bauman, "Profile: Catching Up with Ben 'Creature' Chapman," The Astounding B-Movie Archive, www.bmonster.com.

CHAPTER 27

1. Howard Thompson, "Revenge of the Creature," *New York Times*, May 13, 1955.
2. Murray Horowitz, "Revenge of the Creature," *Motion Picture Daily*, May 15, 1955.

CHAPTER 28

1. Bob Furmanek and Ron Palumbo, *Abbott and Costello in Hollywood* (New York: Perigee Books, 1991).
2. Ethan Alter, "Memories of Abbott and Costello: Chris Costello Talks 'Who's on First,' Frankenstein, and Growing Up in Old Hollywood," http://ethanalter.tumblr.com.

EPILOGUE

1. Brock, Swinson, "Mel Brooks on Screenwriting," *Creative Screenwriting*, January 14, 2016.

BIBLIOGRAPHY

BOOKS

Beckoff, Matt. *Confessions of a Scream Queen*. Albany, GA: BearManor Media, 2010.

Brunas, Michael, John Brunas, and Tom Weaver, *Universal Horrors: The Studios Classic Films, 1931–46*. Jefferson, NC: McFarland, 1990.

Furmanek, Bob, and Ron Palumbo. *Abbott and Costello in Hollywood*. New York: Perigee Books, 1991.

Hitchcock, Susan Tyler. *Frankenstein: A Cultural History*. New York: Norton, 2007.

Lamparski, Richard. *Whatever Became Of? Tenth Series*. New York: Crown, 1988.

Mank, Gregory William. *Karloff and Lugosi*. Jefferson, NC: McFarland, 1990.

———. *Women in Horror Films, 1930s*. Jefferson, NC: McFarland, 1999.

———. *Women in Horror Films, 1940s*. Jefferson, NC: McFarland, 1999.

McClelland, Doug. *The Golden Age of B Movies*. New York: Hippocrene Books, 1978.

McGillian, Patrick, ed. *Backstory 2: Interviews with Screenwriters of the 1940s and 1950s*. Berkeley: University of California Press, 1991.

Miller, Jeffrey. *The Horror Spoofs of Abbott and Costello*. Jefferson, NC: McFarland, 2000.

Nollen, Scott. *Boris Karloff: A Gentleman's Life*. Parkville, MD: Midnight Marquee Press, 2005.

Paszylk, Bartlomiej. *The Pleasure and Pain of Cult Horror Films*. Jefferson, NC: McFarland, 2009.

Price, Victoria. *Vincent Price: A Daughter's Biography*. New York: St. Martin's Press, 1999.

Riley, Phillip K. *Cagliostro: King of the Dead*. Albany, GA: BearManor Media, 2009.

Russo, Vito. *The Celluloid Closet: Homosexuality in the Movies*. New York: HarperCollins, 1981.

Skal, David J. *Hollywood Gothic: The Tangled Web of Dracula from Novel to Stage to Screen*. New York: Faber & Faber, 2004.

Vieira, Mark A. *Hollywood Horror: From Gothic to Cosmic*. New York: Harry N. Abrams. 2003.

———. *Sin in Soft Focus: Pre-Code Hollywood*. New York: Harry N. Abrams, 1999.

Warren, Bill. *Keep Watching the Skies*. Jefferson, NC: McFarland, 2010.

Weaver, Tom, Schecker, David, and Steve Kronenberg. *The Creature Chronicles*. Jefferson, NC: McFarland, 2014.

———. *Monsters, Mutants, and Heavenly Creatures*. Parkville, MD: Midnight Marquee Press, 1996.

———. *A Sci-Fi Swarm and Horror Horde*. Jefferson, NC: McFarland, 2010.

ARTICLES

Bell, Ernest. "Screaming Success." *Hollywood*, April 1942.

Edwards, Kyle. "Morals, Markets, and 'Horror Pictures': The Rise of Universal Pictures and the Hollywood Production Code." *Film & History* 42, no. 2 (2012).

Florentino, Dominic. "The Monster and Me." *Monster Kid Magazine* #5.

Johnson, Erskine. "Hollywood Newsreel." *Hollywood*, February 1943.

Staff Writer. "Child Ban Is Put on 'Werewolf' for K.C." *Motion Picture Daily*, May 28, 1935.

York, Cal. "Cal York's Inside Stuff." *Photoplay*, February 1943.

REVIEWS

Crowther, Bosley. "The Ghost of Frankenstein," *New York Times*, April 4, 1942.

———. "The Mummy's Hand." *New York Times*, September 20, 1940.

Hall, Mordaunt. "Dracula." *New York Times*, February 13, 1931.

———. "Frankenstein." *New York Times*, December 5, 1931.

Horowitz, Murray. "Revenge of the Creature." *Motion Picture Daily*, May 15, 1955.

"House of Frankenstein." *Independent Exhibitor's Bulletin*, January 15, 1945.

"House of Frankenstein." *Motion Picture Herald*, December 23, 1944.

McCarthy, James. "Dracula's Daughter." *Motion Picture Herald*, May 1936.

McNamara, Helen. "The Mummy's Curse." *Motion Picture Daily*, December 22, 1944.

Nugent, Frank. "Dracula's Daughter." *New York Times*, May 18, 1936.

———. "The Invisible Man Returns." *New York Times*, January 16, 1940.

———. "Son of Frankenstein." *New York Times*, January 30, 1939.

———. "Werewolf of London." *New York Times*, May 10, 1935.

Sennwald, Andre. "The Mummy." *New York Times*, January 5, 1933.

Staff Writer. "Creature from the Black Lagoon." *Variety*, March 9, 1954.

———. "The Ghost of Frankenstein." *Motion Picture Herald*, March 1942.

———. "House of Dracula." *Film Daily*, December 3, 1945.

———. "The Invisible Agent." *Film Daily*, August 7, 1942.

———. "The Invisible Agent." *Photoplay*, October 1942.

———. "Is He the Second Chaney?" *Silver Screen*, January 1931.

———. "The Mummy." *American Cinematographer*, December 1932.

———. "The Mummy's Ghost." *Harrison Reports*, July 8, 1944.

———. "The Mummy's Tomb." *Film Daily*, October 19, 1942.

———. "The Mummy's Tomb." *Motion Picture Herald*, October 24, 1942.

———. "Son of Dracula." *Motion Picture Herald*, November 13, 1943.

———. "Son of Dracula." *Film Daily*, November 22, 1943.

———. "Werewolf of London." *Silver Screen*, June 1935.

Thompson, Howard. "Revenge of the Creature." *New York Times*, May 13, 1955.

Variety Staff. "Bride of Frankenstein." *Variety*, May 1, 1935.

———. "Creature from the Black Lagoon." *Variety*, March 11, 1954.

———. "Dracula." *Variety*, February 18, 1931.

———. "Frankenstein Meets the Wolf Man." *Variety*, March 11, 1943.

———. "The Invisible Man Returns." *Variety*, January 21, 1940.

———. "Son of Frankenstein." *Variety*, January 31, 1939.

Weaver, William. "Abbott and Costello Meet the Invisible Man." *Motion Picture Daily*, March 7, 1951.

Weiler, A. H. "Son of Dracula." *New York Times*, November 6, 1943.

"What the Picture Did for Me," a series in *Motion Picture Herald* featuring theater exhibitors indicating how movies went over with patrons at their establishments. Random issues were consulted for responses to some of the movies contained herein.

ONLINE

Alter, Ethan. "Memories of Abbott and Costello: Chris Costello Talks 'Who's on First,' Frankenstein, and Growing Up in Old Hollywood." http://ethanalter.tumblr.com.

Bauman, Marty. "Profile: Catching Up with Ben 'Creature' Chapman." The Astounding B-Movie Archive. www.bmonster.com.

Deutsch, Keith Alan. "Curt Siodmak: The Black Mask Interview." www.blackmask magazine.com.

Di Fate, Vincent. "The Fantastic Mystery of Milicent Patrick." www.tor.com/2011/10/27/the-fantastic-mystery-of-milicent-patrick.

Internet Movie Database. www.imdb.com.

Weaver, Tom. "June Lockhart on She-Wolf of London." http://classic-horror.com/newsreel/interview_june_lockhart_on_she_wolf_of_londonClassic-Horror.com.

INDEX

ABOUT THE AUTHOR

James L. Neibaur is a film historian who has written hundreds of articles, reviews, and essays, including over 40 entries in the *Encyclopedia Brittanica*. He is the author of *The Fall of Buster Keaton: His Films for MGM, Educational Pictures, and Columbia* (2010), *Early Charlie Chaplin: The Artist as Apprentice at Keystone Studios* (2011), *The Silent Films of Harry Langdon* (2012), *Buster Keaton's Silent Shorts: 1920–1923*—with Terri Niemi—(2013), and *The Charley Chase Talkies: 1929–1940* (2013), all published by Scarecrow Press.

Neibaur is also the author of *The Elvis Movies* (2014), *The James Cagney Films of the 1930s* (2014), *The Clint Eastwood Westerns* (2014), *The Essential Mickey Rooney* (2016), *Butterfly in the Rain: The 1927 Abduction and Murder of Marion Parker* (2016), and *The Essential Jack Nicholson* (2016), all published by Rowman & Littlefield.